More Praise for *Beyond: Create ‹*

"A great book filled with question: Ultimately this gives you a significant road map of topics to consider in your life. I loved the format with each author giving their personal perspective on a topic. Written by women at a seasoned stage in their lives with comments coming directly from their hearts and life experiences."

—*Melissa Foles, mother of MVP Nick Foles of Super Bowl 2017;*
Co-Founder of Eddie V's Restaurants; Encore for Empty Nesters

"I love this new resource for all of us over 50 who are still hungry to grow and learn. The women who speak here are beautifully wise. The format is efficient, lending itself to quick bursts of guidance just as we need it. Congratulations on creating a book that is sure to bring clarity and inspiration to the later chapters of our lives."

—*Leslie Leyland Fields, author/editor of 14 books including*
Nearing a Far God: Praying the Psalms with Our
Whole Selves *and* The Wonder Years: 40 women Over 40

"Wouldn't it be wonderful to sit down with some wise female friends and have some real talk about the issues you're facing in the second half of your life? *Beyond* is a print version of those conversations. The Q & A format of the book welcomes readers into honest and lively discussion about life's second act that is both practical and grounded in faith."

—*Michelle Van Loon, author of* Becoming Sage: Finding Meaning, Purpose;
Spirituality in Midlife, Translating Your Past; *and* Moments and Days

"This is one of the most practical, honest books I have read. It answers hard questions on dealing with conflict in different types of relationships and situations; a virtual "encyclopedia" of dealing with the changes in life (including sex and body image); and daring the reader to dream at every age."

—*Diane Strack, author of* New Start for Single Moms;
founder of She Loves Out Loud; co-founder of Student Leadership University

"Wisdom, wisdom, wisdom. That's all I kept thinking when I read an insight, a suggestion or a perspective by Judy, Carol, Lyn, and Mary. This is a needed field guide for those believing their best years are still ahead."

—*Beth Guckenberger, Co-Executive Director, Back2Back Ministries; author; global speaker*

"I am thrilled to endorse *Beyond!* The authors honestly share their life experience with readers by responding to questions and wisely offering suggestions for everything from creating a vision for life to handling complex issues. For those of us upwards of age 50, these years can be the most insightful, productive, enlightened, growth-inducing, and educational of our lives. The authors of *Beyond* want us to live them to the fullest!"

—*Judy Allen, writer for* Reimagining Retirement, Fathom Magazine, *and* The Sage Forum; *Connecting Dots to God* blogger

"This lovely book reads like a conversation between authentic friends. *Beyond: Create a Life You Love After 50, 60, 70 and More* dives deep into the real issues women face as they age. The experiences, questions, responses, and resources shared by the authors will help you understand there is much to look forward to as you age."

—*Pamela Henkelman, Empty Nest Coach; host of the Midlife Momma Podcast*

"A book written by several friends as they answer questions that both women and men over 50 have about life! And it comes with a bonus of the focus on one's relationship with our Creator. How great to have this all together in one place. Well worth keeping handy on one's shelf for reference and periodic review."

—*Janet Beal, affiliate faculty of Kairos University; Latin America Human Resources Team at Cru Global; author; international Spanish teacher*

"The authors feel like our close friends as they share their hearts on the challenges and discoveries of our latter years. They ask—and answer—the questions bubbling up in our souls and nudge us forward to understand the good and not-so-good aspects of the seasons ahead."

—*Elisa Morgan, speaker; author; regular contributor to* Our Daily Bread Ministries; *co-host,* Discover the Word *and* God Hears Her; *president emerita, The MomCo by MOPS International*

"Beyond is a thought-provoking resource for wise people in transition with practical advice and memorable metaphors. May we all consistently strive to fill our life jars properly—with rocks, then pebbles, then sand—and seek such great counsel throughout our life journeys."

—*Kim Laughton, former SEO of Charles Schwab and Co. Inc.; president of Schwab Charitable*

BEYOND

Create A Life You Love
After 50, 60, 70, and More

JUDY DOUGLASS

MARY HENDERSON

CAROL DODDS

LYN ALEXANDER

ISBN: 979-8-9856046-3-4 (Paperback)
ISBN: 979-8-9856046-5-8 (ebook)

All scripture quotations are from the New International Version, unless otherwise indicated

thebeyondbook.com
https://thebeyondbook.com/Contact.html

Production Management: Weaving Influence, Inc.
Cover and Interior Design: Stephanie Jordan, Lori Weidert
Copyediting: Becky Antkowiak
Typesetting: Lori Weidert
Proofreading: Keri Hales

Printed in the United States of America

Dedicated to our husbands,
children,
daughters-in-law, sons-in-law,
and grandchildren now and to come.
May you live BEYOND with joy and purpose.

CONTENTS

FOREWORD

How old were you when you first recognized a bit of who you are?

Five? Fifteen? Twenty-five?

My self-recognition came in stages. At eight, I wrote plays for the neighbor kids and started my only novel. By high school, I knew I wanted to write.

I graduated with a degree in journalism, confident I would write for a magazine and eventually be the editor. I thought I would marry my college sweetheart, have a couple of children, write books, and become an influencer (before that was a thing).

Some of my hopes and dreams came true. Some didn't. There were unexpected twists and turns, disappointments, joys, and lessons learned. I broke my engagement to my college sweetheart and went on to become the editor of two magazines for fourteen years. A man I had been dating and grown to love finally asked me to marry him. Steve was so worth waiting for.

As our two wonderful daughters arrived, I discovered more challenges, more joys and more understanding of who I was. We adopted a nine-year-old boy. He brought joy, hurdles, and pain into our lives—and taught me more than I could ever have imagined.

I have traveled the world, spoken to thousands, and written six books as I partnered with my husband in our work and in parenting. Our three children married, enriching our lives with their friendship, their spouses, and our ten grandchildren. Steve and I enjoyed doing meaningful work with less pressure—but then, without warning, he had a reaction to a cancer treatment and died. Even in grief, I am again discovering who I am and finding new opportunities and paths.

Some pathways become apparent early and seem to flow naturally. Others are big surprises which come as we reach an age of new freedom and opportunity. I'd never even listened to a podcast when I was asked to start one. I'm now in my fourth year of encouraging and giving help and hope to weary parents.

Maybe you wonder, "Is a purposeful, meaningful, abundant life possible as I get older?"

Let me give you a quick reminder of some people who have found it is possible. Some are names you know. Others are more like you and me.

- Julia Child learned to cook at forty and collaborated on her first French cookbook at fifty.
- Vera Wang first began to think about fashion design at forty. Becoming the icon she is now took many years.
- Margaret Ringenberg completed a round-the-world air race at seventy-two.
- Diana Nyad swam 110 miles from Cuba to Florida at sixty-four.
- Alice Mathews went to seminary at fifty-seven and became a professor and speaker in her sixties.

However, the possibilities don't have to be beyond your imagination.

- You could be like my friend Jane, who took up knitting in her sixties and made many stocking caps to give and to sell.
- Or Carol, who took classes to become certified as a spiritual director and is touching many lives.
- Or Susan, who got a realtor license at fifty and has a thriving business.
- Or Jackie, who became a travel agent and fulfilled her dream to see the world.

Bringing along all your life experiences, strengths, and desires, what do you see in the days and years ahead? Are you ready to retire, to take it easy? Do you have dreams from the past that have resurfaced?

Maybe you're filled with questions: Who am I now? What will life be like with my husband around all the time? What will I do since my children and grands live so far away? Who will be my family, my community? Do I have enough money? Do I have a future? What will the rest of my life look like?

If you have similar questions, you have come to the right place. *Beyond* is filled with life realities, experiences, resources, and perspectives. In this amazing collection, my three friends—real women—share rich, practical wisdom regarding what they have learned and are still learning.

Let me introduce them to you.

Mary Henderson loves helping people learn to experience a more enriched, meaningful life, helping them to overcome obstacles along the way. To this end, she has taught and mentored for over forty years with Cru, a multinational non-profit organization. She's lived and worked throughout New Zealand, Eastern Europe, and the United States.

Mary has written three books: *Breaking Free, Retrain Your Brain for Joy*, and *Rest for Your Soul*. She travels worldwide, speaking on a variety of topics.

Mary graduated from the University of Texas with a bachelor of fine arts degree in theater and from Hope International University with a master's degree in counseling. Mary and her husband, John, have three grown children and two grandchildren.

Carol Dodds is the founder of Encore, an organization for "empty nest" women (50+) who are ready to "take the stage," impacting their communities and the world through their God-given passions and desires.

A graduate of the University of Texas, Carol was a member of Kappa Kappa Gamma sorority. Since 1982, she has served alongside her husband, Stuart, with Cru and Athletes in Action in Colorado, Costa Rica and Texas. Carol and Stuart have three grown children and a granddaughter. Carol is a certified personality trainer and a life coach.

Those who know Carol best describe her as engaging, energizing, and passionate. She strongly believes she was called by God for a purpose and is thrilled that those who read this book will understand their lives and callings in an expanded way.

Lyn Alexander served for many years as the Executive Director of TruCare, a non-profit organization that provides services for couples facing unplanned pregnancy in Austin, Texas.

Growing up in a military family, Lyn moved nineteen times. She graduated from the University of Texas with a radio/television/film degree and moved to Los Angeles, planning to become a VJ (Video Disc Jockey) for MTV. Even though this goal was not realized, Lyn gained great experience and later ran the marketing department for McDonnell Douglas. As a young adult, Lyn managed a new wave punk band and an avant-garde movie theater.

She has been married to her teenage sweetheart, Dan, for thirty-six years, and they have three adult children and three grandchildren. Lyn is committed to developing deep, lasting relationships with her family and those she mentors. She loves helping women live to their fullest potential.

As these women have progressed past age fifty, they have brought their own experiences, along with input from many friends, into what I might call a Book of Wisdom for the Latter Half of Life.

They have asked the questions we all ask, as well as the hard ones we are hesitant to ask. With honesty and vulnerability, they have shared advice from their own experience.

In these pages, you'll discover

○ who you are and what you bring for the years ahead;

○ wisdom for navigating all the relationships in your life;

○ thoughts on finishing well; and

○ amazing resources.

Let's explore how the later years may be our best years.

—Judy Douglass
Author, Speaker, Encourager
Shaped by God: Words for Life
When You Love a Prodigal (book and podcast)

INTRODUCTION

Welcome to the adventure of life after fifty! We've come a long way and experienced much, which will serve us well as we journey onward.

We've covered a lot of ground in relationships, jobs, education, finances, physical endeavors, emotional ups-and-downs, and spiritual journeys. In each of these, we've climbed difficult mountains, forged emotional jungles, endured heartbreaking storms, and survived desert conditions. Perhaps you're still in the midst of some of these.

We've gained a lot of experience and wisdom to draw upon, to enrich ourselves and others. In light of all this wealth, isn't it strange that our world sometimes refers to life after fifty as *over the hill, past our prime,* or *out to pasture*? Instead, this can be a time of new beginnings, just getting started, and the golden season.

We invite you to experience life after fifty as an exciting adventure filled with new possibilities and purposes for each decade. You have many options in this season of life that may cause you to become either better or bitter, healthier or declining, fulfilled or dissatisfied, peaceful or gloomy. *Beyond* provides encouragement, ideas, information, support, and resources. Together, let's explore how to choose the options that will result in joy and peace of mind throughout this season.

Maybe you don't feel so revved up, and that's okay. Perhaps you're in the middle of serious difficulties, a downward trajectory, or a barren wilderness. By now, we know that life can be very hard. Our goal is to provide you with tools and motivation to make the best of your current circumstances. Embracing our new opportunities can be difficult for a number of reasons.

For one thing, society tends to speak negatively about these years. We may accept this self-defeating mindset without even realizing it, then live out this pessimistic reality.

Also our physical bodies begin to experience more problems as we age, though this downward decline can be greatly reduced by our lifestyle choices before and after fifty. Nutrition, exercise, sleep, emotional health, good relationships, and spirituality can drastically affect our physical and emotional realities. If we aren't proactive in these areas, physical problems may arise, potentially leading to a downward spiral.

Working less, either because of retirement or health challenges, can create problems if our income or activity level decreases as a result.

Relationships change. When our kids become adults with families of their own, we may not know how to manage the ups and downs and new dynamics these factors create. As our own parents enter their later years, many new difficulties can arrive at our doorsteps.

This list of reasons for pessimism versus optimism may seem overwhelming, but we don't have to give in to a downward emotional and mental pull. We can actually become more fulfilled and joyful as we advance in years in spite of various challenges. Journey with us to learn how to choose positive options for yourself. We've gathered information from others who have vast experience in the topics we'll cover, and we can't wait to share their inspiring stories and resources with you.

This book is designed so you can read it straight through and also use it as a reference when you need help with different topics. Toward that goal, we've written in a question-and-answer format, with each of us taking turns in the book's conversation.

Our hope and prayer is that your golden years—your season of new beginnings, your fresh start—will be a time of joy, peace, and fulfillment. That reality is possible for each of us as we make wise choices at each turn in the road.

Let's advance onward and upward, embracing the adventure ahead!

Warmly,
Mary, Carol, and Lyn

YOUR LIFE: YOUR VISION AND GOALS

We each get only one life. We have learned the importance of significant people and wise choices. Moving forward in the after-fifty life phase, how will we fuel our passions and pursue our priorities? Living with intentionality is our best friend—let's not miss out!

1

AN EXCITING VISION FOR THESE YEARS

Vision is planning your future with wisdom and imagination in light of your goals and priorities. Will we trudge aimlessly through these years or stride confidently with intention? Let us help you create a vision statement that fits your personality and purpose. Then, let the following chapters help you plan your goals and activities to accomplish your hopes and dreams.

CREATE YOUR CONCISE VISION STATEMENT

What is a vision statement and why do I need one?

MARY: Those are great questions to start our adventure! A vision statement is a short, written description of what you want to accomplish in your life. Use your mission statement as a guide when you're determining how to use your time, making important life decisions, planning how you'll accomplish goals, and realizing your life dreams. The mission statement acts as a guide when you encounter challenges. It inspires and motivates you toward what you want to accomplish.

CAROL: A vision statement includes the dream, the long-term goals, and the guiding principles to direct a person in life. When these areas are in place, I know my daily decisions can align with what is most important to me, what I feel my life is called to be.

LYN: If you aim at nothing, that's exactly what you'll hit. Without vision, we do the next thing that seems necessary; we don't know if we are accomplishing anything of importance to us. A personal vision statement is a filter to determine why we will do something and with whom.

When I was a high school student, my family moved five times. I drifted through many years without any plans or understanding of what or who was important to me for growth, joy, and purpose. We must have a vision. I don't want to aim at nothing and hit that!

MARY: My Aunt Margaret couldn't wait to retire, but then she watched television most of the day, took her dog for walks, and complained about being bored and out of shape. Aunt Kate, on the other hand, determined her overarching purpose was to help people and bring spiritual meaning to their lives, while having fun along the way. She lived in a retirement home for over a decade and used her time leading study groups, volunteering as a chaplain, and spending quality time with her kids and grandchildren. She was filled with intentionality and purpose—laughing and loving her way to the end. As you think of these two women, which life sounds more appealing?

Creating a vision takes imagination and planning. I don't know exactly what I want out of the years ahead. Where should I begin?

CAROL: Start with your interests, goals, strengths, dreams, and values. By now you probably know where you want to invest your time, energy and finances in the years ahead. Who do you hope will receive the benefits of your time and energy?

Write down all your thoughts about the *what* and the *who*. Synthesize those thoughts into a few sentences about what you hope to accomplish overall. Word it in a way you can get excited about.

LYN: A conversation with a good friend or family member can help get your ideas flowing. Write down your ideas as you talk. Now that we are over fifty (many of us *much* older), it's important to really take notice of how far we have come in this life, and to consider what we want to accomplish before we die.

What are some examples of vision statements for this season of life?

MARY: Here are some simple and complex examples that people have written:

"My vision is to help my family, friends, and others live the most abundant life possible for them."

"My vision is to love God, love people, and enjoy life along the way."

"My vision is to help create change and a positive environment in my family, my work, and my community. I will utilize the talents God has given me and participate in my life with energy, purpose and gratitude, while providing a positive role model for my children and grandchildren."

CAROL: I created a personal vision statement back in college. I internalized the idea of making my moments and days count for that which outlasts me. This vision has endured through the years: "To daily live my life connecting everyone I meet to God's love and purpose."

Can you give some practical steps for getting started with planning my vision?

MARY: An internet search might help you consider different approaches to writing your personal vision statement. Here are some simple steps I like.

1. Answer these questions about yourself:

    ○ What personal qualities do you most want to emphasize in yourself?

    ○ What strengths do you have?

    ○ What life values do you consider important?

    ○ How can you use and display these qualities, strengths, and values in areas like family, work, community, and spiritual life?

2. Visualize yourself five or ten years from now. What qualities do you hope to possess, and what would you like to have accomplished with the people and areas of life most important to you?

3. Using the information above, write a few sentences describing what you'd like to be and achieve during this time. Write as many drafts as necessary. Take time to get it just right for yourself. You might have a friend or family member help you. You'll know your vision statement is right when reading it makes you feel excited and inspired.

My vision statement seems too general and vague. How specific should it be?

LYN: As you begin planning your vision statement, consider both who you are at this moment and who you want to be in the future. In the following chapters, you will have the opportunity to crystallize your overall thoughts and musings into specifics—to bring what is deep in your heart into reality. You'll process moving from your generalized vision statement into specific goals, then into individual activities.

MARY: Your vision statement should be broad and non-specific.

Devoting myself to things of eternal value is important to me. How can I reflect this in my vision statement?

LYN: Knowing what eternity means to you is critical in phrasing your vision. As you work through the approach Mary described, be sure to incorporate eternal outcomes.

MARY: Use wording that expresses and includes eternal purposes. Consider phrases like "to have an eternal impact," or "for God's purposes," or "spiritual influence."

CAROL: A mentor of mine always filtered his decisions through the grid of "loving God and loving people, with the goal of impacting the world." A lot of normal things can be eternal when we approach them with an intentional mindset.

I love the illustration of filling a jar with rocks, pebbles, and sand. I must put my big rocks (things that have eternal value like growing my relationship with God, serving his purposes, caring for my family, etc.) in the jar first in order to pour the pebbles (i.e., job, minor goals) in around the rocks. Finally, I add the sand (material possessions, hobbies). If I start with the sand, I won't have enough room left for the pebbles and big rocks. Your vision statement would emphasize your overarching goals, especially regarding the "big rocks" in your life. For example: "I want my life to make a spiritual impact for God's purposes in my family, at work, in my community, and in all my endeavors."

What season am I in? Each decade—fifties, sixties, seventies, eighties, and nineties—seems so different. How do these differences affect my vision and planning?

LYN: Aging brings significant life changes. We experienced developmental changes of life from zero to fifty and will continue to do so. In each decade, wisdom calls for us to be intentional about what we want to accomplish in ourselves and with regard to others in our sphere.

MARY: Work, retirement, health, grown kids, grandchildren, finances, and other factors will affect each decade. With significant life changes, specific goals and activities may change, but your vision will likely remain solid. Our core values and strengths change little over time. This is why your vision statement should be broad and non-specific. Let's say your vision statement is simply "to love God and love people." That would play out one way when you're in your fifties working as a realtor, helping people find a house with great care and skill. As a retired person in your seventies, you might live out that same vision by spending time with your grandchildren, visiting sick people in the hospital for your church, and writing your memoir for future generations.

I'm barely paying my bills. My work, family, and home chores take up all my time. How can I fit in anything else?

LYN: Although these areas take up time in your life, you can make changes in the ways you approach them and the people involved. These changes can determine how rewarded or discouraged you will feel in your final days. This is why reflecting on your goals and creating a vision statement is so important.

When I turned fifty, I decided to approach everything with gratitude and wonder. This mindset shift does not add anything to my schedule, but it shapes how I fulfill my goals and tremendously enhances my life.

CAROL: Instead of being overwhelmed by the list of things I must get done, I ask the Lord, "Is this mine to take?" This week, an acquaintance came over to meet with my houseguest. Instead of sitting outside talking with them, I chose to get something done inside the house. It's a small example of accomplishing things with the mindset and values most important to me.

How does the priority of family balance itself out in my vision statement?

MARY: We must each order our priorities so we know where to focus our time and energy. I always say I wish I had three separate bodies to live through because there's so much I want to do. I overextended myself for many years and my health suffered, so I don't want to do that again! God is my top priority. My family and self-care practices come right after that. My vision statement includes loving God and loving people, so family is at the top of that list of people. The way that plays out in my schedule varies since many people in my family live in different states.

CAROL: I need to learn to prioritize myself. As flight attendants say, "put the oxygen mask on yourself first so you can put it on others." One of my friends calls me "The Juggler." Keeping all the balls in the air is a challenge. Two balls I often drop are self-care and reserving energy for my husband after a long day. My top values in life are God, self-care, my significant other, my family, and my life calling. My family is tremendously important to me, but it is one high priority in my life among others. Since God is my starting point, all other priorities flow from there.

LYN: For over fifty years, a major part of our focus has been our parents, children, extended family, and significant others. While those values don't change, many of us find we have more time in this season to include other things we've really wanted to do. I've always been concerned about meeting others' needs or dreams. It is high time I allot focus to my own needs and dreams. Having launched my children, they now want me to focus on myself (and not always try to micromanage their worlds). Knowing I serve others in this season by being the best person I can be is marvelous.

MARY: Our vision statement might be different than earlier phases of life because we now have more time to do things we want to do. For example, my vision might now include serving people in my community and pursuing my creative endeavors, so the priority of my family might be included in my vision like this: "I want to express love to my family, to my community, and through my creative endeavors."

UNCERTAINTIES

I prefer to live one day at a time. I'd rather not create a "vision statement."

MARY: I completely understand your feelings, and I believe that living one day at a time is very important.. However, desires we'd like to see fulfilled exist deep in each of our hearts. If we don't identify these and make some type of plan to accomplish them, we won't feel satisfied and at peace.

CAROL: I don't think that these ideas exclude each other. When we know what we are aiming for through a vision statement, we can relax and live one day at a time with purpose and influence.

LYN: After my first fifty years of life, I am now able to look back and see those times I didn't consider what was going on or what was coming up—I *only* lived one day at a time. I didn't think about how I wanted to impact that season. As a result, I have many regrets. Living one day at a time with intent is a healthy mindset, and after we have determined where to focus our time and energy, we can be fully present.

Once I've decided upon my overall vision and hope for this season of life, can I change it?

CAROL: Yes. Life is messy and personal growth is a process. I have experienced moments and seasons that clarify my desires and goals. At those points, I tweak, add to, or change my vision statement.

LYN: Absolutely. We must always be aware of significant changes in our lives and be ready and willing to make some modifications. As Mary shared before, our vision statement reflects our values, goals, dreams, and strengths. If any one of these areas gets fulfilled or changes drastically, a change of vision may be required.

How much influence should my significant other have on my dreams and future?

MARY: Let's consider two aspects of this question. First, "Should I communicate with my significant other about my vision statement?" Second, "Should my significant other be included within the scope of my vision statement?"

To the first question, I would answer "yes." Hopefully, your relationship is such that you talk about the important things in your life. Input from people who know you well and have your best interests in mind is always helpful. If your relationship isn't healthy enough for this type of interaction, you might pursue counseling so that you can enjoy your relationship more fully.

As far as including your significant other within your vision statement, I would say that he or she might fall into a general category like, "loving people," "loving my family," or "influencing everyone around me." You could then write specific intentions concerning your significant other in your goals and create activities that flow out of your vision.

CAROL: When I made my vows to my husband Stuart, our lives became one. I still clearly have my own life, choices, passions, and strengths. However, since my relationship with Stuart is a high priority, I share and process my dreams and decisions with him on an ongoing basis. I listen to his responses and value his input. We make most major decisions together based upon wisdom that we each contribute.

When we evaluated going overseas to work in a collegiate ministry, we were conflicted. I decided to write a very specific "pros and cons" list while Stuart worked in our basement. I walked down to show him my list. Lo and behold, he had written a "pros and cons" list at the same time. We spent five wonderful years in Costa Rica ministering to college students and eating gallo pinto.

My spouse has a disabling chronic illness that requires most of my day. How can I have any other vision than caregiving?

MARY: This must be a very challenging time in your life, and I commend you for your devotion and self-sacrifice. It's normal to go through our days completing tasks, checking things off lists, and doing what needs to be done. A vision statement elevates us above the mundane tasks of life, giving us renewed purpose and inspiration. It helps us to be the best version of ourselves, a person we can be proud of. Possible vision statements in a situation like yours might be:

- ○ "I will live my life with love, peace, and joy as I give to the well-being of others, especially my spouse."
- ○ "I will love God with all my heart, soul, mind, and strength, and will love people with God's self-sacrificing love."
- ○ "I will live for the good of others, particularly my spouse, while placing a high priority on my own self-care."

CAROL: A vision to successfully care for your spouse is honorable, admirable, and worth every ounce of your time, money and effort. If you have extra time and energy, think about how you want to approach other interests, family relationships, finances, etc. These can provide refreshment to keep you going through difficult days.

My sweet friend Wendy has a grown daughter, Katie, who has many special needs. Wendy created a home-baked treat business which allowed Katie to push a cart through office buildings offering breaktime snacks. Wendy combined her caregiving role toward Katie and her strengths in home baking to provide a productive and impactful service toward others. Is there anything involving your strengths and values that would be possible, and maybe even life-giving, for you? It doesn't have to be as big as what Wendy did, but perhaps it would involve your caregiving in some way.

LYN: Kind treatment toward a spouse speaks volumes about love, responsibility, and hope to family, friends, and medical staff—as well as to the spouse. We never know who may be watching us and what kind of impression and impact we will leave. Keep your vision statement nearby to infuse your mundane activities with energy and purpose.

I will be in a nursing home from now on. Does having a vision even apply to me?

CAROL: Absolutely. Whether you are a twenty-year-old college student or an eighty-year-old living in a nursing home, everyone benefits from having a vision for their lives. We all need motivation, focus, and inspiration to keep moving forward. Your vision may be as simple as focusing on other people in the nursing home to keep your thoughts going outward and not too inward. People who isolate themselves have a harder time staying positive.

I know of an elderly woman in a nursing facility who asked people to email her their prayer needs. While she was restricted in her physical movement, this lady would pray specifically for needs in her community and family. Someday I might have the privilege of that high vision of praying for others full-time.

LYN: So much of life is lived within our hearts and minds. Many caregivers and people around you desperately need to be noticed, encouraged, or prayed for. We are often unaware of the impact we make on others. Even with a deteriorating diagnosis, we can develop our inner life and character. This can increase our sense of well-being and peace. If we are still alive, there is purpose for our lives.

I long to feel confident about my future, but I'm worried about many things in the world and in my own life. How can I be excited about planning the future when everything seems to be going downhill?

CAROL: This reminds me of a time I dated someone I really liked. I was devastated when we broke up. A co-worker reminded me I still had many unbroken areas to focus upon and enjoy, even though this area of my life was broken. This is true for all of us. Do we dwell upon the part of the glass that is half-empty, or half-full?

Truly, you are not the only one worried about the state of the world. Many people struggle to keep a positive mindset in our current times. Try to remember you can only control certain things that pertain to you, and the things you can't control are not worth your energy. Continue to go about your planning with an optimistic mindset, working toward your desired goals and objectives. In this way, you will improve the things you can control and move forward in areas important to you.

LYN: Ongoing trials and troubles will always exist in our world. With the plethora of media options available, it's easy to fill our minds with all the bad news and become overwhelmed.

When I watch too much news or study negative topics, doubt and fear begin to fill my mind. However, I've also realized many sources cover good things that are happening.

For one month, I chose to not watch or listen to the regular news. I substituted positive news and input. This incredible exercise produced peace in my heart, and I was able to regain my excitement for my future. I continue to be very careful with what I allow into my mind.

People talk about reinventing themselves. How can I do this?

MARY: Reinventing yourself is an interesting idea. Our culture defines this concept as identifying things you don't like about yourself and replacing them with better options. It can involve external characteristics, like your job, hobbies, appearance, relationships, and location. It can also mean changing how you think and behave. It might mean breaking bad habits, adopting a new life skill, or making a major career change.

Truly reinventing yourself usually involves making major changes in your life. When this is the case, people should consider why they want to make the changes, and be sure that their reasons are healthy, wise, and best for the long haul.

CAROL: What if reinventing is actually maturing in who we already are? It's like a little chick inside an egg who eventually bursts out with freedom and energy, ready to go in new directions. Reflection and quiet have helped me reinvent areas of my life. We continually grow and learn new things, becoming new versions of ourselves.

Compared with younger people, individuals in later decades of life sometimes seem to have outdated ideas and goals. In light of this, how should we adjust our vision and planning?

LYN: Awareness of the trends and changes occurring in younger generations is important, since these factors may affect our adult children and grandchildren. We don't need to try to be young again, but we have wisdom and valuable life experience to offer younger families and friends. We have seen trends come and go. We can recognize which trends are unwise and which are a matter of preference. This is an opportunity to realize our worth and become intentional in the lives of those who are younger.

MARY: We want to stay relevant and able to relate well with the people and spheres of influence important to us. When we seem outdated or uninformed, we lose credibility with those we most want to communicate with or influence.

To your point about a vision statement, you could add something about this area as a specific goal. For example, if my vision includes having a positive impact on my children and grandchildren, one of my goals might be to stay current with the ideas and trends in their age groups. A related activity could be to regularly read a magazine or website for that age group—or one that helps my generation to relate in their context.

Since we can never know the future, why should we try to plan and predict? Our hopes and dreams may not matter if things change.

CAROL: If we wander through these years with no plan or intentionality, we won't accomplish the things most important to us. As Lyn wrote previously, if we aim at nothing, we will hit it every time.

In life, there is my part, and then there is God's part. I am responsible for doing my part and controlling my focus in life. God is in control over everything that happens, even amidst the continual changes.

MARY: God ultimately weaves our storyline into his masterpiece plan. Like an air traffic controller at an airport, God sees all the aircraft and coordinates their activities, even amidst apparent unexpected changes and chaos.

LYN: I will add that even though our future is not known, certain realities are. Winter will always follow fall. After your fifties come your sixties. We may not know the actual circumstances of the future, but we do know that our significant people will need unconditional love, and that we will leave an impression on anyone we come into contact with. If reality doesn't meet our expectations, we will still be there and will still need to bring hope and love into the world. Planning allows us to be intentional about who we are in any given situation.

I feel my life is almost over. How can I plan what to do with my life?

CAROL: Jim Elliot said, "Wherever you are, be all there! Live to the hilt every situation you believe to be the will of God." We need to live to the fullest whatever moments, days, and years we have. This means being present where I am: focusing upon the people and specific opportunities that surround me, even in my final stretch.

I have a succinct list of priorities I live by every day: My faith in God; my relationship with my husband; my relationship with our grown kids and grandkids; and the specific ministry to which I'm called. I pray daily for the needs that surround me, including key relationships, my community, and those who are suffering. When my body grows weak, I can grow stronger as a prayer warrior, praying fervently for others.

This is the way I hope to live my life, even through my last days on this planet.

LYN: It's important to realize that the present is a gift—a present. Even in our final years, weeks, or days, we can plan to stay present in our final moments and live them for our values and goals. Often life gets so hustle-bustle that no one feels seen or heard. As we near the end of our series of life events, we can make our ultimate finish strong and impactful by focusing on what's most important to us. Remember, as long as we are alive, we have opportunities to touch others with what we say and do.

As a grandmother, I live the truth that I can easily enjoy my granddaughters, stay right in the moment, and accomplish goals for my time with them. I answer their questions thoroughly and look them right in the eye, encouraging and connecting with them. I give them the *present* of staying present with them while living out my vision.

What if what I intend to do is wrong and I miss out?

LYN: Being wrong, experiencing failure, and making mistakes—these are all part of a life well-lived. As a young mom, I wanted to do everything exactly right. I became legalistic and small-minded. My family worried about me, but I just thought they were the problem. Once I realized I was alienating many of the key people I wanted to influence, I was able to see my mistakes, ask forgiveness, and become more balanced.

Feeling we've "missed out" is always hard, but we can glean a lesson from the situation and become a better person for the next time. Learning from circumstances of regret allows us to become much wiser and able to mentor others in that area. I can also model giving myself grace when I feel I've made a mistake.

CAROL: As we embrace our faith and the overarching plan of God, we are assured that even our greatest failures will work together for good. Like my mother-in-law used to say, "It is good to be humbled by life." I have experienced this often in my well-intentioned parenting journey. The amazing thing is we can make changes even after falling short. The experience makes us more receptive to others' pain because we understand our own shortcomings.

MARY: We will all need a course correction at times. A few years ago I got very excited about my involvement in theater and over-committed my time. I loved the performances, rehearsals, and classes, but after a while I realized I was missing out on more important priorities. Self-correction wasn't easy, but I am happier giving more time to areas significant to me in the long run.

Part of life is trying things and then re-calibrating when needed. I hope my children and grandchildren can learn as I model making mistakes, self-correcting, and giving myself lots of compassion and grace along the way.

BEFORE WE COMMIT: THINGS WE MUST KNOW

How do I live out my vision daily?

LYN: Reviewing and pondering your vision will inspire you. Write your vision statement on small cards or sticky notes to post around your home and workplace. Create a computer screensaver or a picture for your bathroom or bedroom. Meditating on the commitment you have made to yourself will renew your thoughts and help keep you on track for what you hope to accomplish in life.

CAROL: I write my vision statement in my daily journal so I can look at it and pray for it regularly. Also, acrostics have helped me through the years to keep my mind focused on what is important to me. This is the one I've been using recently:

Savior God and Stuart

Healthy boundaries in daily life

Authorship of this book, Athletes in Action, Mom's Alzheimer's, Adult children

Real grandparenting

Eating, exercise, and Encore group

How should I proceed if my vision depends on others to help me?

CAROL: Your vision will often depend upon others. Mine definitely does.

MARY: I've sometimes realized my vision requires too many people. You can always alter your vision to be more realistic.

LYN: Once you feel certain of your vision statement, it's important that you remain faithful to your vision no matter what someone else does or doesn't do. When we persist in what we said we were going to do, we often inspire others to do the same.

CAROL: My response is my responsibility. I can only control my part. If I'm faithful, I do what I can do regardless of how others respond.

MARY: Hudson Taylor said, "God's work, done God's way, will never lack God's supply." When we live in sync with what is supposed to happen, the resources and people will be there. When we try something over and over, and the people and resources aren't there, that's a signal to pause and consider whether we're going in the right direction or whether things need to be done differently than we originally envisioned. We can pause, pray, then proceed accordingly.

How do I communicate my vision to family and friends?

LYN: First, I want to commend you for wanting to communicate with your key sphere of influence. That's so important.

MARY: Communication involves two categories of people: family and friends we simply want to inform, and those who will be involved in the fulfillment of our vision.

LYN: For both of these categories, here are some strategies you might use:

1. Intentionally discuss your vision and what you want to accomplish with the people who will be affected. They will have an understanding of your choices going forward and will possibly be motivated by what you communicate. When we verbally express the reasons for our behavior to our intimate community, we are more likely to be successful in our commitment.
2. If you think it would be helpful, write your vision or a version of it and post it on the refrigerator and other key locations for others to read and think about.
3. In conversation, begin to use phrases and sentences that motivate yourself and others to work toward your vision.

CAROL: Jo is a friend whose life has deeply impacted mine. Ten years ago she buried her twenty-five-year-old son. Two years ago she buried her sixty-eight-year old husband. She has five other adult children and seven grandchildren. She has inspired her family by communicating her vision. "I can grieve and move forward, knowing that my lifelong goal is to live one day at a time doing what God has called me to." This succinct statement has a powerful influence on others, especially amidst her grief.

Also, I think of the phrase "a lot more is caught than taught." How we live will be very important and it will reflect our vision clearly to our family and friends.

MARY: People become inspired and motivated when they see us living something out, and especially when we've explained what we are doing. Our words and actions combined can make a powerful impact.

TAKE ACTION

1. Visualize yourself five or ten years from now and answer these questions:

    o   What personal qualities do you want to have developed?

    o   What do you want to have achieved during this time period?

    o   What do you want to be remembered for?

    o   Who do you want to impact?

    o   What is on your bucket list—what are the things you've never done but want to do before you die?

2. Now, write your vision statement. It's okay to write and rewrite it over several days. Try to use no more than three sentences. Write it so you feel excited and inspired when you read it. Ask others for their help and input as needed. Then use it to live your best life.

3. Look through the resources in Section 4, Chapter 1. Write down any that would be helpful for you. Make a plan to use the resources and add them to your calendar.

2

REDISCOVER YOUR PASSIONS AND STRENGTHS

Let's dive in and explore your passions and strengths to help clarify your goals and activities.

WHAT MAKES YOU TICK?

How can I discover my passions and strengths?

MARY: Great question! Many helpful tools and exercises are available for this purpose. We've included a lot of them at the end of this book, in Section 4: Chapter 2.

CAROL: Think about what is easy for you. Determine what doesn't feel like it takes effort or produces stress. Olympic track athlete Eric Lidell once said, "God made me fast. And when I run, I feel his pleasure." Have you done something that made you feel God's pleasure in you, his blessing on you? If so, what were your strengths and passions in that experience?

MARY: Think of experiences throughout your life that you really enjoyed or did well, even back in elementary and high school. What strengths and passions did you experience in those times? They were probably part of the core of who you are. Write them down.

LYN: Become your own Sherlock Holmes. Everything you do reveals aspects of your personality puzzle. Your concerns, opinions, feelings, and actions are clues to discovering your strengths. The strengths and passions that bring you joy and peace are also critical parts of your innermost equation.

I've asked my husband, children, and very close friends what they think I'm good at. Knowing how I come across to others has given me great insight into what my unique, God-given purposes are.

How can I find what I feel strongly about?

LYN: The ways we use our time reveals what we care about. Review your experiences, from your first job until now. Think through how you felt during each of your time frames and projects. What did you especially enjoy or feel committed to? As you give yourself time to reflect upon your life, you may recognize your natural gifts, talents, and values. You probably gained skills and knowledge in those areas along the way.

CAROL: These questions help me: What do I wake up thinking about because it's important to me? What would make me pound my fist on the table because I value something so much?

MARY: Here are a few more ideas:

1. Make a list of things you love to do.
2. Determine your values—what is most important to you in life? Do an internet search for the word "values" if you don't know where to start.
3. Consider the achievements you are most proud of. What do they reveal?
4. Journal for a week regarding "What am I passionate about?" Write down whatever comes to mind.
5. Have a conversation about your thoughts with a family member or friend. Ask what they see in you.

What are some ways I can inspire myself to have more passion?

LYN: There are several practical things to consider. Take great care of yourself physically. Your physical body tremendously affects your emotions and mindset. We often neglect some of the most important choices we can make, like getting plenty of sleep, exercising regularly, and eating correctly. If I am exhausted or hungry—or have too much junk food, sugar, or alcohol—I find that I am not passionate about anything. Instead, I'm prone to grumble, see the world's shortcomings, and ignore my goals because I just don't feel motivated.

Another way to increase your passion is to surround yourself with people who are passionate about your interests. Their enthusiasm may rub off on you, and they will provide new ideas for you to ponder and incorporate into your life.

CAROL: I have a quote by Moliére hanging in my office: "Passion is a powerful force that cannot be stopped." I love the idea of living for something beyond myself, of being a significant part, though small, of the big picture of this life I am living. This inspires me to step out and contribute the part that only I am made to do.

MARY: We all have such different personalities. Some people experience very strong feelings while others are laid-back. I think the important thing is to be motivated. Motivation comes in a variety of ways. If you're looking for motivation, try doing an internet search for "how to get more motivated." You will find a plethora of articles, YouTube videos, etc. Look through those to find information specifically helpful for you.

THAT'S ALL GOOD BUT . . .

When I think about my strengths, I compare myself to others, and I come up short. What can I do about this?

MARY: Many of us have compared ourselves to others all our lives, making us feel insecure. Insecurity can be even more of a problem after fifty because our culture tends to value individuals less as they age, a perception filled with faulty thinking. Therefore, we must proactively renew our minds with the following truths:

- Every human is infinitely valuable regardless of age.
- There are things only I can do, and I should do those with all my might.
- Each person has her own individual strengths and weaknesses.

When we focus upon someone else's strengths, we sometimes overlook our own. Even the great apostle Peter compared himself to the apostle John when they walked down the road with Jesus. Jesus simply said to him, "You must follow me" (John 21:22). We each have to follow our own calling and focus upon that.

CAROL: God created me uniquely, and he has unique things he wants me to do. Yes, I have weaknesses, and so do the people I'm comparing myself to. I like the analogy that our physical bodies are made up of many parts that are all valuable. Each part has its way of functioning to contribute to the whole. The same is true with the body of God's people. When I compare, I work to redirect my thoughts to these truths. Reframing thoughts can be difficult, and I'm often tempted to stay in a negative thinking pattern, but I experience such freedom when I choose to create the habit of remembering these positive truths.

My mom is seventy-five and chronically ill. She can't leave her house
much. How can I help her evaluate her strengths, passions, and vision?

MARY: Many people find it difficult to believe I was an invalid for an extended period, barely able to leave the house. That's another story, though, and I now live a normal life with a full schedule. But I can identify with your mom.

She may not have a lot of energy or desire to think about these things, but even the smallest shift of focus toward her purpose can help her. You could reminisce with her about things she's been good at and loved doing in her past and discuss how those could play out in her current situation. She can pray for people who do things she's interested in—my background is in theater, so I pray for performers and artists—along with praying for loved ones. Perhaps she can write notes to loved ones, call them, or leave voicemails.

Also, our strengths, passions, and vision are not all about productivity. They can include our own personal growth. Does your mom like to read or sit quietly in God's presence, getting to know him more? She can grow through books and audiobooks, or even take a course. Your willingness to collaborate may enable your mom to live her final years with the peace and joy that come from living with a purpose—a blessing for both of you.

CAROL: Your mom can have a unique impact on one life at a time from her home. Can she invite friends and family over with the intentionality of reflecting God's love through her words and prayers? This would bless them and be a blessing to her as well.

Events and people tend to drain me. As I live out my passions, how can I
avoid exhaustion?

MARY: It sounds like you might be an introvert. If that is the case, you'll want to plan time to refresh and recharge before and after being with people. I love the true definitions for introverts and extroverts, which many people don't understand. Introverts are refueled and energized by having time alone, while extroverts are refueled and energized by being with people. One is not better than the other. One does not like people more than the other. Each has its own advantages and purposes, allowing you to accomplish what you were uniquely created to do and be.

One of the advantages of introversion is the ability to be by yourself for longer periods of time without requiring the presence of people. Whether you're an introvert or extrovert, taking care of yourself physically in terms of nutrition, exercise, and sleep is important. When we lack these things, we get drained more easily.

CAROL: Several years ago, I searched for treasures at the Round Top Antique Festival in Texas and came across a sign that would change my life: "Be fearless in the pursuit of what sets your soul on fire." I see this sign every day on my bathroom counter and the reminder continually recharges my battery.

We can refuel ourselves in practical ways through daily practices like devotional time, interaction with significant family and friends, involvement with personal groups of various types, and church commitments. Noticing and surrounding ourselves with things of beauty can revitalize us and bring refreshment to our souls.

A wise friend once noted we will inevitably get tired in life, so why not get tired doing things that outlast us and leave an impact on others?

LYN: Sometimes it helps me to remind myself of why I am doing something, like an event. Thinking through what my presence and input can provide gives me motivation to be interested and mentally present.

I had the privilege of leading an organization. I traveled a great deal for speaking engagements and activities, explaining the mission and goals to potential donors. When I felt I could not do it another moment, I reminded myself of the precious people who needed help. The knowledge that I was the conduit to rally others to action on their behalf fired me up and took away the doldrums.

In addition to keeping my commitments, I always have a pre-planned exit strategy to help me feel safe and able to leave when I'm ready. Because of all these things, I have been able to keep going with cheerful grace and laser-focused energy.

I am passionate about and want to accomplish many things; how can I fit them all in at this age?

LYN: I'm a huge believer in keeping a calendar as a planning tool to keep track of my daily, weekly, and monthly goals and activities. When I just keep priorities and ideas in my head, I forget and am easily distracted. Writing and planning with my calendar locks them down.

Also, we must allot sections of our day for our own personal non-negotiables. This will include our exercise and rest as well as personal times of mental, spiritual, and physical engagements we are passionate about. As we regularly review upcoming events for the next few days or weeks, this discipline allows us to be cognizant of our goals and intentions.

During review, I often choose to move entries to other days to ensure I am not expecting more than I can do. Margin in your schedule leaves room for personal rest times and allows for unexpected things to come up without causing you stress.

MARY: Margin and boundaries are both crucial. Boundaries require knowing when to say no to things. You may even have to say no to yourself. You can only accomplish a certain amount before exhausting your inner resources.

CAROL: Check out the resource in Section 4, Chapter 2: *At a Glance Yearly, Monthly and Daily Calendars.* It's a very practical way to accomplish the things Lyn and Mary talked about.

My budget is limited. How can I live passionately without money?

MARY: Some of us barely get by each month, some have a little extra financially, and some have plenty. Regardless of income, living passionately means approaching whatever is in your schedule with a mindset that prioritizes what is most important to you in life. Once you determine your values and overarching goals, you can use these as mental filters and motivations for approaching daily activities and other people. This is what we mean by living with vision, rather than simply going from task to task each day.

Let's say my vision and passion is "to live with spiritual depth and demonstrate love for people, changing the lives of those I encounter." If my job is cleaning houses, I can pray for the people who live in them. I can serve my employers with purpose. I can go home and eat with my family, intentionally interacting with love and concern for their best. I can write an encouraging email to my lonely friend and lovingly call my sick father. I can talk to God with thanks and love through it all.

LYN: Wise management of whatever money we have, however small or great, will maximize the fulfillment of our passions. Budgets provide a great picture of how we want our lives to be lived and what is most important to us. We can ask ourselves, "Am I spending in proportion to my passions?"

A monthly review of where we are in our goals, monetarily-speaking, is important. Monthly reviews show us the details of what we allowed to become important. If your spending hasn't reflected what you are most passionate about, tweak it for next month.

And don't forget that saving a little money each week can be applied toward your passions. Small amounts add up and can help make your dreams come true.

TAKE ACTION

- o What achievements in your life are you most proud of? What do they reveal about your strengths and passions?
- o What strengths and capabilities do you see in yourself?
- o When do you feel part of a group or team? How are your strengths apparent in these situations?
- o How can you develop your strengths and habits to fulfill your passions?

Look through the resources in Section 4, Chapter 2. Which ones will you utilize? Make a plan to use the resources and add them to your calendar.

3

DEFINE YOUR GOALS

Now that you've created a vision for this season of life, and know your passions and strengths, it is time to clearly define your goals and activities to fulfill your vision. Start creating your plan of action!

INSTANT FOCUS-BOOSTERS

What's the difference between my vision, goals, and activities?

MARY: This is a great clarifying question. Vision is your general, overarching plan. Specific goals flow from your vision, and you plan activities to reach those goals. The formula looks like this:

$$\text{Vision} > \text{Goals} > \text{Specific Activities}$$

CAROL: They are similar but one difference is that goal setting comes from knowing your vision well. Your specific activities will be an indication of how accurate and concise your goals are in relation to your vision. In most cases, reaching your goals means you are accomplishing your vision's purpose.

Can you give some examples of vision, goals, and activities, as differentiated from each other?

LYN: Let's say my vision is simply to love God and people. One of my goals might be to show God's love in my workplace and to intentionally connect with each person. Finally, a specific activity could be to invite one coworker to have our lunch break together each week.

Or, maybe my overarching vision is to experience joy, love, and peace, and extend this to others. One of my goals under this is to experience life with joy—and with willingness to look at trials as opportunities to grow and learn. A subsequent activity might be to read a specific book about suffering that leads me to grow and learn.

I know my vision and I've discovered my strengths and passions, so how do I go about planning my goals and activities from here to accomplish my vision?

CAROL: Try asking yourself these questions:

- ○ "What specific goals will help me achieve my vision?"
- ○ "What activities am I most passionate and excited about?"
- ○ "What do I love to do because of my strengths? How could I use my talents to accomplish my vision?"

Nothing in life is more exciting and fulfilling than seeing your vision realized as a result of careful planning, hard work, and perseverance.

Should I try to achieve certain markers in this season of life?

MARY: Many view a human's lifespan as having expected human developmental goals or themes that happen along the way.

Renowned psychologist Erik Erikson developed what is called the "Stage Theory of Psychosocial Development." He believed in the years from 35 to 65, the major focus or "marker" of a person's life is contributing to your family, community, and world. When you think about it, this is the overall goal everyone tries to achieve in these years, evaluating and readjusting to fulfill this. According to Erikson's model, in the years from 65 until death, a focus or "marker" is reflecting on your life to determine whether you are satisfied and fulfilled with your lifespan and making changes as a result.

CAROL: One of my personal markers is to live one day at a time faithfully. I try to do "the next thing" with integrity day by day. Living this way brings increasing peace to my heart.

LYN: Yes, one of the most important markers of achievement is peace within our hearts. For me, another marker is living successfully as the matriarch of my clan, which helps to determine the routes I take and the memories I initiate for my family. Leading well is one of the ways I want to make my mark.

How can I prioritize my goals and activities?

CAROL: Set a time, like Sunday night, to make sure your calendar represents the things you must do. This practical session can be serious but also fun and life-giving. Does my time and the way I spend my finances represent what is most important in my life along with the dreams and goals I want to achieve?

LYN: It's critical to take intentional time to review the upcoming week. It's also critical to review our upcoming months, which will make up our years, to ensure we're fulfilling all we want in life.

Planning our values and vision must be a prioritized activity. I spend time in December preparing for the year ahead. This key activity ensures my hours and days truly accomplish what is important to me.

I consider goals in several categories for the hours and days ahead.

Spiritual

Health

Family

Friends

Career

Philanthropy/Ministry

Home

I've tried listing goals before but never complete them. Do you have any ideas or tips for making them happen?

MARY: Ask a friend to be your accountability partner and meet regularly. Enter this in your calendar as a recurring scheduled activity. Otherwise, it's easy to forget. Meeting with an accountability partner keeps your hopes and goals at the forefront of your mind, and this can be a fun time over coffee or lunch as well.

Another approach is to consult a life coach, someone trained to help people with exactly this. A life coach is also beneficial if procrastination is your difficulty.

LYN: I struggled with not accomplishing my goals for many years. Through trial and error, I learned to plan specific activities to achieve my goals, and then to write them down in my calendar—including exactly how much time I needed for each goal and activity. I didn't give up, and now, it's great to have accomplished so much.

Be sure to leave margin in your days since we never know what unexpected things will come into our lives. We need to leave enough time in our schedules for unforeseen circumstances. Otherwise, we become tired or overly stressed when things happen, or we give up on prioritizing what is most important to us.

CAROL: Someone taught me the SMART acrostic when thinking through my goals and activities. Make each one:

S-Specific

M-Measurable

A-Attainable

R-Realistic (am I aiming too high or too low?)

T-Timely (create deadlines for myself)

What is a strategy to include all the items on my lists of plans?

LYN: As we said before, it helps to review daily or weekly where you are and where you want to be. Review and tweak. Review and tweak. Don't just let life happen; instead, determine to be focused and wise with your energy and time. Make sure you are living your calling and not just dealing with everyone else's wants or emergencies.

MARY: A friend of mine worked in a large, busy office, and he had this sign on his door: "Excuse me if I don't let your lack of planning interfere with my carefully prepared schedule." It's so easy to live according to the interruptions and plans of others. I still remember a small booklet from my college years entitled "The Tyranny of the Urgent." The seemingly urgent can become the dominating factor driving our lives, even though these things are not priorities for us.

Also, be sure you're not trying to accomplish too much. Howard Hendricks, a well-loved and respected theologian and professor at Dallas Theological Seminary, asked, "What is it you *must* do?" Weed out the good priorities and focus on the best. It is possible to have too many ideas, and we need to eliminate the ones which aren't of utmost importance to us.

If I have ideas that seem unrealistic, should I still try to make them work?

CAROL: A goal can be realistic and yet challenging at the same time. That balance is sometimes hard to find but it can also be very motivating.

In my prayer journal, I keep a list of things that seem unrealistic to hope for in my life. I've learned that God may answer "yes," "no," or "wait," using a variety of methods. I pray for God to guide me through circumstances, conversations, and my own thoughts. Over time, I learn whether to proceed with an idea or leave it behind.

LYN: Sometimes an idea seems unrealistic because it has multiple parts that need to be broken down and planned individually. Review the idea and determine what steps will be needed to accomplish it.

Think through how you will break up the idea into small sections and what needs to be done before something else can be addressed. Consider other people you may need to include in each task. Be sure to plan realistically, allowing margin in your life and schedule, as we addressed previously.

Ideas with substance will often need to be stretched through many months or years because they are big and will make a huge impact one day. Don't shrink back just because it feels like a lot. Visions and goals are often bigger than we are. Take small steps and you will find yourself having accomplished many grand purposes for your life.

MARY: Get input from others about whether your ideas are realistic. Ask two or three trusted people to give you their honest feedback and to help you tweak your ideas if needed. Don't hinder yourself by becoming defensive if they tell you things you don't want to hear. This practice of getting input from others has helped steer me through many seasons and decisions of life. If your advisors feel an idea is totally unrealistic, ask them to help guide you as you consider alternative options.

What if I only have one or two goals?

LYN: There is no competition or comparison here. This is your life and your callings. One or two goals is wonderful. List the specific activities needed to accomplish those goals, and you are off to a wonderful life.

MARY: Some goals are so big, they will require a substantial amount of your time and energy. For example, let's say your overall goal is to "help others, using my specific gifts." Fulfilling that could take up a great portion of each day. It might require a multi-faceted plan, encompassing many years.

How does maintaining my financial lifestyle fit in with planning my vision, purposes, and goals?

LYN: A wise CPA friend of mine once said, "Our budget is the skeleton on which our vision hangs." Living within our means is critical to living with peace and integrity. Your money allows you to realize what your limitations may be. It allows you to plan monthly and yearly to know when you can begin things, and when you need to wait and save for that goal.

MARY: God will always fund work he wants completed. When we live in sync with what is supposed to happen, the money will be provided. Our finances can be a helpful guide, showing us which paths to follow and which paths to avoid.

I'M IN, ARE THEY?

Often it feels as if the people who I want to be my priority don't feel the same about me. What can I do?

MARY: I'm not sure if you're talking about family members that you'd like to spend more time with, or potential "helpers" in achieving your goals. I'll talk first about the family members.

It's frustrating when one of our highest goals is to enjoy and influence our children, grandchildren, and other family members, but they don't seem as interested. We're going to address this thoroughly in Section 2. For now, I'll say that if this is your goal, assess each person's receptivity and availability to you. If there are problems with this, an "activity" in your plan could be to get input from books, assessment tools, or a counselor. You may need to change things about yourself, including your expectations, in order to move forward with your heart's desire. All of us need to change things about ourselves and our expectations to have good relationships with loved ones. It requires us to be non-defensive and humble, which are two necessary qualities in successful relationships.

CAROL: I'll pick up the baton and run from here, addressing your potential "helpers" in achieving your goals. It's important to talk to prospective supporters while you're planning your vision and strategy. If they're not interested, ask others or reassess your plan. Choosing the right people is a key factor in your own overall enjoyment of your venture. It's okay and even advisable to recognize from the start when someone is just not interested.

Sometimes my significant others are draining to me as I try to meet my goals. How should I handle this?

MARY: People can be divided into four categories: those who are motivated by tasks, those who are motivated by goals, those who are motivated by vision, and those who are motivated by relationships. You may be most motivated by tasks, goals, or vision, rather than relationships.

This doesn't mean that you aren't motivated at all by relationships, but tasks, goals, or vision inspire you more. When this is the case, we can feel drained by people or put them as a lesser priority. It's important to be aware of this and decide which relationships really are your top priority. Then, you won't want to give them second-best in terms of your energy and time.

For me, my immediate family—my husband, my children, their spouses, and my grandchildren—comes before everything else. I want to always make sure I'm giving them my best in terms of energy and time, even though other tasks, goals, and visions are very important in my life. I want to continually keep my internal reservoir full enough, and my schedule available with margin, for these prioritized relationships.

CAROL: Friendships and family are a high priority for me. Friendships can be lifegiving, as can family, and we need to be careful to not push them aside if we are too goal-oriented. It's never worth straining a relationship in my desire to see my goals met.

LYN: This is where life's balance comes in. As we live with others, if we are task-oriented, we can focus on what we are doing with little consideration for another's feelings, thoughts, or needs. People are our most important asset within our family, friends, and work.

Remember, when we get to heaven we cannot take anything with us. We can only take people!

I like to work alone. Why do I need to include people in my plan when I'm more effective on my own?

CAROL: When you have the right people involved in your plan, the end result will usually be a better product.

LYN: An African proverb says, "If you want to fast, go alone, but if you want to go far, go together." Going fast is not always best.

At the end of life, people often find themselves asking, "Who did I influence or impact?" It's important to be proactive now so that we aren't disappointed later with our answer to this question.

MARY: Even a true introvert, who is most energized by being alone, needs people in order to be her best. Even the most isolated task, like being an author, requires the input of others to bring writing to its highest level, to be published, and then marketed. We all need support, encouragement, and input. If being with people is difficult for you, which is not uncommon, you might seek counseling to be able to live your most fulfilled and rewarding life.

TAKE ACTION

It's time to write your specific goals for the coming months or year. Use your vision statement, and from that plan your goals. Take some time to do that now, or after reflecting upon the questions that follow.

- o How would you like to look back on your life and how you spent your time 5 years from now? 10 years? 20 years? What goals do you want to have accomplished?

- o How do you need to change your schedule to focus on the goals that are the most important to you? When do you have trouble saying "no" to something that would interfere with more important goals? How can you change this?

- o How will you measure your ongoing progress in regards to your goals?

Look through the resources in Section 4, Chapter 3. Which ones will you utilize to help you? Make a plan to use the resources and add them to your calendar.

4

YOUR JOB, CAREER, AND COMMITMENTS

What does it look like to make the most of our days? Those days turn to years before we know it. How will you turn your goals into specific activities that can be scheduled into specific days on your calendar?

Remember this formula from Chapter 3?

Vision > Goals > Specific Activities

This chapter guides you in the final step of turning your dreams into precise, identifiable realities.

Can you give an example of turning a vision into a goal and then into a specific activity?

MARY: Okay, let's say my vision is "to help my family, friends, and others live the most abundant life possible for them." One goal from this might be to help my elderly mother, who is in a nursing home, to live a more fulfilled life. An activity to reach this goal could be to have lunch with her once a week in the facility's public lunchroom and help her to develop relationships with the other residents.

My days are filled with my job and furthering my career. Am I supposed to fit in a vision and goals beyond that?

CAROL: Not necessarily. A vision and goals can provide focus and motivation in what you are already doing. You might want to consider setting goals for your whole person, not just the job. These might include the physical, social, mental, and spiritual areas of your life, which will ultimately enhance your work. You can integrate these types of goals into what you're already doing or fit them into your schedule, spaced out through your month or year.

MARY: I'm a big fan of doing some things only once or twice monthly when normally they would be scheduled more often. Another time-saver is to remember this axiom: "Work expands to fill the time allotted." When I think, "This activity will take the entire afternoon," it takes that long. If I think instead, "I'm going to do this in an hour," I work more efficiently and quickly. It's a little game I play, constantly reminding myself during the hour to keep moving along.

Can you describe a schedule where I fit in my job and also fulfill a separate vision and goals?

MARY: One example is my friend Megan. She has a full-time job, but also has a vision to influence and shape the next generation. She volunteers to teach a children's class at her church on Sunday mornings on a rotational basis, so she teaches twice a month for an hour. Those hours add up, and she's impacting children's lives. In this way, she fulfills her vision while maintaining her full-time job.

LYN: It can also be helpful to track your free moments, as well as your job hours, in order to identify time slots where you can fit a separate vision into your schedule.

I have done this by getting a twenty-four-hour calendar (see the *At a Glance* resource in Section 4, Chapter 4.) I like to use colored pens designated to my life's categories. For example, I have one color for my job, one for my family, one for myself, and one for my vision.

I fill out the whole month ahead of time with the hours I'm working. I include travel time to and from home. Next, I fill in my sleep, aiming for seven to eight hours. Then I can see the openings to add the other categories of my life, including my vision and goals. You may have only a few hours monthly, but you can live out what is most important to you.

Every night I fall into bed exhausted. Am I doing something wrong?

MARY: I've had times like that, and usually I'm doing too much or not allowing myself enough down time. Each of us has to find our own individual balance between work, play, and rest, so take a good look at that. Also, I get tired when I'm not eating right and exercising regularly.

LYN: Sometimes I become exhausted and discouraged because I haven't allowed enough time for what I'm trying to accomplish. For example, I expect something to be accomplished in a month, when I should have planned for six months.

I try to balance my home life and work, but it's hard. Do you have any tips for doing this?

CAROL: Using my former analogy, I have to put the big rocks in my jar first. This includes vision-focused activities involving my faith, self-care, significant other, family, and job. Then the pebbles fit in around the big rocks: other aspects of my vision, goals and relationships. Finally, I fill in with the sand—hobbies and material pursuits.

LYN: Carol's analogy is brilliant. It helps us realize that if we aren't intentional with where we invest our energy and time, we will find ourselves out of balance. We will also find that weeks have gone by and nothing but the most urgent has been addressed.

Home life is just as important in our long-term vision as our work, but since we don't have a boss paying or holding us accountable for home life, it's tempting to leave family, home, and self-care out of the equation just to save time or energy.

Just as I fill out my calendar ahead of time, I also review and analyze later how my days and weeks actually went. Your past weeks can inform your choices for coming weeks. Staying on track with our goals and living out our visions doesn't just happen. We can use our calendar as a tool to help us find a better balance in the future. Make time to review your past weeks to ascertain how you balanced home life, work, and other priorities, and evaluate ways you can improve your use of time going forward.

TAKE ACTION

It's time to write specific activities to fulfill your vision and goals for the coming months or year. Take time to do that now, or after reflecting upon the following questions. Allow margin in your life for rest and for the unexpected things that come up. Don't forget to create a weekly or monthly time slot to continually evaluate and modify your plans as needed, perhaps with an accountability partner.

- o What are the non-negotiables in your work and life?
- o Review the aspects of your job within your control. Are there mental or practical adjustments you want to make to better accomplish your goals and manage your energy levels?
- o In life, we often have many careers. Is it time for you to consider a career change? If so, how will you begin this process?
- o Write down goals for your top priority people. How will you specifically work these into your schedule?

Look through the resources in Section 4, Chapter 4. Which ones will you utilize in your job, career, and commitments? Make a plan to use the resources and add them to your calendar.

We'd like to introduce you to people who shine in areas we've covered in the preceding chapters. These "Spotlight Stories" highlight a role model we can all learn from.

SPOTLIGHT STORY

HOLLY WILLIAMSON

Founder and Director of The Women of Pader Uganda

"What am I going to do with the rest of my life?" Holly Williamson asked herself this question after her two sons graduated from high school in 2011 and 2012. She had been providing care for her own father, as well as for her husband's father, who both died around that time. In addition, Holly had just spent five years caregiving for a friend before her death.

At fifty-three, Holly wondered where to focus her time and energy. A blog post about an American woman who was helping people in Africa tugged at her heart. Her heart was further moved in 2013, when Holly heard about an opportunity to go on a group trip to Uganda. She signed up and saw firsthand the beauty and the devastation of Uganda. Later that year she visited the town of Pader in the northern region of Uganda. Warlord Joseph Kony and his guerilla "Lord's Resistance Army" had abducted over 20,000 children, killed 100,000 civilians, and displaced 1.5 million people in that area of the country. The Ugandan government set up camps in Pader for people to live protected from Kony, but the camps brought additional problems and deaths due to starvation, rape, and disease. The region was now not only devastated, in extreme poverty, and desperate for help, but the people, whose lives were in ruin, did not trust anyone.

From that point on, Holly was determined to help. She calls herself an ordinary woman, but her story is extraordinary. She took the first small steps of what became The Women of Pader Uganda (TWOPU) by starting The Bead Project. She taught the town's women to make jewelry—though she herself had never made any. Holly took the jewelry they made and sold the items in America. This little beginning has grown in eleven years into an organization with a multitude of programs and projects. TWOPU now has its own campus in Pader, bringing employment, financial help, education, and personal development to the people in that region. These programs include businesses that now sell jewelry, maize, pigs, and other items. The programs provide education and personal growth opportunities. Holly had no previous experience or training in any of these areas—she simply took the next step and enlisted the help of others.

Now in her sixties, Holly oversees the work from her hometown in Austin, Texas. She makes three trips a year to Pader, staying for a month each time. Of course, email and internet meetings make up a great deal of her time in Texas. She relies on a team of people in Pader and in Austin as together they carry out everything that makes this significant undertaking possible.

To find out more about Holly's story and The Women of Pader Uganda, check out www.thewomenofpaderuganda.org.

With Holly's background in mind, let's hear from her regarding the topics we covered in Section 1: our vision, passions, strengths, goals, jobs, and commitments.

Holly, how would you describe your overall vision for this season of life, and how did you arrive at it?

After my sons graduated high school, my husband and I discussed my future. I knew I didn't want to just earn money—I wanted to do something meaningful. My vision and mission started by simply looking into areas where my heart was drawn to help people. I would say my vision statement is "to help people in deep need to get through their problems and come to a self-sustaining place." I'm drawn to people with the highest and loudest needs.

When I first visited Pader, Uganda, one of the leaders of their church said to me in desperation, "I have people starving to death right now and I need help." I saw that the women were already making simple jewelry, so I told them I would take a bunch of necklaces and sell them in America, sending the money back to them. That's how The Women of Pader Uganda started.

How did you discover your passions and strengths? What part do they play in fulfilling your vision?

I discovered my passions and strengths as I went along, going where my heart and the needs led. One of my strengths is being willing to try new things. I'm not an expert pig-raiser, businessperson, jewelry-maker, etc. But as I saw the needs, my strengths came into play to help solve problems. I didn't realize what my strengths were until they emerged.

I guess another of my strengths is asking people to help me, because I've done that and received a lot of assistance along the way. This overall project is not something I could be doing on my own.

I had already learned that giving care in practical ways is one of my gifts and passions as I raised our children and provided care for relatives and friends. The Women of Pader Uganda is all about giving help through tangible actions. I love helping people who have deep needs.

How do you compensate for your shortcomings and weaknesses when it comes to living out your passion and mission?

I reach out and ask for help. I get educated. For example, early in the process I realized I needed to learn how to make beaded jewelry. I searched online for "bead stores," then drove around town to various shops. I told the employees what I was doing, and asked if they could help. A young woman in one of the stores helped by teaching me the process. Now she designs new jewelry each year and shows us how to make the items.

I also hire good people who are trustworthy and do their parts well.

Please share tips you've discovered for fitting everything into your schedule—practical daily things you must do, family goals, other opportunities, and your various projects and passions.

I carry around my large paper calendar, and I have everything written down: appointments, family times, exercise, my goals, to-do lists, etc.

I must exercise four to five days a week to be my best. I have a set time every day, and this helps me mentally as well as physically amidst a demanding schedule. It helps me to be more effective.

With family, we plan ahead and put definite times into our schedules for both casual get-togethers and events. I leave work early to do things with my kids and grandkids. You can't be all things to all people all the time. I've had to learn to be at peace about that.

When you have felt overwhelmed by life and too many commitments, what has helped you?

Every morning, first thing, I sit alone quietly with God in thought, prayer, and reading. If I don't, my day is disorganized and disoriented.

I also take a bath every night and read in the bathtub—I love to read all different kinds of books. I live with a lot of pain in my joints. The bath, chiropractor, doctors' appointments, etc., all keep me going. When I get discouraged, it helps me to get out of myself and do something for others.

If I'm totally overwhelmed, I try to stop and walk away. It just doesn't work to keep pushing, and amazingly, when I go back to it later, everything works smoother and better.

One final thing—I've learned to live with low expectations, which brings increased peace and fulfillment. Life is not so overwhelming when I lower my expectations of myself, other people, and various endeavors.

What advice would you give to the person who is in this later season who wants to be more purposeful in life but doesn't know where to start?

I would say to look around, observe people, and see what needs strike your heart. Maybe you want to help people with limited resources, or those without homes. You could do simple things like making your own bags of bottled water and food to hand out or join a group in your community that is already assisting people in need.

I remember a little boy in Pader, now a teen, who lived most of his life tied to a tree. He had tremendous mental and emotional problems, too great for the community to handle. The young man always took off his clothes because he did not like to wear them, and behaved in disturbing, destructive ways. For the good of the community at large, they limited his difficulties by tying him to a tree.

When we saw this need, we began to provide food and medication for him and his family. This has improved the boy's life—and the whole family's life as well. We are in the process of building a property where the young man and a family member can live. We discovered a need and have begun to meet it with whatever means we have available.

This principle is something anyone can do: see a need and ask yourself if there is a way you can help, even with something small. The Women of Pader Uganda grew by taking little steps to assist someone, which ended up helping people in big ways.

YOUR RELATIONSHIPS

Nothing enriches our lives more than the relationships we pursue with God, our significant other, kids, grandkids, extended family, and friends. The priority we place on each of these as we age will determine the impact and fulfillment we experience in our individual lives.

5

YOUR SIGNIFICANT SOMEONE

How do we continue to cherish and enjoy life with our spouse or significant other? What does it look like to navigate our communication and conflict, finishing well with our soul mate? And if we are alone, we might ask, "Can I find a significant someone in this life stage?"

ENJOYING LIFE TOGETHER

What are some enduring habits we can establish to make these years together the best and the most fun?

CAROL: Almost every afternoon when we finish work, my husband and I sit under our big live oak trees for about half an hour to enjoy a refreshing drink and review our day, often with laughter. We briefly pray for things we have discussed and for people in need, and we give thanks for specific areas of God's provision. We look forward to this time each day.

We usually give each other the gift of travel for birthdays and Christmas. Sometimes we simply go to a nearby Texas town. Habits like our weekly dinner date night and daily touchpoints have kept our relationship fresh and fun even in the darkest of days.

MARY: John and I try to continually build our connection and emotional intimacy in various ways. You might make a date with your sweetie and talk about implementing some of these ideas:

1. Seek out new and novel experiences together. Our relationship gets a boost when we do new things as a couple. Take a class together, try out new restaurants, explore tourist spots in your area, or read a book together in a different location each week.
2. Make it a goal to be vulnerable with each other regularly in your communication. This means sharing your hurts, fears, worries, and joys, having established a relationship where it is safe to do so. Some couples establish a habit of sharing one high and one low from their day over a meal. The goal is to talk openly about our feelings with each other as a way of life.
3. Share your spirituality. Wherever you are in your spiritual lives, plan ways to talk about your journeys. You could have a designated mealtime each week to explore this topic, read a book together and discuss it, or set up a regular time to pray together.
4. Share common tasks together, like yard work, cooking, washing your cars, etc.
5. Share physicality. Make it a goal to touch each other lovingly throughout the day. If your sex life needs help, try reading a good book on the topic together or seek counseling. We've listed some resources for this in Section 4, Chapter 5.
6. Set up a daily, focused time to talk about your day, even if only for a few minutes, and have a date night each week. This adds spark and spunk to your relationship.

LYN: Habits are actually made up of moment-by-moment choices that create our lives.

Dan and I make it a point to greet one another when one of us comes home. We also drop what we are doing and walk each other out to the car when one of us is leaving. In doing this, we stay close in the moments of our lives and acknowledge to each other that there is nothing more important.

In addition to this, we often honk the horn when we are leaving and wave until the other is out of sight. It's silly but also romantic. The point is, every "last" moment together is a time of encouragement and young love . . . even though we have been married thirty-six years.

How can I continue to cherish my spouse or significant other after many years together? How can we keep our relationship fresh?

LYN: I have always thought of my husband as God's son, and with that I experience a sense of honor and gratitude to "get" to be around him. With that mindset, even though we have been married for over three decades, I continue to value my husband's preferences and experiences as if he is new to me— it helps me to stay intrigued by him and not take him for granted.

Dan is my friend, my date, and my comrade throughout this life. When he struggles, I am sad. When he is delighted, I am thrilled. One day my husband will be gone. I hope my treatment of God's "son" will be such that God will say to me, "Well done."

CAROL: Sometimes Stuart and I reflect together on our journey from the beginning to the present day. We seek to remember the blessings and specific ways God has guided and provided for us along the way. We also acknowledge that suffering within and outside our families has brought us closer, even through sadness.

Being intentionally kind to one another is key when it comes to developing safety and a sense of feeling cherished. Selfishness is the enemy of kindness. Small acts of kindness add up to create a fresh, secure, lifelong relationship. We continually pray for insight into the mystery of each other as well as abundant love for one another.

My wife and I have different expectations for this season. What can we do about this?

LYN: Understanding our spouse's beliefs and expectations is important because resentment, fear, and anger can result from unfulfilled expectations.

We need to have some specific conversations to get on the same page before problems pop up.

MARY: Here's an exercise that's been helpful in our marriage:

1. Working separately, write a series of short sentences that describe your personal vision of a deeply satisfying love relationship. Write each sentence as a positive statement in the present tense, as if it were already happening.
2. Then share your sentences. Underline the ones you have in common. If your spouse has written sentences that you agree with but did not think of yourself, add them to your list.
3. On your own lists, individually rank each sentence with a number from 1 to 5 according to its importance to you, with 1 indicating "very important" and 5 indicating "not so important." (Don't argue about why one of you ranked an item higher than the other.)
4. Circle the two items most important to you.

5. Work together to design a mutual relationship vision of your expectations, as in the following example. Start with the ones you both agree are the most important.

OUR RELATIONSHIP VISION		
Michael		Deborah
1	We have fun together	1
1	We settle our differences peacefully	1
1	We are healthy and physically active	1
1	We communicate openly and easily	1
2	We have a satisfying physical relationship	3
2	We are each other's best friend	3
3	We work well together as parents	1
2	We share important decisions	3
3	We meet each other's deepest needs	2
2	We are financially secure	4
4	We have adequate "private" time	2

Post this list where you can both see it. Once a week, briefly review together how you're doing. If this exercise reveals major differences in your hopes and expectations that you can't resolve, seek help from a spiritual advisor, mentor, or counselor.

CAROL: You could also discuss ways to incorporate these things into your weekly and daily schedules. You might come up with an acronym, phrase, or motto that serves as a reminder for what your lives are about, moving forward.

How can I become my spouse's best friend?

CAROL: Best friends share the deepest parts of one another's lives. That idea can feel daunting in light of the complexities of marriage, at least from my experience. Deep discussions may feel easier with a girlfriend with whom I am not sharing a bed or managing finances.

Deep friendship is built upon the daily deposits of being present with one another, caring about the little things of each day, and sacrificial forgiveness. This is lived out especially when it comes to fully accepting the other, even when difficult patterns seem to never go away. When we embrace each other with all our faults, "warts and all," we experience growth and safety, which brings increasing closeness. Our souls become melded together over many years of intentionally investing in one another.

LYN: Webster's dictionary tells us that a best friend is an especially close and trusted companion.

That kind of loyalty is built upon knowing all of a person's flaws, weirdness, unmet goals, outright mistakes, and desires—and still having their back. Does your significant other know beyond a shadow of a doubt you will be there forever, no matter what? That kind of faithfulness is what we all long for in a spouse and is what builds a deep friendship. This takes a lot of personal growth on our part. The rewards are well worth the effort.

MARY: People have different definitions and expectations of a "best friend." Some of these are realistic and some aren't, given the personalities and backgrounds of each person in a relationship. Unrealistic expectations can set us up for disappointment. Discuss and explore your expectations and friendship. You could use the exercise in the previous question. Some spouses are very different from each other. Accepting our loved one's differences and weaknesses can bring us peace.

No individual person can meet all our emotional and relational needs—understanding this is important. We each need several friendships, along with community, to satisfy our relational needs.

How much time should we spend together and apart to be healthy in our relationship and in ourselves during these years in our lives?

MARY: This varies from couple to couple. John and I experienced tension during our early years together as we navigated and negotiated this area. Part of the answer came when we realized this wasn't about whether we liked each other, but about our own individual differences and needs, which have varied throughout the seasons of life.

It's important for each person to feel satisfied with their amount of time alone, together as a couple, and with other people. Explore your preferences together. I've learned the hard way that communication goes better when I don't become defensive and when I realize his needs are often more about who he is than a reflection on me.

CAROL: Everyone will require time alone, no matter how extroverted or introverted you are. As we have grown as a couple, my husband and I can sense when the other needs more or less time together to keep our relationship enjoyable and meaningful.

It was clear from the beginning that we were opposites in so many areas; how can we continue to grow when we don't ever seem to like the same things?

CAROL: I try to take an interest in Stuart's pursuits while continuing to enjoy my own. It can be fun, and most of all, knowing you are willing to do your part, to take the initiative to learn and even participate in their world, is encouraging to your spouse. It also sets an example for them to do the same for you.

MARY: Many couples find it helpful to start a list of things they might enjoy doing together, then slowly work through the list, trying those things. It's okay to realize that some aren't right for one or both of you. Agree ahead of time not to get upset when the other doesn't like something. Just keep working through the list and adding things you've never done.

John and I have discovered hiking, weekend festivals, and dancing at this life stage. We've developed the motto "Too much fun is just barely enough." It's fun to experiment together!

I read Gary Chapman's book The Five Love Languages: The Secret to Love that Lasts. *How important are the five love languages in a relationship?*

MARY: You're talking about words of affirmation, quality time, receiving gifts, acts of service, and physical touch. Gary Chapman describes these love languages as different ways that people give and receive love.

Discovering a loved one's "language" and relating specifically in that way can be helpful. This enables us each to express love so that it's truly felt and appreciated by the other. Otherwise, we tend to give love in a way that is meaningful to us, missing the mark for our loved one.

CAROL: My husband and I first have to focus upon loving, respecting, and accepting one another. Then the love languages can be a guide for how to focus our expression of these things. One of my mentors wrote, "How do you spell love? True love is spelled G-I-V-E. It's not based on what you can get but on what you can give to the other person." The five love languages can be helpful in carrying that out.

How can I find a significant someone in this life stage?

LYN: I have many friends all over the world who have used internet dating to find their mates. It has proven to be a success because it keeps people out of bars and environments that are often filled with people only wanting short-term connections instead of deep, loving relationships.

MARY: Yes, I too know many people who have found their lifetime companions through dating apps. You do have to be consistent and persistent with these, and not give up when some of the first connections fail to be "the one." Of course, choose reputable dating sites, following diligently all their recommendations for success and safety.

Also, don't forget about your place of worship, faith-based groups for singles, or a city-wide singles group based upon your faith or other interests.

CAROL: One of my daughter's co-workers found her significant other later in life through connections. She simply asked ten dear friends to think of a quality person who was single and in her age range (for her, that meant seven to ten years younger or older). During those years she was set up on dates with numerous prospects. Eventually, she met the right one and they are now enjoying a purpose-filled life together.

COMMUNICATION

What does it look like to navigate our communication and conflict, finishing well together?

CAROL: Conflict will happen for the rest of our lives. It helps to accept that truth and prepare ourselves to resolve disagreements as quickly and effectively as possible. Stuart and I are still learning to avoid getting stuck trying to win an argument, and also not to withdraw from the problem. We both tend to be strong-willed. We are intentional about addressing the problem quickly, seeking to hear and understand each other, expressing our hearts, and making the needed changes. When we do this, we experience healing, growth, and increased intimacy.

LYN: A book and website called *How We Love* is a top-notch resource. The authors, Milan and Kay Yerkovich, are counselors who are also a married couple. The main point of their approach, which is based upon psychological research, is that we all have different attachment styles because of our different upbringings.

Varying experiences in our childhood homes often dictate the burdens, misunderstandings, and expectations we bring to our marriages.

There are five different styles of connecting in this approach: avoider, pleaser, controller, vacillator, and secure connector.

When Dan and I were first married, we knew we came from very different upbringings, but we didn't think our backgrounds would matter. Love does that to a couple.

Dan's dad was seventeen years older than his mom. It was his mother's second marriage, so Dan had three stepbrothers. All his life, he lived in one house in Austin, Texas.

My dad was a high-ranking military officer, and we moved nineteen times while I lived at home. My mother had a PhD, was a stay-at-home mom, and stayed very active as a military spouse. I was an only child until I was ten, when I got a younger brother, who I adored.

Dan and I were opposites . . . surprise!

We have different opinions on almost everything. At first, it was upsetting and mysterious. Now, it's interesting and allows us to understand a wide range of life, circumstances, and people. We know each other's weaknesses, but more importantly, we know our own weaknesses. Don't be afraid of being different from your spouse. It's not a cruel joke of the Creator—it is a gift in disguise.

The relationship tools that *How We Love* provides have made all the difference in the world.

What is the healthiest way to communicate with your spouse about their weaknesses?

CAROL: First, my husband and I ask for permission to share some observations about the other's weakness. For example, "Hon, could I share an insight that I think could be helpful for you?"

If permission is granted, we share our observations.

The sandwich approach to communication is also helpful. You start by verbalizing a specific strength you have observed recently in your spouse. Next, you gently fill the sandwich with one area that has been difficult for you, for example, "I wonder if you would consider your tone of voice when we are in a hard conversation?"

To complete the second piece of "bread on the sandwich," you finish with another positive. For example, "I really appreciate that we can sit down and talk about this. You have such a caring and teachable heart to grow—it really draws me to you." Of course, be sincere with your compliments so they don't seem manipulative or fake.

LYN: Yes, a positive statement to begin and end can make the other person feel safe and valued. I try to remember it's a privilege to speak into my husband's life, and to be sure he knows that I only want the very best for him.

Often I have topics I want to cover with my significant other that might put him on the defensive, but I feel would make us so much closer. How can I phrase sentences to help our conversation to go better?

MARY: Here are a few that have worked well for my husband, John, and me:

"We are both such great people, but like everyone, we have weaknesses. Can we talk about something I think is holding us back from all that we can be?"

"Let's talk about this in a way that our relationship gets even better as we discuss it."

"I'd like a do-over." (When I've said something that made things worse.)

"This doesn't work for me." (Instead of "I don't like it when you do this or that.")

Use "I" statements instead of "you" statements. For example, "I struggle when anyone raises their volume with me," rather than, "You always yell at me."

In addition, don't use "always" or "never," because these words automatically make people defensive. Rarely do things *always* or *never* happen.

LYN: It really does help to phrase things in a way that keeps the other person's defenses down. When someone feels they are being criticized, deep inside they're afraid they're not enough. Then they want to guard themselves. Knowing this about human nature helps me to approach Dan with the intention of keeping his dignity intact, even if he must admit a shortfall.

The right timing of a hard conversation is important. It's critical to be sure the other person has eaten and is relaxed and not trying to watch a favorite show, work on the computer, etc.

Something else I've found helpful is to use a word picture to describe my feelings instead of a direct accusation. For example, I wanted to express to Dan the lonely sadness I felt when he came home exhausted from work and didn't want to engage with me. I used this approach:

"Dan, remember last week when you made your lunch and then left it in the car? It sat in the hot car for several days. When you finally brought it home, you threw it into the trash. Sometimes I feel like that lunch. I know you are very busy and giving your job and the family all you've got. But I often feel scrunched up and forgotten."

Dan hugged me and apologized. We now have this as an inside joke. And now he comes straight to me when he gets home, not out of obligation, but because he empathized with my experience.

CAROL: Here's another approach that has helped me. Lead into your statements with:

> I feel . . .
>
> when you . . .
>
> because . . .

For example, "I feel unseen when you don't listen, because my dad didn't value what I tried to share with him while I was growing up."

Those three transitional phrases can be applied to difficult topics and interactions with your significant other.

My mate is an introvert who processes life alone. I am an extrovert, who needs to process out loud. It seems to me he uses up all his energy talking at work and there is none left for me. What should I do?

LYN: As an extrovert, I've found I need to have other friends to verbally process with. Then I can determine what is really important to talk about with Dan, who is (no surprise) an introvert.

Dan has made a commitment to ask me to come outside to talk on Saturday mornings over coffee. I know this is not natural for him, so I feel loved and connected when he makes this a habit. I'm learning to listen when he shares. Not everything an extrovert wants to say must be said. Also, since I have debriefed enough with others, I can be clear and concise with him instead of going on and on.

This difference has taken years for us to understand, and these are skills we're still working on.

CAROL: My husband is also an introvert. We meet for lunch once a week, and it's so fun and interactive, even after being married over thirty-seven years. We discuss topics we are both truly interested in. An introverted person is often glad to talk about subjects they really enjoy, even if their energy is low. We love to travel. Dreaming of ideas together and looking to the future with our family and friends excites us both.

As Lyn said, friendships are valuable. Though my husband is my closest confidant, I also process with a handful of women on a regular basis.

MARY: Introverts truly want and need to have good conversations and connections with others, especially with their significant people. Introversion simply means that a person is energized by spending time alone. Everyone falls on a spectrum in terms of how much they are energized by being with people versus energized by being alone. This knowledge can help us determine when and how much to talk to our significant people. If an introvert feels the need to be re-energized by alone time, that's not the best moment to expect a lengthy conversation. Likewise, extroverts can meet refueling needs by spending time with a variety of people.

I know everything about my wife after so many years together. What is left to talk about?

LYN: When we've lived with someone for a long time, we know their opinions, perspectives, and expected patterns of behavior. But the events of life provide new opportunities to explore together, to process our thinking, and to develop different perspectives and opinions.

Life events might include kids launching into adulthood, grandkids, health issues, finances, and our parents' end-of-life stages. Sometimes we don't even know what we think, so we need to explore and discover together. That's why our partner is so special and is a true gift to us from God.

If we make a habitual choice to draw out our mate by asking questions and listening with a compassionate heart, we can learn together through our various seasons. Marriage is a lifelong learning adventure and our loved ones won't always be there. We need to make the most of our time together.

CAROL: I like the idea of thinking about the mystery in each other. As we get older, life may feel harder, and we can seek to understand one another's hurt. We can ask how the other's upbringing affects their current feelings and experiences. When we take time to listen from the heart, we can have conversations that draw us closer and make life richer and more meaningful.

MARY: Sometimes this type of communication is difficult. *Why Am I Afraid to Tell You Who I Am?* by John Powell is an excellent book for learning to communicate with the significant people in our lives.

CONFLICT

What are some general tips for resolving conflict in this life stage?

MARY: If we find ourselves becoming more negative, judgmental, or particular as we age, we can be proactive to address these tendencies. This will enable us to choose our battles wisely, which is so important in conflict resolution. The opposites of these detrimental qualities are positivity, acceptance, and grace (unconditional favor). When I'm proactively growing in these characteristics, I find I don't have as much to be disgruntled about.

I remember a time I was very irritated with John. I forced myself to think about things from his viewpoint, and I realized I was more at fault in the issue than he was. This technique caused me to be filled with acceptance, humility, and grace toward John.

CAROL: My husband and I have been slow learners in this area. Our learning styles are different, and we have gradually learned how to dance together. When conflict arises, we take time apart to calm ourselves and try to see things objectively. We try to see the other's perspective instead of attempting to win.

LYN: Validating the other person's thoughts enough for them to feel safe can help. You might start with phrases like, "I can see your perspective, that …" or "I understand how you feel that …"

Conflict can feel scary for the moment, but it's really part of life. In this world, we will have misunderstandings and differences of opinion. I try to be an ongoing example of restoring friendly relations with my husband and others. My family and the outside world are watching, and I hope to point them to what is life-giving and true.

How can you love your significant person even in areas you disagree about?

MARY: Even in the best marriages, couples agree on about seventy to eighty percent of issues. That means it is normal to disagree about twenty to thirty percent of issues. Realistic expectations are important. Unrealistic expectations lead to disappointment, and it's hard to love someone when you're disappointed with them.

"Let's agree to disagree" is a healthy statement and attitude to incorporate into a marriage. I don't have to agree with John about everything to love him deeply. I can respect his right to differ from me and can ask him to do the same toward me.

LYN: When Dan and I disagree, we often make it an inside joke. For example, he is a Type B. I pride myself on being a Type A. We tease that he is looking for a support group of Type Bs that are being pestered by Type As. This silly joke helps us describe our union and not be bothered that we are so different from one another. The "Type" differences have become an asset to us.

CAROL: Talking about our general differences can serve to defuse the tension and allow for compromise, even in issues like setting the thermostat. As we have gotten older, we need to be especially comfortable with the temperature in order to sleep better. Though Stuart is frugal and helps us stay within our budget, he has heard my heart and made adjustments in this area where we are so different.

My spouse's family were yellers and door slammers, and he allows himself to continue this tradition. Mine, on the other hand, discussed everything calmly and kindly. What can I do?

MARY: Your question is concerning because yelling and door-slamming are associated with abusive behavior. Often, victims of abuse have gotten so used to it that they don't recognize it as abusive and unacceptable.

Even if your husband's behavior is on the milder end of the spectrum and not frequent, this type of thing can escalate over time—emotionally or physically, or both. Either way, you shouldn't tolerate these patterns.

It could be helpful for you to educate yourself about abusive words and actions, even if his behavior isn't "that bad" in your opinion. As you navigate this situation, you might need a counselor's help in learning how to talk about this and to set your own boundaries for how you will be treated.

Also, do some internet research about abusive speech and behavior in a relationship and what to do about it. Your journey through this will lead to a happier, stronger you. If you need resources immediately, check out the the ones listed in Section 4, Chapter 5.

My husband irritates me at times. How can I continue to be patient and at peace, knowing he'll probably never change?

CAROL: My husband sometimes irritates me, but I can also irritate him. Remembering my own weaknesses that are difficult for my husband levels the playing field and provides understanding. Also, focusing on all that I am grateful for in him gives me a different perspective and more patience toward him.

LYN: Think back to the time you weren't irritated with your husband. In the beginning of our relationship, we felt romantic and loving. To remind myself of the time when we were young and falling in love, I have put pictures of my husband by my bed, where I dress, by the kitchen sink, and in the laundry area. When I feel frustrated, I look at those pictures. I remember why I love him. I remember that I did not want to live without him.

I'm teaching myself to dwell on what is good about my husband, what he has done right, and how I can praise him. Every time I choose to do this, my irritations diminish.

Is it possible to be my spouse's greatest cheerleader, even knowing all his faults from so many years together?

CAROL: We have intimately experienced our spouse's greatest strengths. What if we set our minds on those instead of on their faults? I love this quote: "Above all, have fervent and unfailing love for one another, because . . . [it overlooks unkindness and unselfishly seeks the best for others]" (1 Peter 4:8, Amplified Bible). I have to call out to God for the ability to do this—to think of my husband's strengths even amidst his weaknesses. This is not easy and is beyond my own limitations, but God enables me.

My spouse has had an affair. Can I ever love or trust again?

MARY: I highly recommend seeing a counselor who specializes in marriage counseling. Affair recovery is possible but requires guidance from a trained professional to successfully navigate the complex dynamics. If your spouse isn't willing to go, you can see a counselor first and ask for guidance about your partner's involvement. If it's financially difficult for you to see a counselor, contact 211 by phone or online (https://www.211.org/about-us) to find reasonably priced counseling and other resources. 211 is a gold mine for finding health and human services in your city. This resource is also listed in Section 4, Chapter 5.

CAROL: The situation will take time and lots of "baby steps" to heal, trust, and forgive.

LYN: Sometimes affairs are a cry for help from the partner. As the areas of hurt are addressed—and as you rebuild and transform as individuals and as a couple—you might even become a beacon of light to others going through the same traumas. This has happened many times, so take heart.

My husband plays golf with a close friend from childhood. They are very close. When he comes home, he acts like an immature high school jock. It takes him days to shake off the poor influence his friend has on him. What can I do?

CAROL: I would start by journaling my thoughts and concerns about this, or talking to a mature friend, to become clear in my thinking. Then I would pray and look for an opportunity to ask clarifying questions in a spirit of love and listening. In this way, he might reach his own conclusions regarding the influence of this friend. After asking and listening, you could share how it affects you. Finally, you might ask yourself how you could be at peace with accepting him and this situation if it never changes.

LYN: When I get together with a particular friend, we can really affect one another—sometimes in raunchy ways. I begin to act and talk like her. There's truth in the saying, "Show me your friends, and I'll show you who you are." Each of us has to evaluate our friendships.

Often, we don't realize how we affect others by our behavior. It's important to not shame our spouses but to encourage one another to a higher level. Carefully choose your timing and speak candidly to him about this. In the end, you'll need to find the path to your own peace if he continues with choices and behavior you don't like. Resources in Section 4, Chapter 5 can help you.

We seem to fight about such petty things. How can we stop this frustrating pattern?

CAROL: Honestly, I feel this has been a trap in our marriage. Even after forty years, immaturity overtakes one or both of us sometimes. After we decided together we would not speak negatively in front of our grown children, or with meanness or sarcasm in private, we experienced far greater peace.

LYN: I have a really good friend who fights with his wife over petty things when they are with other people. It's hard to be around them, because they are always correcting each other. They seem so adamant about being right.

Could you talk together about considering your relationship to be more important than calling each other out for small things? It's always better to strengthen our friendship in marriage than to be right. This is a good choice to model for our children. More is caught than taught.

SEXUALITY AND AGING

MARY: Sexuality is such a multifaceted topic. We've added significant resources from the experts in Section 4, Chapter 5. We'll address a few questions here, but please check there to find the most information on this subject.

What are the biggest challenges with sexuality as we get older and how can we respond to those in our desire to keep sexual intimacy?

MARY: Well, I have some bad news and some good news. Our sexual drive and capabilities are affected as our bodies age, but healthy lifestyle choices like good nutrition, exercise habits, and maintaining positive spiritual and mental health can help. However, our risk for health problems increases as we live longer, and our bodies typically decline in various ways.

Conditions like arthritis, heart disease, high blood pressure, diabetes, obesity, and depression can make having sex more challenging. Narrowing and hardening of the arteries can change blood vessels so blood does not flow freely. These and other health issues can make physical intimacy difficult in a variety of ways.

Also, for couples married a long time, boredom and predictability can be a problem.

Sounds bleak, doesn't it? That's why it's important to make extra efforts to establish our physical, spiritual, and emotional health. We can form habits and practices that help us to thrive inwardly regardless of circumstances. I love what the Apostle Paul wrote amidst a life of hardship and suffering: "Though outwardly we are wasting away, yet inwardly we are being renewed day by day. For our light and momentary troubles are achieving for us an eternal glory that far outweighs them all. So we fix our eyes not on what is seen, but on what is unseen, since what is seen is temporary, but what is unseen is eternal" (2 Corinthians 4:16–18).

Growing strong in your spiritual life is crucial at every age.

Another part of the solution is learning the multifaceted world of acceptance: "Lord, grant me the ability to accept the things I cannot change, courage to change the things I can, and the wisdom to know the difference" (The Serenity Prayer).

I can change myself: my spiritual life, my mental health, and my ability to be at peace amidst challenging circumstances. Be encouraged; we can achieve a lot through our own personal inner growth, along with attention to physical health.

Is it normal to want sex less frequently as we age?

LYN: That is what society seems to think. Dan and I have realized it's more about not getting bored or just predictable. Try to make encounters together exciting and different occasionally. Flirt with your spouse. Meet each other at the door with hugs and kisses. Dress nicely to show that you care about the other. Listen well when they are speaking.

What if you greet your partner at the front door wearing something very unlike you? (Make sure your children or others are not going to arrive any time soon.) If he seems to be in shock, you can take the lead. If you've set up a room with candles and music, all the better. The point is to be creative.

CAROL: Dressing in cellophane and greeting your spouse at the door is one example of what Lyn is talking about! That is creative and the price is right. Sustaining sexual intimacy as we get older is a choice and a habit we can navigate with our spouse. It's a balm that we put over our marriage even as we are aging.

How can I stop feeling insecure as my body begins to age and I don't look as young as I once did?

LYN: This made me laugh when I read it: "If you met a person in real life who had a Barbie-doll figure, she'd never be able to walk upright with such tiny feet, rounded hips, and a top-heavy bosom!" Be sure not to buy into the fallacy of an unreal person. Having said this, we do want to present ourselves in the best way we can to our mates. Often people get dressed nicely for company or to go out, but then they become lazy at home. Try to spruce up for your partner. Also, don't forget that your partner is aging as well. That perspective can equal the playing field in your own mind and help you to not be so hard on yourself.

CAROL: Don't forget that when we committed to our spouses, it was a body, soul, and spirit covenant. As we age, that total-person connection needs to remain our emphasis and focus. This brings me security and confidence even with the challenges of an aging body.

LYN: Over the years, my husband has helped me realize that he really does love being close to me as a total person. For him, the desire for physical intimacy flows from this no matter what I look like.

Why does my husband just turn everything we do into a push for sex?

LYN: Our culture has encouraged both men and women to see one another as sexual objects. It's important to help your partner realize that you both need to engage emotionally and spiritually to have the most satisfying physical relationship. It's also vital to slow down and honor your differing needs for a gradual build-up at the beginning of sex. Intimacy takes time, not only within the moment but also over the years you are together.

CAROL: We don't want to forget the physical component of sex drive. In some ways, this can be likened to the desire for food and water. Some people simply have more of a sex drive, and we each have to learn to honor and work with our partner's differences in this regard.

The idea that we are united body, soul, and spirit through our sexual relationship helps both partners in this desire for intimacy.

LOSS

My spouse died three years ago, and it's been difficult. What can I do?

MARY: One of the strange realities of life is that we often have to feel worse in order to feel better. This is definitely the case when we grieve a loss. While we might let ourselves feel bad for a little while, we can hurry on to other things because we don't want to have negative feelings for too long. What most people don't realize is that if we take the time to truly feel and process our feelings, we'll feel better faster.

Grieving involves feelings of denial, anger, yearning, and sadness—represented by the acronym DAYS. We must allow ourselves to process through each of these to get to a peaceful acceptance of our loss. Otherwise we get stuck in the negative feelings.

Here are some ways to process your grief:

o Talk about your feelings with someone who is a good listener—possibly a counselor.

o Write about your feelings in a journal.

o Talk out loud about your grief when you are alone.

o Talk to God about it.

o Listen to, sing, or write a song that expresses what you are feeling. Repeat these things over and over as long as you need to.

CAROL: After experiencing loss, I participated in the GriefShare program (grief-share.org), which is offered by many churches all over the world. It was and is extremely practical when those in grief feel undone and unable to think. Processing with wise people and keeping ourselves in community is essential.

LYN: Finding a hobby that gets you around other like-minded people can be life-giving and lead you to new friends. Perhaps you don't ever want to get remarried, but it's okay to have fun again. Often we need someone to give us permission to let go—you have permission! Remember this: you are still being faithful to the vows you made to your spouse, even if you go and discover another part of yourself. You can begin a new season of life.

My wife and I divorced last year after 28 years of marriage. It was hard for both of us, but we fought all the time. Do you have any advice for handling the unique challenges of divorcing after 50?

CAROL: DivorceCare (divorcecare.org) has had a tremendous impact. This organization can help you move outside your own limitations and learn from those who have gone before.

LYN: Divorce is never easy and I commend you for trying your best for twenty-eight years. A couple I know well struggled for so long, even their children begged them to get a divorce. Their incompatibility made everyone miserable, and they finally divorced.

After a lot of counseling, they were each able to see their own issues that needed improvement. They did a lot of work on themselves individually and focused upon healing from all that had happened.

MARY: It's vital to take a significant amount of time to heal, learn, and grow as an individual after a divorce, and to mend and rebuild any family relationships that have suffered. In these ways, you'll be able to move into your coming years with strength, peace, and wisdom.

It's so hard being in a long-term caregiving role with my significant other. Do you have any tips for this part of my journey?

LYN: I watched my mother faithfully serve my dad through COPD to his death. I then served my mother through her journey with COPD; they were both heavy smokers since the 1950s. After she died, many people were beside themselves with grief, but I was at peace.

I learned that this long-term caregiving assignment feels unbearable and often boring and inconvenient. Yet if we lean in and serve with commitment and God's wisdom, we will have no regrets when they are gone.

CAROL: I love that idea of having no regrets. One of my best friends has been a caregiver to her husband for thirty years through his journey with muscular dystrophy. She has reminded me that she always expected suffering in this fallen world. As a result, she feels this is just a normal part of life. Her faith has been an incredible example to me as she serves her husband all day long and also still works in a sports ministry impacting college students through phone calls and virtual appointments. She has kept herself healthy in her caregiving by focusing on her life calling to influence and mentor the next generation. At the same time, she embraces her suffering and, out of love for God and her husband, serves tirelessly. This is not easy but it is possible when one draws on the love and strength God offers.

I've lost my husband to Alzheimer's, even though he's still alive. How can I handle this ongoing distress and loneliness?

MARY: It's important for you to allow yourself to grieve through each stage of your husband's illness. Mourn the losses you feel, and process your sadness, denial, anger, and yearning for what has been lost. As you grieve these, you will feel more acceptance and peace about what is going on.

Surround yourself with supportive, loving people—friends, family, and your spiritual loved ones. Join an online or in-person support group that is specific to what you're going through.

Learn more about God through this journey and lean heavily upon a personal friendship with him. I love the Bible verse that says, "God is our refuge and strength, an ever-present help in trouble" (Psalm 46: 1). I have found this to be true during so many troubled times in my life.

LYN: The journey with our loved one through illness is so very hard. Though in our hearts we truly mean the words, we usually don't realize how difficult things will be when we say in our wedding vows, "For better or worse, richer or poorer, in sickness and in health, I will stand by you." Now is the time you are living out "in sickness." You won't regret being there for him. I have found that grieving loss while my loved one is alive helps after they pass on. I don't struggle as much because I've already completed much of my grieving.

Take heart; there is a light at the end of this tunnel. Also, you may be strengthened by the realization this struggle as something that will equip you to help others in the future. Your distress and loneliness will have been worth something.

My husband came back from the Gulf War a different man. He is always irritable and wants to be alone for long stretches of the day. How can I break into his heart and win him back?

LYN: PTSD is very real and not something a man or woman can just shake off. War can be brutal and traumatizing. Coming back to normal life afterward is challenging in so many ways, including the tormenting flashbacks that attack many veterans.

You and your loved one can go together to counseling or a support group. There you can each find others who are going through, or have experienced, your role as either the spouse or the veteran. If he is not yet willing, you can avail yourself of these resources, which can help you to help him and yourself.

This is a lifelong journey, and the Gulf War was only a part of your lives individually and as a couple. It may be that one day you both will be able to help and support others, which might give meaning and value to your current sufferings. God is with you, my friend. Lean on him.

SPECIFIC PROBLEMS

What do you do in this life stage when your significant other makes upsetting choices? For example, how do you respond when you discover there has been a pattern of lying about spending?

CAROL: This is so hard. My husband and I have learned a lot by not doing it the right way many times, when the other has made choices that are upsetting. We've learned to start by not drawing conclusions until we have all the information, instead of immediately believing the worst. We avoid thinking of the other person as "all bad." We seek to make sure everything is on the table.

Our desired goal is to talk through things in a calm and mature way, seeking not only to be understood but also to understand. When things are beyond us, we have the choice to seek wise counsel and make corrections that are often painful but ultimately help us heal and remedy the situation.

LYN: Often we lie because we fear getting caught, or because we don't know how to handle something, or we fear the other will be displeased. Our partners need grace and may respond better if we approach them in a calm and encouraging manner. If you can solve a huge difficulty together, you will have a stronger, trusting relationship for the rest of your lives. You can also be mentors to others in similar predicaments. First, though, you have to walk through this together.

We married three years ago after we both turned 65. What can couples do together in their later years that doesn't cost a lot of money?

MARY: It may sound obvious, but my husband and I like to use the internet for this. Try searching for something like, "Fun cheap dates for senior couples." Then do a search with the same words but add your city: "in Boston," "in Lansing, Michigan," etc. When I searched with the first phrase, here's a sample of what was suggested:

- Hit a garage sale.
- Organize a stargazing picnic.
- Play tourists for the day.
- Plan a photo shoot together.
- Break out your board games.
- Do crafts together.
- Go to a local trivia night.
- Attend a local band performance.
- Take a long walk.
- Go fishing.
- Visit an art gallery.

There are so many possibilities—have fun!

My spouse looks at porn a lot, and it's not okay with me. We've talked about it, but nothing has changed. What can I do?

MARY: You are right to be concerned, and there is help around the corner for you. Our culture likes to think that porn is harmless, but a vast number of studies show this is not true. Porn is highly addictive for the brain. As with other addictions, the users are commonly in denial, even to themselves, about their addiction and its harm to themselves and others.

Seek out experts and resources to help you. We've listed some in Section 4, Chapter 5.

God bless you on your journey. He can be your guide into peace and even joy as you utilize these valuable resources.

How should I handle areas of ongoing pain in my relationship with my significant someone?

LYN: Ongoing pain seems to indicate that your relationship has reached a block. Many times, when Dan and I couldn't solve issues, differences, and disagreements, we went to counseling. Having another individual who is trained to listen and ask the right questions has helped us tremendously. At different times in our marriage, we have both had counseling separately as well. Dan often says, "Every person should go to counseling about every five years to get a reset on various issues." Counseling really is a wonderful tool for closeness.

MARY: I agree wholeheartedly. If your partner isn't ready to go as a couple, begin counseling yourself. Not only will this help you personally, but your counselor can suggest ways you might get your partner to join you.

CAROL: Professional input can be tremendously helpful. As my husband and I have operated through the decades of our lifelong commitment to one another, we've discovered that things can get messy and painful. We've had to learn how to communicate honestly, respectfully, and openly in sensitive areas. Through this, understanding and growth have been the result.

MARY: For John and me, part of that understanding and growth has been learning to forgive: not holding something against the other, but instead, extending unconditional love and grace. Remembering my own faults in our relationship that have been hard to change is helpful. I can forgive another because there is so much that needs to be forgiven in me.

My husband's mother is in a nursing home and is so lonely. He was wounded by a great deal of abuse in his family and has no desire to go and see her. What should I do?

LYN: This question is very near and dear to my heart because it is the circumstance Dan and I faced. His mother's health was failing; it was time to find her a home. There was way too much unresolved pain and hurt in his heart to have her come to our home, so I took it upon myself to find her a place. She did not want to go, so she was mean and fought the whole way.

I went to see her every week—often several times a week—until she died. I took her grandchildren to see her as often as I could. At the end, my husband was able to muster the strength to go and see her, pray with her, and hug her. She was so happy

It's important to visit those who are captive in their own bodies as they deteriorate. Even if it is inconvenient or they are hardened by life, you will never regret being kind, going to the nursing home, and doing what you can for them.

How should I handle telling our grown kids about our ongoing relationship struggles? I shielded them while they were growing up, but it seems different now.

LYN: Yes, our kids have become adults, so we relate to them differently than when they were younger. From an overall perspective, I think it's important to speak of our mates with respect and honor, even through all our weaknesses. You might be surprised at how much they already know just by watching the two of you. There is always conflict between partners. This requires each of us to grow in our abilities to love, forgive, and resolve conflict well. Growing in these abilities will help you communicate about your struggles with your adult kids.

Try not to gossip. You're a role model for how they talk about difficult relationships within your family and for how they might even talk to others about you.

MARY: I think it's okay to say something like, "There are difficult areas in any relationship, especially in our closest ones. I always want to respect your dad and our relationship by being careful with what I say." You could then share some generalities without being too specific, if you think they need to know more. You might also let them know that you're getting help, like counseling or mentoring, if that's the case. This can be calming and comforting for kids of any age.

DAILY LIVING

What if your spouse habitually makes poor financial decisions? I'm afraid for our future at this stage of life.

LYN: Obviously this is a biggie because it affects so many things. Here are some ideas that can help:

1. Ask your spouse if you can be the accountant for the finances. If they agree, set a brief time to keep them up-to-date weekly and to check in about each of your spending activities.

2. Have a monthly budget meeting to go over your goals and plans for the next month.

3. Notice their spending activities—is there a pattern? Initiate a kind and respectful conversation about both of your patterns. As we purchase things, we are sometimes trying to fill a void, to escape, to bring excitement to our lives, or something else. Could you each share a vulnerability and talk about that?

4. It's nice to have a third party to point out issues; we don't feel as attacked. If you cannot do any of the above, ask if you two can go to counseling. Often we only need a few sessions to address issues and move forward.

5. Don't forget the outstanding financial resources at ramseysolutions.com. Their Financial Peace University is an effective course that has helped thousands of couples. You can take it online or in person.

My husband has had a drinking problem all of our marriage and it is getting worse since the kids are gone. I find him passed out in front of the TV almost every night. Is there anything I can do?

MARY: I know this is very difficult. Most people with drinking or substance problems are in denial and extremely resistant to becoming aware of this or getting help.

An outstanding resource for you is Al-Anon. This organization is for any loved one or friend of someone with a drinking problem. They offer articles, books, and meetings—both online and in person. I highly recommend that you attend their meetings. Sometimes people have to try two or three different meeting groups to find one that is right for them, but it's well worth the trouble.

You will find experienced companions on your journey who have been where you are and have the answers you are looking for. They will guide you in how to talk to your husband about his problem and how to have peace and joy even before his drinking habits change.

Al-Anon is listed in Section 4, Chapter 5, as is Alcoholics Anonymous, the organization that can help your husband.

What can I do when my spouse doesn't relate to me as an adult? Sometimes he speaks to me as if I were a child.

MARY: This is a relational dynamic many women and men experience.

Tell your husband you've discovered a resource that you think will make your relationship better. Explain that you've noticed times when the two of you interact in a way that doesn't work for you, and you think the following exercise will help. Read the following sentences together and do the exercise as suggested:

It's common for couples to fall into a pattern of relating to one another in the manner of a parent or child, rather than as adults. This ends up making one or both frustrated. From the lists below, circle the words that describe what you notice in yourself and in the other when communicating. You might use one color of pen for yourself and a different color for your spouse. Consider not discussing them in depth at this point, but simply looking at each other's list and taking in how you each experience your relationship.

Next, talk together about the words describing the "adult" that would be preferable for each of you.

Finally, talk about a strategy in which you can choose the "adult" ways of relating, and some type of signal you can lovingly convey to the other when they are relating as a "parent" or "child."

One approach for drawing the other into an adult way of relating is to proactively do this yourself. When one person begins relating as an adult, this can change the dynamic so that the other also relates in this way. Conversely, when one person is relating as child or parent, the other can unintentionally revert to relating as either a parent or child.

Don't forget that it's hard to break patterns, so give yourselves a lot of patience as you're transforming your relationship in this way. Here are the lists to circle and then discuss:

Child: Argumentative, Rebellious, Pouter, Withdrawn, Selfish, Self-centered, Rude, Hitting, Stubborn, Hopelessness, Lost, Lies, Exaggerates, Impatient, Ignores, Passive-Aggressive, Tattles, Reactionary, Tantrums, Revenge, Holds Grudge, Defensive, Sneaky, Blamer, Manipulates, Swears, Addictions, Hot-headed, Yells, Worrier, Compliant, Threatens, Exaggerates, Cheats/affairs

Parent: Self-appointed Teacher, Drill Sergeant, Hovering, Over-protective, Smothering, Controlling, Argumentative, Impatient, Punishing, Demanding, Permissive, Enabling, Shamer, Co-Dependent, Hot-headed, Yells, Threatens, Abusive, Critical, Bossy, Lectures, Worrier, "You" statements

Adult: Goal-stater, Polite, Truthful, Hopeful, Loving, Joyful, Communicates, Peaceful, Honorable, Resourceful, Secure, Humble, Generous, Responsible, Forgiving, Trusting, Patient, Kind, Good, Faithful, Considerate, Loyal, Gentle, Self-controlled, Persevering, Clarifies, Apologizes, "I" statements

I am a morning person, and my spouse is a night owl. How can we ensure we connect every day?

CAROL: It helps my husband and me to have emotional touchpoints throughout our days:

○ Calling each other in between work or other commitments.

○ Catching up on our day before dinner whenever possible.

○ Going on walks.

○ Traveling together for work.

○ Socializing with friends and our grown kids.

Connection can be found if you are intentional and seek to understand what your spouse values. You can do all of these things in the middle of the day whether you are a night owl or a morning person.

When do I know that I personally need to change in our relationship, or even pursue therapy?

MARY: It's healthy and normal to need therapy at various times in our lives. The stigma for going to counseling has slowly diminished, but some still feel it means that they are significantly flawed. In actuality, each one of us as humans will need to get expert input to navigate life's hurdles. Here are a few signals that you need therapy individually, as a couple, or with other family members:

○ Ongoing anxious or intrusive thoughts

○ Apathy

○ Hopelessness

○ Ongoing relationship problems, negative patterns, and tensions

○ Overwhelming fatigue

○ Disproportionate rage, anger, or resentment

○ Alcohol, substance, or porn issues

○ Extreme overuse of screen devices

○ Significant changes or disruptions in sleep or appetite

○ Ongoing difficulty adjusting to a new job, role, location, or situation

○ Feeling incredibly overwhelmed

○ Avoiding social situations

○ Inability to control your emotions

○ You just don't care about anything

○ Significant work issues

○ Depression

○ Attention Deficit Hyperactivity Disorder (ADHD)

○ Trauma

○ Grief

There are resources listed in Section 4, Chapter 5 to help you find a professional counselor if you don't know where to start. One resource that people overlook is to call a local place of worship and ask for recommendations.

TAKE ACTION

○ Describe a couple of things from this chapter that you definitely want to apply. What are your next steps?

○ What dreams do you have together that the busyness of earlier years prevented you from fulfilling?

○ In this season, what expectations do you each have for your relationship? Write down yours, and ask your partner to do this as well. Be concise and try to state things in a positive, kind way. How can you navigate expectations that are different from each other? (You can utilize the exercise in this chapter.)

○ Would you and your significant person benefit from counseling in any area? If so, what's holding you back from setting up an appointment? How will you proceed?

Look through the resources in Section 4, Chapter 5. Write down any that would be helpful for you. Make a plan to use the resources and add them to your calendar.

6

YOUR KIDS

Relationships make the world go round, and they can definitely make our heads go round. There is nothing more dizzying than navigating relationships with our grown children, through all their various phases and romantic attachments. From the time they leave our homes to attend college or start jobs, through all their adult connections, romantic alliances, and other challenges, we can find ourselves puzzled about how—and how much—to be involved. Things become more complicated with each new person they form a bond with, or when problems like addiction, mental illness, or criminal activity enter the picture. We learn in new ways to live from a place of wisdom, grace, and truth.

YOUR BEST POSSIBLE RELATIONSHIP

What should I be aiming for in my relationship with my adult kids? What is realistic in terms of an overall vision?

MARY: I think it's twofold. First, we want to maintain a loving, kind, supportive relationship with them through their ups and downs and to show unconditional love in many ways. Apart from maintaining a respectful and caring rapport, it can be challenging to achieve another hope that most parents have: to influence and guide our grown children, helping them to overcome difficulties and reach their fullest potential. This relationship can be complex and multifaceted, requiring wisdom and skill.

How can we build healthy relationships with our adult children and also as a family unit?

CAROL: It's crucial to intentionally build a good one-on-one relationship with each person, which ultimately strengthens our entire family.

MARY: I invite you all to learn from my many mistakes! Following are some things I've discovered.

Through the various seasons of their adulthood, my time spent with each adult kid looks different. I've learned to adjust this according to their desires, availability, and boundaries. If they don't want to spend as much time as you do, guess what? You probably need to change—in your expectations, boundaries, communication style, or even your likeability. Sometimes we have to work to become the kind of person they want to be with and do the kinds of things they like to do. We can learn to be interested in things that interest them.

We must respect one another's boundaries. Usually this means that we as parents need to accept our kids' boundaries if we want them to like being with us.

We can't smother our kids with questions about their lives, nor try to control or manipulate them. To avoid this temptation, we can help ourselves by focusing upon and pouring ourselves into our own lives.

Often, we have to adjust our expectations of our kids and time spent with them. You may discover you have expectations you never knew you had. I love principles like "Live and Let Live," "Let Go and Let God," and the Serenity Prayer. These are foundational perspectives in many recovery programs. Study the thinking behind these principles so that you will be more peaceful and your relationships can be healthier.

Give your adult kids verbal affirmation. Support their decisions. Only offer advice when asked. One of my adult kids started avoiding my husband and me during a period when we were giving him a lot of input because he was going through a difficult period. We realized that our advice-giving was keeping him away, so we stopped, and guess what? He started coming around again. As we simply listened to and loved him, our relationship grew and blossomed.

Avoid the perception or reality of favoring one child over another. Even older adult kids notice things and can feel slighted, even when that truly isn't where you're coming from.

Don't gossip about your adult kids, especially to others in your family.

Adjust your way of communicating to fit their styles and "world." Be a good listener. When we seem out of touch, they don't want to spend time with us or talk to us as much. Remember how it used to be with "old Aunt Mabel?" You tolerated her presence and tried to be around her as little as possible. Don't be Aunt Mabel.

Plan times when your entire family can be together. This may involve work and intentionality on your part, but it's worth it.

Enjoy your adult kids through the decades and love them unconditionally in your attitudes, words, and actions.

LYN: It's important to have a strong relationship with their dad, so that the family sees your love and respect when issues come up. This may result in our grown kids wanting to learn from us. When we set this type of atmosphere, our family unit will be strong and lasting through the ups and downs of life's predicaments.

What should I do when I have different expectations for our relationship than my grown child has?

CAROL: I've learned to not push for things I want that are different from my adult child's desires. I follow their "red light, yellow light, and green light" signals. When I sense a "red light" from them, I don't proceed. When I sense a "yellow light," I proceed slowly with caution in my words or actions. If I push for a "green light," they resist. If I don't push, a "green light" often comes at the right time. This has been a challenge for me, but I'm growing through my mistakes and victories.

MARY: It's usually us as parents who must adjust our expectations, whether those expectations are for the quality of our relationship, amount of time spent together, or choices our kids make. One way to adjust your expectations is to list all the positive things you can think of that go along with lowering your expectations, and to find things to be thankful for within that list. For example, when my kids have to live far away from me, I've learned to focus on the fun things we can do when I visit them. I've plunged into creative ways to stay in touch. I've also learned to focus more upon my own life apart from them, including the worthwhile, fulfilling things God has given me to do.

How much should I share of my own life struggles and joys with them?

MARY: Sharing these things can cause your adult child to feel much closer to you and greatly enhance your relationship. As in all things, balance is the key. Be aware of whether you tend to overshare or undershare and adjust in the opposite direction. In some life seasons, your child may not want or need to hear as much from you. Be patient—other seasons may provide more in-depth conversation opportunities.

What can I do when my relationship with my adult child isn't what I had hoped for?

LYN: Having a grown child is an opportunity that can last for many decades. My husband, Dan, always tells me, "Let some time go by." After thirty-seven years together, I have learned to follow this advice. People—especially our grown children—need space to live and they don't always want to check in with their parents or discuss every decision they make.

Our grown children have left the nest, and they get to decide things without our input or approval. Our expectations can breed unspoken anger, and no one wants to be around someone who is miffed with them.

MARY: You might try having an open conversation with them about their hopes and expectations for your relationship, in a way that makes them feel safe and non-defensive—but be ready to adapt yourself to what they want. You can't force them. Be ready to examine yourself and make changes that will help them want a closer relationship with you.

How do I know when to proactively address problems with my adult child or even seek therapy?

MARY: If your child is open and ready to discuss problems, then proceed carefully according to Carol's previous "red light, yellow light, green light" principle. If you find yourself "stuck," unable to make progress, that's a good time to seek therapy. You can get counseling for yourself about the relationship, whether or not your child is ready to go together. The therapist can help you know what to do next, and your grown child may decide to join you in sessions. Either way, your own therapy may resolve the issue you're experiencing.

FRIEND, MENTOR, OR PARENT?

How do you gracefully make the transition from the role of parent in authority to that of friend and mentor? Is it okay to want to be their "friend?"

CAROL: As our three kids have launched, we've let them know that we love and pray for them, but we want them to live their own lives. If they want our help or advice, we will always be available to them. Having this as a foundation has brought the right order to our adult child-and-parent relationship. We've moved from being their authority to being a supportive, loving parent and sometimes a mentor.

In our family, I've found it wise to wait on our adult children to pursue more of a friendship connection. There are obvious transitional times in our children's lives like college, the start of jobs, marriage, and having children themselves. Through these seasons, their needs and desires change and evolve. When we keep building a supportive relational foundation, adult friendship and mentorship may happen. It works best when we allow time for maturity and readiness to take place in the heart of each adult child.

MARY: I think that in many ways we can be our child's friend as an adult, but we will always be in the unique, prized role of parent. This is a special, one-of-a kind role that we don't want to lessen or abandon. For each parent, each child, and each relationship, this can mean different things based upon personalities, cultures, and life stages. As parents, we want to strive to be someone they can look up to and honor in a way that is different from a mere friend. A parent role also has different boundaries than a friendship, for both the parent and the child. These are things we have to think about as we navigate our various roles through the decades with our adult kids.

How much should I be the initiator in getting together with my grown child? What about overall communication when it comes to calling or texting?

CAROL: We've learned to allow our grown kids to go with their own rhythms of communication. In other words, we've learned to wait until they actually want to talk or text with us. The opposite is to apply pressure, expectation, or guilt from the parent to the grown child. Does anyone really want a relationship with someone who creates pressure or guilt?

I had to learn this the hard way as I tended to push too much.

After all, we're trying to build a relationship where they truly want to communicate with us. As your relationship with each adult child matures, it may allow for more freedom in the back-and-forth of who initiates. Our grown children find it important that we have our own lives and are not dependent on their affirmation or connection.

Our daughter lives with her boyfriend. Do we relate to him as if they are married and he is our son-in-law?

MARY: This can be a tough one, based upon each parent's individual values, beliefs, and goals. I've seen different parents approach this in various ways. It might help to ask yourself questions like these:

- How important is it to me to have an ongoing relationship with my son or daughter?
- Will my beliefs or values be compromised if I continue a relationship while they are living together?
- Could my relationship, love, and support be life-changing for my daughter and her partner over time?

I know one set of parents who accepted the situation and kept building the relationship without referring to them as married or in-laws. The young couple themselves did not use these terms, so it worked.

Another parent couple made it clear that they disapproved of anyone living together without marriage, and they didn't have contact with the young couple for several years. When their daughter had two children in the relationship while remaining unmarried, the parent couple decided they did want a relationship with their daughter and her children. They now spend a lot of time with the young family, hoping their beliefs and values will have a positive influence.

For help with this and other tricky questions, you might search the website https://www.focusonthefamily.com. This resource has many articles, audio recordings, and books that address difficult issues for faith-based parents.

CAROL: In daily life, it might help to relate to her partner as you would if they were in a relationship but not living together. You could be friendly and respectful, knowing that your relationship might have a positive impact on him and your daughter.

What do you do if your grown child rejects your input into her life?

CAROL: I think this happens to most parents in some way. Rejection can take various forms, including silence, disagreement, anger, or even rebellion. Based on this, instead of giving input, I seek to love them and avoid arguments.

MARY: When I experience some form of rejection, I begin by asking myself if I could have done something differently in the situation. Maybe I shouldn't have given input, or maybe it was the way I did it. I try to learn from my mistakes so I don't keep repeating them to my own detriment. Jim Burns says it well in the subtitle of his book, *Doing Life with your Adult Children* (Zondervan, 2019). The subtitle is "Keep Your Mouth Shut and the Welcome Mat Out." Their response often tells me I need to keep my mouth shut and simply build our relationship. As I wrote previously, it works best to wait to give advice until it is asked for.

How can I tell when I am being too controlling?

MARY: Ask yourself, "Do I want to change, control, or manage my adult child? Do I feel I will only be happy or at peace if my child does this or that?"

If you answer "yes" to these questions, you probably have a control issue. Learning about codependency may help you to overcome this and to be a happier individual with healthier relationships. You might start with *Codependent No More* (Hazeldon, 1986) by Melody Beattie.

When I find out my grown children are struggling, I want to rescue them, and they seem to appreciate my support. Why shouldn't I help them when I have the means and ability to do so?

CAROL: In many cases, part of loving a grown child is choosing to help by not enabling them. Even though it's painful for parents to watch their child struggle, in the long run it will help them more to let them figure it out for themselves. Some examples of what not to do include helping them inappropriately when they are making unwise choices, protecting them by seeking to cover up their mistakes, and approving their bad decisions because we fear confrontation or desire their approval.

MARY: We all learn by struggling and failing. We don't want to deprive our kids of valuable opportunities that will help them more in the long run than our rescuing efforts.

It's so hard to see our adult kids struggle and not help them. And yet, in many cases, that's the exact thing to do if we want them to learn, grow, and not repeat the same mistakes over and over. This includes issues involving relationships, employment, grandchildren, finances, substance abuse problems, and so much more. Knowing when to help them and when to let them struggle to learn on their own can be confusing at times.

There are things we can do when our kids are teens to help them slowly transition to their full independence in their twenties. We can allow them to struggle and fail along the way, while teaching them appropriately while they are still under our care. When our kids are ten to eighteen years old, this includes things like jobs, checking accounts, and what helps or hinders relationships. We can share our own failures in these realms and our lessons learned. This builds the relationship while letting them learn from our mistakes.

An internet search such as "When should I help my adult child?" or "How to help my teen grow into an independent adult" can produce helpful articles. Of course, be sure to consider the reliability of the resources you find. Don't forget to check out Section 4, Chapter 6 on this topic.

WHEN YOU WANT YOUR CHILD TO CHANGE

How can I continue to parent my adult child, affecting her character and choices in life?

MARY: For the first two decades of our children's lives, we had a great deal of influence and responsibility, affecting their choices and character. Once they become adults, they take responsibility for all that we have given them. If you continue to cultivate a good relationship with your adult child, you may still have opportunities where she wants your wisdom and influence. But you have to be careful because too much input can hurt your relationship. The result may be that she won't want advice from you and may even want less contact with you. As with any adult relationship, we don't want to be around someone who gives us a lot of advice. We want to be around people who enjoy us and support us.

My daughter, who is 36, won't listen to any of my advice, even though I'm a lot wiser and more experienced. What can I do to make her more open to what I say?

CAROL: More is "caught than taught." We are each responsible only for our own choices. We have to live our own lives, focusing upon our own growth and self-improvement. We need to wait for opportunities where our kids initiate a time to process and dialogue about their lives. This feels challenging but it is the right and most effective thing to do.

MARY: Welcome to the "parent of grown kids" club! Our kids have to make their own mistakes, just like we did, and our focus can't be upon changing them. Our focus needs to be upon building a good relationship with them, supporting them, affirming them, doing things together that bring mutual enjoyment, talking about things that interest them, and loving them self-sacrificially. If you're a person of faith, pray for them and trust God to work in his timing and ways.

LYN: This life is lived in seasons and decades. It's probably time for you to stop giving your thoughts on her choices. You may have offended or hurt her without knowing it. They say that "time heals all" and sometimes that is true. You may need to give your daughter some space in which to live her choices without having to argue about them with you.

She needs to live her experiences—like you did—to gain her wisdom. Let some time go by, and in the meantime, be praying.

Now that my kids are adults living on their own, they've embraced beliefs and values very different from mine. It's hard for me to understand or relate to them. We've grown further and further apart. What can I do?

MARY: Jim Burns has a good chapter on this in his book *Doing Life with Your Adult Children.* He gives ideas on things like how to "maintain a climate of openness and grace," "refuse to beat yourself up," and how to "continue to influence them." Keep nurturing your relationships with your kids. The phrase "don't stop the story too soon" is a source of help for many parents. This means that you are in one chapter of the book of their lives, and there will be many more to come. You don't know where that story is going to end, so don't let yourself become discouraged. Keep living one day at a time—one experience at a time—with your kids, focusing on your own life's path and decisions.

CAROL: It sounds simplistic, but love does cover a multitude of errors. This means that your love is like a blanket surrounding them, regardless of how they differ from you. Finding common ground can be a powerful bonding agent, even in your differences. (For example, "I like movies … you like movies … let's enjoy them together.") They are not at their destination yet. And neither am I.

LYN: When I was young and doing foolish things, my dad once said, "I do not condone what you are doing, but neither do I condemn you." He was loving in his tone of voice even while acknowledging that he would not do what I was doing—living with my partner, who later became my husband. Dad never avoided spending time with me. I never felt him to be angry, disgusted, or displeased. He always seemed to be excited to see me and he seemed to like me. Looking back, I realize he was a very kind, wise man.

Our kids are grown, independent adults, so we need to treat them as such. Let's not break our relationship over difference of opinion.

What is the right way to respond to the issue of entitlement in an adult child?

MARY: The word entitlement can mean different things. In our current culture, entitlement is the mindset behind the actions of people who believe they deserve to have things and special privileges given to them. They feel they have a right to certain things, and that their perceived needs and wants should be met. This usually happens on a subconscious level; they're probably unaware this is their underlying perspective.

LYN: Depending on the issue of entitlement, I think it helps us as parents to realize that we may have helped to create it. We may have done this by providing finances for them as adults, so that now they expect it. We may have excused their inappropriate behavior many times in the past when we should have talked to them about it. It's important to be kind as you say, "In the past I paid for x, y, or z, but now that you are an adult, this needs to be taken over by you. I'm sorry this may feel as if it is coming out of left field, but since this bill is your responsibility, we have to start somewhere." Admitting our part of the problem can help them to own up more quickly and to realize there is a change coming, but it doesn't have to become an argument.

CAROL: This has been a long, hard lesson for me, but I've grown and gained a lot of understanding. When the opportunity presents itself, talk gently about specific challenging areas when you see entitlement in one of your kids. If they argue or become defensive, don't get pulled into destructive conflict. Take the high road. We are older and have experienced more of life, so we can respond with wisdom and grace.

I've finally realized that my 32-year-old daughter is an addict. She lives in an apartment about thirty minutes from me. What can I do to help her?

MARY: Addiction is a complex, multi-faceted issue. First, educate yourself on what to do and what not to do to help a loved one with an addiction. Al-Anon is an organization devoted to exactly that, and we've listed it in Section 4: Chapter 5, along with other addiction resources. You could also consult with a counselor who specializes in helping families with addictions. Your church may utilize services provided by an addiction program, so check with them. Often, what we think will help our loved one is the exact opposite of what actually helps them when it comes to addictions. This is why it's vital to educate yourself on all aspects of helping a loved one who is addicted.

TRICKY NAVIGATION

What are some typical "tricky navigation" issues with grown children at this stage?

MARY: The bad news is there can be so many different issues with our grown kids. The good news is you're in great company with the rest of us.

Some issues?

What should you do when they move away from home for the first time, and you suspect that they're involved in an unhealthy dating relationship? How much should you get involved?

Or when you suspect their anger issues have become a problem, but now they're married with two kids. What should you do and to what extent?

Or maybe they're closer to their spouse's parents than to you, and they seem fine with that. All of these require new information on how to proceed.

CAROL: We all have hopes and dreams for our kids we don't even know we have until they are not fulfilled. This includes areas like their marriages, their career choices, and the quality of our relationships with them. I never realized how deeply I desired to have a true friendship with my grown kids. Like all relationships, it takes continual hard work to understand that each grown child is different and requires varying elements of care. A lot of the solutions involve my own self-awareness in how to proceed.

I'm having trouble letting go because I care so much about my child and worry about him. How can I let go of worrying and caring so much?

MARY: Care and concern for our kids is a normal part of loving them. It's so hard to see them struggle as they're going through difficult times. For some parents this becomes an obsession, to their own mental and emotional detriment.

I've had to deal with worrying many times, like when my son was fighting as a Marine in Iraq, or when my daughter was pregnant, and tests revealed possible abnormalities in my unborn grandchild.

There are a variety of helpful approaches and techniques for dealing with this topic of anxiety. Check out our resources in Section 4, Chapter 6.

Why can I relate so well to some of my children but not others?

LYN: There are many personalities and temperaments within a family. Each of us reacts differently because of our God-given traits. It's important to understand your own, your husband's, your children's, their spouses', and your grandchildren's dispositions. Understanding their temperaments, needs, and goals will help immensely in your relationships. Learning how to tailor discussions and plans can become a fun family journey.

Even though some temperaments don't like quizzes or personality tests, they ultimately help us decipher what may be going on in another's head.

MARY: We've listed several helpful references in Section 4, Chapter 2. These will help you to understand varying temperaments, strengths and weaknesses. Even if you are the only one willing to start this journey of understanding, it will be immensely helpful, and the others may want to join you as they see your positive results.

CAROL: I think the adage that "opposites attract" is often true, even in relationships with our children. When we are a lot like someone else, there can be a repelling effect, which can be navigated as we all mature and remain open to growth and awareness in our family unit.

Also, strengthening your one-on-one relationships can strengthen your entire family. Knowing this motivates me to keep leaning in and developing our relationships, even when things feel difficult with an individual. My goal and passion is to keep our family unit strong through the ups and downs of life.

How do I navigate the tension of having a difficult relationship with one child and an easier relationship with another child? I try not to compare them, but I think they notice the differences in how I relate to them, and it's hard on me as well.

MARY: This brings us into the old topic of sibling rivalry. It shows up in many forms, for them and for us, even when our kids are adults. Some personalities go well together, and some don't. It's important to intentionally keep your focus upon each individual child's strengths and valuable uniqueness. Never gossip to one child about another or their family, and do not extol their different strengths and accomplishments too much to the others. These things will breed resentment, competition, and further struggles for everyone.

Each child will go through difficult seasons, and while one person may be difficult this year, another will be difficult the next. The very person I struggled with during one season may be the most supportive and understanding in another season of life. Most parents innately love and treasure their kids unconditionally. Sometimes, though, we must give time and effort to grow as individuals for our kids' sake, to be filled with grace in our hearts and actions toward them. Be sure to do this through reading, classes, or counseling. Your own growth will help you to navigate difficulties well with your adult kids. We can serve as a role model and leave a lasting legacy.

Why are some of my children grateful and others dismiss the things I do for them? Am I doing something wrong?

LYN: This might be due to having different individual love languages. Remember that the five love languages are words of affirmation, receiving gifts, acts of service, quality time, and physical affection. A person feels loved when she receives in the area of her love language. We tend to give to others based upon what makes us feel loved, rather than upon what makes them feel loved. This is true for significant others, our children, our grandchildren, etc. It's important that we realize each person is different in this way and provide what that person longs for. See Section 4, Chapter 5 for Gary Chapman's *The Five Love Languages*.

When do I help my kids and when am I enabling them? I'm thinking of things like financial matters, babysitting, etc.

CAROL: Helping is doing something for someone he is not capable of doing himself. Enabling is doing for someone things that he should and could be doing himself.

I know of one family who faced this challenge when their adult daughter was a college graduate and continued to live under their roof. I'll call her Emma. After a few months, the parents realized that Emma was not actively pursuing a job. As a result, they had a conversation with her, discussing specific options and deadlines for how Emma could transition to a new living situation. This included finding work and obtaining enough money to move out by a specific date. They lovingly let her know that continuing to live at home was not an option and explained that continuing to do so was detrimental to her own personal growth.

This type of conversation takes careful navigation but is prudent for the child emotionally, relationally, and financially. This type of love is intended to put your grown child on a journey toward healing and wholeness.

MARY: None of us is exempt from the trap of enabling. We can become overly involved in our kids' lives, which causes us to lose sight of our own needs, values, limitations, and life callings.

When you concentrate on living your own life, boundaries with your kids happen more naturally because your focus and energies are directed elsewhere. In other words, staying involved with your own mission can help prevent you from enabling.

When is it okay to help my adult kid financially?

LYN: This is a common question: "How involved should parents get with their adult child's finances?" We can become so involved in their mishaps that we take to rescuing or giving them a "reset" check, trying to make all their financial problems go away. This is dangerous behavior on our part because, although we mean it to be loving assistance, it can hinder their growth. They need to learn through experience that poor choices have dire consequences, so they don't keep making those same choices over and over. Helping them financially can also breed laziness and entitlement in our grown child. We have to let them learn to live within their budget.

Ideally, parents help their kids learn to create a budget before they leave home. Even after they have launched, we can guide them in this to an extent. If they have issues with managing money, Dave Ramsey has many resources geared for all ages of launching adults.

My adult child has been living with me for two years. Is this okay?

CAROL: There are seasons when having an adult child live with you can be appropriate. When we had two adult children preparing for non-profit work, our home was a base from which they could raise their needed funding until they moved to their new job locations. On the other hand, we can be doing them a disservice, and in some ways causing them to regress, if we are enabling our kids' unhealthy or inappropriate choices.

MARY: We wrote previously about enabling, and that applies here. As the saying goes, "Give a man a fish and he will eat for a day. Teach a man to fish and he will eat for a lifetime." We want our kids to learn to live on their own and to provide for themselves—we won't always be here. It's important for you to think through the reasons your child is living at home, and what steps need to be taken to help him transition to living independently. You can seek the help of a counselor or other professional to assist you in thinking this through.

How should I handle feeling disrespected or marginalized by my adult child?

LYN: Often an adult child is working through a past trauma or trying to learn to set a new boundary. We want to keep our eyes on our future relationships with our kids and their partners. When we feel disrespected or marginalized, we may need to give them time and space. Sometimes staying silent and stepping away will allow them to think through the situation. They may come back to us with an apology or even with newfound respect for us. We can decide what's best to communicate to them about our own feelings and perspectives, keeping the long run in mind.

Not calling out my grown kids on rude behavior all the time has given us some inside jokes later in life that the kids like to bring up. Our home has become a safe harbor, knowing people can make mistakes and won't be immediately "thrown under the bus" by others.

MARY: Yes, sometimes silence speaks louder than words. When I have felt marginalized or disrespected within our family, I look for the right timing and have an honest, authentic conversation with the person. When I was neither accusatory nor defensive, the conversation caused our relationship to become better than ever.

CAROL: This reminds me of the story of a domineering husband who continually pressured his wife to do household tasks. This couple lived on a ranch in the country, where flies were daily visitors. When her husband gave her a list of unending tasks, this lady learned to mentally "flick the fly" off her arm. In other words, "I will do what I can do but this is not going to rob me of inner peace."

The same can be true of our grown kids and the things that bother us. In many cases, we are responding to those who are less mature and perhaps unaware. We can address our own issues, pray, and wait. When the timing is right, we can also take opportunities to share our hurts and desires with our kids. We must remember we cannot control their responses, but only our own. We can turn to friends and family members, who maturely accept and care for us, to experience support and encouragement.

How do I handle significant events with my grown kids (Christmas, Easter, weddings, etc.) when I'm in a difficult relationship with my ex? My daughter is upset because she wants both of us to be at her house for a holiday. This would be meaningful for her, but hard for me.

MARY: It sounds like it's time for an authentic, loving conversation with your daughter about the depths of this. When we reach an impasse in a disagreement with someone, sometimes it's because one or both parties have a deeply rooted dream that's not being fulfilled. You might ask your daughter what dream is at the heart of this. It may stem back to the lost dream of having the three of you back together as an unbroken family. Try to listen to her and even grieve with her the loss that she experienced in the break-up of your family. You may need the help of a counselor to work through it successfully, because this can be hard on you. Have lots of compassion for yourself—and for your daughter—during this part of your journey.

Our twenty-somethings have begun experimenting with vaping and marijuana. Since both are legal in many states, how should we as parents respond?

MARY: This reminds me of the Serenity Prayer, with slightly altered wording: "God, grant me the serenity to accept the people I cannot change, the courage to change the one I can (myself), and the wisdom to know it's me." Once our kids are adults, efforts to change them usually do more harm than good. We can have a meaningful conversation with them about our concerns, and we can earnestly pray for them. But our efforts for change need to be directed toward ourselves, toward learning to achieve inner peace despite our loved ones' choices.

IN-LAWS

What is the best way to develop a good relationship with a son-in-law or daughter-in-law, especially when we've had disagreements and friction in the past?

CAROL: I've benefited from this summary that Henry Cloud shared in a video (he's speaking to a young couple):

"The relationships we have with our families are important, but when you leave and cleave, that means it's time for making decisions outside of those relationships. Their job as a parent is over because a married unit is now a new family. In-law problems occur when that design isn't followed. The best way is to do it before you get married and talk about where the family of origin ends and where the new family begins. If you're in a situation where this conversation has to happen afterward or problems have occurred, you can still make this work. It's okay to gather wisdom from your family, but you are now in a position to make your own decisions."

MARY: As parents of grown kids, we will save ourselves a lot of trouble if we quickly accept our married kids are now their own independent family unit, even if differences in personalities, values, or beliefs cause friction.

We've written a lot about this in previous questions regarding our kids: if we want to have a good relationship with them and be involved in the lives of our kids and grandkids, we parents have to find ways to make sure they know we love and accept them unconditionally. We have to do things with them and their loved ones that they enjoy. We have to reach out and resolve conflict successfully when frictions occur. We may have to alter some things about ourselves or how we do things.

I've made mistakes when I didn't pick up on the very subtle non-verbal communication that let me know an in-law is uncomfortable or unhappy. When I fail to recognize these things, the person doesn't want to come over or be with us anymore. Then, my son or daughter doesn't come around as much either. I've learned to ask my adult child what I can do—or stop doing—to help their loved one want to be with us more. I'm motivated to change or improve by my hopes for the coming years with my kids and grandkids.

My son-in-law doesn't really like me—we have very different political and spiritual views. Yet, he's the father of my young grandchildren, so do you have any advice as I weather the long years ahead?

MARY: In various relationships throughout life, I've had to pray and research things like, "how to be in a relationship with a difficult person." There are many internet articles and books about this. Try an internet search for "difficult people information." You'll find a plethora of resources to get you started. You might even discover that you are the difficult person, so then you can research how to make changes. Discovering this can be a blessing in disguise, because you may unlock new doors that have been holding you back. It's never too late to change and grow.

We can be role models in our families of what it's like to grow and to extend grace and wisdom when someone significantly disagrees with us. Being an example of these things can benefit our kids and grandkids, leaving a lasting legacy.

CAROL: "When you're in your own lane, there's no traffic" (Ava DuVernay). One of the greatest gifts we give our kids and grandkids is to live our own lives in our own lanes. Though my personal emotions can lead me down a road of wanting deep validation from my extended family, I can be secure in who I am. My identity is not based on their opinions of me. I can relax in this reality.

Family relationships are challenging when we know that others hold strong political or spiritual viewpoints different from ours. However, when we sow good actions and attitudes, we will reap the benefits, and others will as well. Our life-giving ways will reap a harvest in the long years ahead.

How can I respond when my daughter-in-law's parents say bad things about my son in front of their children?

CAROL: In 1985 at a Family Life Conference, we were introduced to three ways people can handle conflict or misunderstanding.

1. Win: "Whatever it takes I will come out on top."
2. Withdraw: "I will run away and hide and avoid things altogether."
3. Resolve: "How can we come together in our differences and reach a place of understanding?"

What might it look like to encourage your son to initiate a conversation with his in-laws regarding their negative talk in front of their grandchildren? What if he told them he cared for them and wanted to reach a place where they all felt heard and understood as much as possible? Again, this is ultimately not our issue or responsibility as parents, but we can certainly stand on the sideline and root for unity and change.

How do I relate to our adult child's in-laws? Are they "family" for us, too?

LYN: When our adult children got married, I feel they left our "clan" and started another "clan." If they have children, our grandchildren will be a part of their "clan," not ours. When we relate to the in-laws, as well as to our grown married kids, we realize they are all independent units. We enjoy their company, we speak the best of them, and we are committed to not bad-mouthing anyone—especially our children's in-laws. This would only breed resentment, confusion, and future offenses, and it could put my adult child in a predicament of having to choose.

My husband and I are committed to not comparing families. We all did the very best we could. We are supportive of their successes and treat them with respect and love.

CAROL: My opinion is that they are my married kid's family, but they are not my husband's and my family. In many ways, we treat them like we would anyone else: with kindness, care, and interest in their lives. We show excitement and encouragement regarding their special times with our married kids. We desire to keep open lines of communication for the long haul.

I'm jealous of the other set of grandparents, because my grandchildren have a better relationship with them. What can I do?

MARY: Jealousy is something most of us struggle with at various points in our lives. One definition describes it as feeling "hostile toward a rival or one believed to enjoy an advantage." I don't think it's uncommon for grandparents to feel this. I've experienced jealousy and its sibling, comparison, throughout my life, and the principles I learn each time serve me well the next time it comes up.

Every person has their own set of great and difficult things throughout life. When I'm jealous of someone's "great thing," I'm not seeing their current, past, or future "difficult things." I'm also not focusing upon the "great things" in my current, past, or future life. I might have three wonderful things happening right now, but all I focus upon is what I don't have.

Two practical things that help me are gratitude and prayer: I make it a habit to thank God for them and to pray wonderful things for them. This can powerfully change my attitude and outlook.

My husband and I are divorced, and we have three kids together. How do I handle the tension I feel with his parents now, since they are and will always be my kids' grandparents?

MARY: Several complexities are involved here. Jim Burns has written a great chapter about this in *Doing Life with Your Adult Children*, titled "In-Laws, Stepfamilies, and the Blend." Also, don't forget to look over the other resources listed in Section 4, Chapter 6, because this topic will be addressed in various ways.

This time in your life calls for you to be the highest version of yourself, exhibiting unconditional love, integrity, kindness, and forgiveness. The apostle Paul wrote,

"If it is possible, as far as it depends on you, live at peace with everyone." You can only do your part to extend grace and kindness, knowing that their response to you is not in your control. But when we treat others with kindness and respect, it often brings out the best in them.

HELP FOR THE FAMILY UNIT

What are some traditions that my husband and I can implement to carry our family into a future of closeness and fun?

CAROL: We plan yearly family vacations that help us to nurture our ongoing relationships. To keep our tanks full as a couple, my husband and I plan quarterly overnight getaways. We take our grown kids and their spouses for dessert or dinner dates occasionally.

LYN: Money is a challenge for most of us. Having said that, we do try to connect with our grown children and our grandchildren as often as their schedules allow. Often my husband Dan cooks, enjoys it thoroughly, and teaches the grown kids some moves. We also reach out intentionally to have family group dates, a favorite event for all.

Another tradition is to celebrate every person's birthday to the hilt. Each child has always been allowed to invite friends over for parties. As the kids have grown into adults, we like to go to a nice restaurant, dress up, and really celebrate the birthday person. A critical lesson that I've learned, often the hard way, is that some of our kids are more introverted than others. For them, it's important not to have the restaurant sing or to insist that we all go around and share what we like about the birthday star. But for extroverts, we engage everyone at the table in the shenanigans. The goal is for the birthday person to be celebrated in the way they feel the most loved.

I enjoy having family gatherings at my house, but as a mom, I'm so aware of how everyone's doing, their interpersonal frictions, and individual problems. How can I be at peace and not worry about these things when we're supposed to be having fun together?

MARY: I practice the principles of the Serenity Prayer. I cannot change other people, but I can change myself. I can learn perspectives and techniques to stay focused on what will allow me to be at peace while offering love and joy to others.

LYN: I have had to learn to stay focused on "my side of the street." Even though our individual lives bump up against one another, it doesn't mean there's a task for me to take action on. People are often in different places: one person may be celebrating a huge goal they've accomplished, another may have had a real kick-in-the-teeth experience, someone else may have PMS, and another has had an extreme fight on the way to our gathering. Moods and attitudes vary, and I've come to realize that I cannot choose how others show up. Instead, I can focus on my own attitudes and actions.

I also try to guard my expectations, because unrealistic expectations lead to disappointment. Time is so short, and I don't want to squander the brief moments of family time by getting offended or worried. Now that I'm older, I've realized that family gatherings come and go so quickly in the larger timeline of life. Enjoy your family now, in this moment, and focus on what is going well.

How do we keep family events safe and inviting for all when some people in the family love to talk and have the capacity to ask questions and discuss personal issues, but others in the family are shy, quiet, or guarded?

LYN: Introverts usually process information within themselves, and extroverts enjoy processing out loud. When the family is getting together, it can be a rich experience for all to be able to share—but some will feel scared to do so.

If there are going to be any questions or expectations of anyone, I've found it best to alert everyone before the event occurs. This way, they have personal time to process and prepare rather than be put on the spot. Dan and I work hard to help anyone in our home to feel safe. My family knows that Dan is an extreme introvert, so when he shares something vulnerable from his life experience, it helps break the ice for others.

Some people aren't in a place where they want to talk very much. Some people are very private and will always be very private. To address this, we have the agreement that it's fine for people to either talk or remain quiet. When a group question is asked, people answer in a random order—we don't answer by going in a circle. That does not feel safe, and we want to be sensitive to everyone.

CAROL: At a family Christmas gathering, I observed that each of our grown children was married to, or in a relationship with, a more introverted and quieter person. At one of our meals, one of the men asked a sentimental question for each of us to answer. It brought me joy to see how these significant others balanced out their one-on-one relationships with our children and our family dynamic. Could we allow everyone to be themselves and to contribute in their own individual styles? That's the beauty of having different personalities in the room. This can work for us and not against us.

My wife keeps taking the side of our grown daughter in things we disagree about, even when my daughter is present. What can I do?

CAROL: You might ask your wife about this privately in a gentle and loving manner. Ask if you could make an agreement to talk about topics of difference privately when your daughter is not present.

Also, when the timing seems right, you could kindly ask your wife why she tends to take your daughter's side in issues of disagreement. Even if she denies that this is true, you have raised her awareness of this issue, which may help to resolve it.

LYN: If your wife doesn't share your concerns and continues forward with this behavior, you can ask if she would be willing to talk to a counselor so a third party could guide you objectively to a resolution.

I have to admit, I've often been tempted to side with one of my grown kids when I feel my husband isn't sensitive to what they are going through. I've learned how to stay in communication with him about this—but not when any of our children are present.

My husband often avoids difficult conversations when our grown children try to address issues. How can I help to facilitate better communication between them?

CAROL: You could go over some particular topics your children have mentioned and kindly talk about how he would be helpful with them. You might point out how his strengths can be beneficial in difficult conversations and issues with your kids.

MARY: We've previously mentioned Milan and Kay Yerkovich's book *How We Love.* You and your husband could each take the simple free tests on the website to determine your individual styles of relating to loved ones. You would come away with a greater understanding of one another and could discuss your perspectives on how to navigate this issue together. I enjoy spending time with my grown children, but each child is so different. How can we have family meals and holidays when their preferences are so diametrically opposed? For example, some like to enjoy alcoholic drinks and some feel alcohol should never be around their children.

CAROL: We can adjust our approach to accommodate those who are present. When everyone is together for one event, try to find some middle ground that is OK with everyone. Encourage them to be flexible and not worry about what other people are doing so everyone can have an enjoyable time.

MARY: This can be especially challenging in our current times when people have widely differing opinions. You might communicate with the family that you're looking forward to a gathering with unity, fun, and positivity—say it in a way that is lighthearted and natural for you. Then be sure to model this in your individual and group times.

LYN: It can be helpful to let people know when a get-together will not be a long event, but just a meal to share space and camaraderie for a little while.

Regarding alcohol, sometimes substance abuse or addiction can be an issue for an individual, even though others don't know about it or consider it. It's important for grown children to learn to be sensitive to one another's preferences. It may be important to alert each family member to the nuances and goals of caring for others.

When my husband, "the patriarch," states a request regarding our time, everyone in our family accepts it more readily. As a parent, I've learned that prayer is a key element in family closeness and difficult issues. Give God time to work.

How do I handle starting a blended family? My new husband has three grown kids, and I have two. My kids don't like him, and I have a struggle with one of his. Do you have any advice?

CAROL: A wise family member shared these helpful ideas with me:

- Respect that the parent-child bond is strong and should remain strong for the sake of everyone involved. The new husband or wife should not disrupt that, nor pit the parent against their child.
- For the sake of your marriage, be very careful about criticizing each other's children. Your role is to support the parent in interactions with their kids, and to remain positive.
- In dealing with your stepchildren, accept that you will never replace the divorced or deceased parent, and do not try to do so. Instead, gradually try to become an "ally."
- Seek to do no harm. Don't discipline or criticize them.

○ If they clearly do not like you, give them space and don't try to force things.

○ Look for ways to gently help them over time in order to build trust and make yourself an ally: make job connections for them, babysit grandchildren or go to their games, stop by the grocery store, etc.

○ Focus on building a happy relationship with your partner and hopefully, over time, the kids will value seeing their mom or dad happy.

○ Be willing to do things and vacation separately in smaller groups with your kids as needed. Don't push large family gatherings or vacations unless people really want them.

○ Be gentle and forgiving with yourself. Seek to do the best you can. Encourage all the kids to do the same.

TAKE ACTION

○ What has your journey been like with each of your adult kids so far? Describe a few high and low points.

○ What next step do you want to take in building your relationship with each of your kids?

○ Is there a problem you need to proactively address, whether in your attitude, thinking, behavior, or relationship? How will you begin to address this?

Look through the resources in Section 4, Chapter 6. Write down any that would be helpful for you. Make a plan to use the resources and add them to your calendar.

7

YOUR GRANDKIDS

Grandkids can be one of life's greatest treasures. How can we build strong relationships with them, whether we live near or far? How do we navigate the new challenges that come up with our own kids and their in-laws when grandparenting? Let's explore the many new issues that come with one of life's greatest pleasures—grandchildren.

A VISION FOR GRANDPARENTING

What is realistic in terms of an overall vision for my relationship with my grandkids?

CAROL: My priority is that they would know and feel they are loved, accepted, and precious to me and to God.

MARY: I want to help them experience all that God has for them.

LYN: We have the opportunity to ensure our grandchildren know they are part of an extended loving family, and that they truly matter.

How much of my grandparent hopes and dreams should I share with my grandkids and their parents?

CAROL: We have to be careful, because our hopes and dreams could be taken as expectations by our adult kids or grandkids. They may feel pressure or feelings of failure if they don't fulfill our hopes; also, they may disagree with our desires. All this might hinder our relationships with them.

One practical idea is to pick a character quality or Bible verse for each child when mom is pregnant and share this with them. As a grandmother, I can pray this verse throughout their lives.

LYN: We have to always remember our grown children's hopes and dreams for their kids will be ever-present. As we stay involved in their lives, we will discover each grandchild's strengths, weaknesses, and opportunities. With this awareness, we can learn what to highlight and pray for (and sometimes even pay for) to help the parents raise their children. I'm thinking of things like ballet or music lessons, art or sports camp, or helping with a special project. As grandparents, we can come alongside the parents in support of the dreams we discover.

MARY: I recently asked one of my friends what she has learned regarding her five grandchildren and their parents, her children. Without skipping a beat, she said, "to keep my mouth shut." I think we have to tread carefully in expressing our hopes and dreams unless we are absolutely sure they will be received well by our kids.

What gifts (material and nonmaterial) can I give to my grandkids that no one else can give them?

CAROL: Time is the most important gift. Share stories with them about your past and particularly your journey to faith. For a tangible gift, one friend of mine made a scrapbook for her four-year-old granddaughter of her young life to that point. The granddaughter loves it because she likes looking at pictures of herself.

My sweet grandmother used to walk on the beach with me and hear about my life. I can share with my grandchild positive stories about her parents when they were her age. Think about what a child enjoys and what might be meaningful to them. Being present and *seeing* that individual child can never be underestimated.

LYN: The beauty of being the "grand" mother or father versus the actual parent is that we have learned, through time and experience, to understand what really matters. Because we are not responsible for their final character, manners, or goals we can engage in a grandchild's life journey in a very different but special and deep way.

Noticing and valuing a person in the season of life they are in—child, middle schooler, high schooler, leaving home—is one of the biggest gifts a grandparent can provide. We can take our time to listen to the grandchild and help them sort out what they may be confused or angry about. We can often help the child understand and accept what the parent is trying to do.

PASSING THE BATON

How can I stay in touch and influence my grandchildren if they live far away?

MARY: I love giving a book to my young grandchild with an accompanying recording of my voice reading it. You can find these on bookselling websites. After visiting my grandchildren who live many states away, I send them laminated photos of our time together. I also make brief videos singing a song to them or showing them something in our house or yard. These are gifts that keep our connection growing across the miles.

LYN: I budget my finances to visit at least three times a year. This allows me to get to know my grandchildren as they grow. While I visit, their parents can go on needed dates or getaways.

I ask my grandchildren these questions to help us get the conversations going across the miles:

○ How has someone helped make your day better?
○ How have you helped make someone else's day better?

This reminds them we have choices to help others—a legacy I hope to leave them.

CAROL: We can ask our children how we can be a meaningful part of their lives. If possible, you could consider moving closer. My dear friend Gail and her husband moved across the country so they could be a strong influence on their grandchildren. Technology provides many ways to grow our connection with grandkids. Learn to use whatever method of communication your grandchildren use.

My husband and I live many states away from our grandchildren. How often should we visit them? How much is too much? Our dream is to be an integral part of their lives.

CAROL: A simple solution is to ask your adult children about their desires for your integration into their lives. Just make sure you have a life of your own at home.

LYN: Having our own lives is critical to continuing to gain respect from our adult children. If we smother them with availability and/or money, we can circumvent their opportunities to discover how they want to operate. Having said this, traveling to their home communicates that they and their events are very important to you.

Not staying too long is key. Leaving soon enough that they still want you to stay is a good rule of thumb. Benjamin Franklin compared houseguests to fish—both stink after three days. Be aware of indications that the parents are tiring of your visit and make an effort to ease the visit for them. For example, you might give the parents a day or night off by taking the children for an outing. Or you might plan an evening to yourself outside the home to give them a little space. Remember that children often become stressed when their routines are altered.

How do we best partner with our kids as we relate to our grandkids?

MARY: I have sweet memories of my dad holding my oldest son Austin's hand when he was a toddler, walking him around and around the yard of our small house. He did this because Austin was so active and loved to walk—and also to give my husband and me a little break. I was overjoyed when my parents loved and treasured my kids. We partner with our grown kids by delighting in their kids and spending time with them; praising and reinforcing their parenting approaches, rules, and choices whenever possible; listening to their frustrations and joys; and being available for babysitting. We partner with them through all of these tangible expressions of love.

LYN: Close communication with the parents is helpful. Learning their plans and goals for their kids allows me to create my action items to supplement their hopes and dreams.

Standing in consistency with the parents is of utmost thoughtfulness. I never want to be that older grandparent sticking her nose into a family's business and causing division. Stress that you know they are working very hard to succeed at molding these little pieces of clay into contributing members of society. Your support will help strengthen the weary stretches of their journey.

We grandparents can help enhance the image of the parent in the child's heart—especially if there is misunderstanding or willful rebellion. Grandparents can encourage the parents to "hang in there—it *will* get better."

My husband and I want to pass on our culture and beliefs to our grandchildren. How do we ensure that each grandchild will receive what they need from us?

LYN: Live your life on purpose and make each moment intentionally rich. We have found that "more is caught than taught," which is especially true for culture and beliefs. As my husband and I simply live our lives when others come over, our legacy is passed on.

Be aware your children may not want to carry on your culture or your beliefs. One of my daughters-in-love once told me point-blank, "You had your chance to raise your children; now it's our turn." Well stated, I must say.

As we continue to live in community with our grown children, natural opportunities may arise for us to express things that are important to us. We can use our words and actions in a way that is well received by all.

MARY: Most grandparents have beliefs and values important to them, and we'd love for our children and grandchildren to embrace these, but we can't force them.

With their parents' approval, we can provide pertinent books and read them with our grandchildren, or we can take them to appropriate events or movies. Busy parents may be glad for us to take this role. We should proceed carefully and prayerfully, modeling the values and beliefs that we hold so dear.

PRACTICAL MATTERS

How do I find balance with my kids about how much time I will help with babysitting?

MARY: Remember evaluating your purpose in life and your personal goals in Section 1? When the blessing of grandchildren comes into your life, you may need to pause and re-evaluate your overarching goals. When my first grandchild was born, I realized in new ways that my family was my highest priority after God. The time I spend with them, the love I show them, the influence I have on them: these lasting legacies are so important to me. With those things in mind, I can figure out how babysitting fits in with my other priorities.

CAROL: I think it works well to talk openly with your adult child about this and agree to evaluate every few months the flow of life and your commitment to help. In this way, everyone's needs and concerns can be expressed and both sides are respected.

Our daughter had the idea of a "grandparent calendar." We send invitations to each other in the same way we would schedule a lunch date or work appointment. The calendar has been a great tool to keep expectations regulated for us all. Rather than assuming what the other person is thinking or needs, good communication helps us to eliminate guesswork and brings peace. I'm learning to seek balance and to understand my capacity when it comes to this great joy of watching our grandchildren.

MARY: Some grandparents regret a weekly babysitting commitment and being locked in. The responsibility becomes wearing for them, especially as more wonderful grandchildren come into the fold. An alternative to weekly babysitting is to be available to provide extra help for when kids or parents are sick, date nights, giving parents a break, etc.

LYN: Each of my parents always "had a life" so my husband and I needed to fit into their calendars—even when it came to babysitting.

While there are positives for being in the grandchildren's lives often, our children carry the responsibility for getting coverage from other support systems to care for their children when the grandparents cannot.

What is the boundary for teaching our grandchildren manners and other behaviors that are important to us? Should we encourage them to speak up when meeting people, follow through on their chores, and speak respectfully to their parents?

LYN: Communicate with the parents ahead of situations whenever possible. Staying on the same page with the parents is critical for camaraderie, trust, and knowing how to handle issues. Regarding manners and behavior, discuss specific situations, expectations, and what to do. When a difficult predicament occurs, be honest with the parents, debrief them, and come up with solutions for the future.

Follow whatever consequences for misbehavior you and the parents decide upon. If things keep becoming chaotic, it may be time for the grandchild (and the parent) to lose the privilege of your visits or babysitting for a while.

MARY: If behaviors occur that you truly don't agree with, like disrespectful language or disruptive actions, try gently and kindly discussing this with the parents. Explain to the parents there are certain things that are uncomfortable for you, so you will need to draw a boundary when the child is with you, just as you would with an adult. You can then negotiate an appropriate consequence or response for when the child violates your wishes. Share your feelings and expectations. The parents may be able to reinforce desirable behaviors at home or remind their kids of your house rules before they visit. Of course, remember to be realistic in your expectations, not overly rigid or unrealistic of what is possible at various ages.

Also, we can teach by modeling behaviors and calling attention to them when we do so, explaining the benefits. When my kids were growing up, I would point out good and bad examples on television and movies, starting a conversation about the positive or negative results of either. For example, when a child acted bratty in a movie, later we would talk about how that made others around them feel, and how unattractive it made the child. I also read age-appropriate books to them about manners, respectfulness, etc.

How much is too much when I want to give gifts for birthdays, Christmas, etc.?

CAROL: First, honor your adult child's wishes—then it's between you, your spouse, and God. Instead of giving physical items, invest in experiences, college savings, and so on. Give them your time.

LYN: When grandchildren are little, the price for age-appropriate gifts can be relatively small. But as they get older, costs increase dramatically. We want to set reasonable expectations for the coming years. Stay in touch with the parents regarding what the children need, then give special items every now and then.

MARY: When I became a grandparent, I constantly saw things I wanted to buy in order to delight my kids or grandkids. I don't experience this dynamic in other relationships. I know that purchasing a bunch of material items isn't ultimately the best for many reasons, including the fact that my kids don't want a lot of stuff around their house piling up. We have to use wisdom, self-control, and communication with our children in this process.

DIFFICULT AREAS

What's the appropriate response when we do not agree with our kids' parenting philosophy or practices?

LYN: A friend of mine answered this question by putting her hand to her mouth and pretending to turn a key to lock her mouth shut. I've often remembered this visual when I am in extended family situations. Another great choice is to quietly leave the room without appearing judgmental.

Never undermine the parent in front of the grandchild. It can be difficult for a grandparent to watch grandchildren being corrected, but our kids must have the room to parent and not be micromanaged by their own parents.

MARY: It might be helpful to mentally step back to see a larger perspective. Parents all around the world, throughout all time, have approached parenting very differently. People with limited parenting skills have produced grown-up kids who do very well in life. On the other hand, good parents have produced adult children with major problems. Think about your situation: did you always parent in the best way? How have your grown kids experienced adult life in terms of having their own problems and issues? Even with our best efforts, things haven't been perfect—this realization can be humbling.

CAROL: Love them and pray for them.

How should we respond when a grandchild expresses a desire to live with us instead of their parents?

CAROL: There are many considerations here. What age is the child? Is this a passing phase, or is something more serious going on? Is their home life abusive? I would try to understand what is in the child's mind and heart. If the home is not abusive, consider that young people may say this when they will miss a grandparent and all the special fun they have when visiting. If this is the case, reassure them of your love even when you're away and remind them that everyday life is not as entertaining as a special visit.

MARY: If the young person is having normal problems at home, help them understand that difficulties are part of life. Bring their parents into the conversation about ways to solve what's going on. If appropriate, help the parents find a counselor for the family, young person, or parents. And of course, in the case of suspected emotional, physical, or sexual abuse, definitely get them to a counselor. A counselor is mandated by law to report abuse, which can help address this difficult situation. You can report suspected abuse yourself, and your name can usually be kept confidential. Check with your state for individual guidelines and laws.

LYN: Sometimes it is in the best interest of everyone for a grandchild to live with a grandparent for a brief or extended time. Taking a grandchild into your home can be very beneficial and even a calling. One word of caution: be careful to bring the parents in on the discussion from the start. Don't go behind a parent's back to drum up a plan with a grandchild. When needed, you can involve an objective third person to facilitate difficult conversations—a family member, friend, spiritual advisor, or counselor.

Each of our adult kids have kids. How do we stop the jealousy and comparison between our kids when our grandchildren have certain talents and successes?

LYN: Discussing in front of others what one child or grandchild has done can create a lot of turmoil, comparison, and jealousy. Our focus carries weight in our family members' hearts. We need a vigilant awareness of what we say and the impact our words have on others. Comparison is the thief of joy, and it hurts people and relationships.

We also have to be careful not to create the perception or reality that we have favorites, which can break the hearts of our grandchildren and their parents. Along these lines, be wise and selective with your gift-giving, not making one person seem more special to you than another based upon the presents you give.

CAROL: Among humans, comparison and jealousy will always exist, and that reality isn't in your power to stop, but you can reduce comparison by focusing your conversation in different directions. For example, find and reinforce the importance of the unique qualities that make each grandchild stand out.

MARY: Prize each individual for being exactly who they are. Undergird their self-image and confidence by stating truths about them and where self-worth comes from. We can provide books about self-esteem, comparison, and other developmental topics, catered to each age group, I like to read aloud, even to older kids, and pause while reading to discuss the ideas. You can also give age-appropriate magazine subscriptions that cover these types of topics.

One final word: we each have to check our own hearts. Do we compare or gain worth through our kids' and grandkids' accomplishments, rather than realize our worth comes from the fact that God created each of us uniquely with great care and excellence? The One who created the universe knows and loves you deeply; nothing can add to or take away from your worth. As we align ourselves with the fact that each person has tremendous worth apart from their accomplishments or attributes, we will be happier, and this will flow from us to our loved ones.

What do you do when you struggle to like your grandchildren?

MARY: Some people are easy to like, while others are difficult to be around. Our grandchildren may go through stages when they are less or more enjoyable. Through it all, grandparents are in a unique position to offer an experience of unconditional love that can be life-changing. No matter how old we grandparents are, each of us can grow in our ability to love unconditionally. When I struggle to like someone, it helps me to look beyond their faults and see their needs, their insecurities, the ways they have been hurt in life, and their personal problems. This often makes a person endearing when their outer traits are unlikable.

I remember a time when I struggled to like some people who I had to spend time with. I began to see myself on a mission to show them God's love and to light the path to him. This larger purpose changed everything for me, as I was part of a much bigger plan. With our love for our grandchildren, we can consistently light the path throughout their lives toward being healthy people who experience all that God has created them to be.

LYN: Sometimes we may be irritated by the faults in others that we see in ourselves. In addition, I must look at my expectations of others: am I hoping for something that they cannot do? Am I missing the good in them and in what they are doing?

CAROL: We can focus upon our grandchildren's good qualities and pray to have empathy for them when they are unlikeable. Look beneath the surface to see what makes them unlikable. Could they be feeling anxious or unlovable? Is there tension at home? What is their deeper struggle? This type of understanding can open your heart to like and love your grandchildren more.

TAKE ACTION

- o How would you describe your overall goal with your grandchildren? At the end of your life, what will you be glad to have accomplished?
- o What do you love doing that you can share with your grandkids?
- o Write three areas of wisdom and life experience that you hope to impart to your grandchildren.
- o What part of grandparenting do you find difficult? How can you begin to help yourself with this?

Look through the resources in Section 4, Chapter 7. Write down any that would be helpful for you. Make a plan to use the resources and add them to your calendar.

8

YOUR AGING PARENTS AND RELATIVES

At this time in our lives, we find unique companionship with those who rocked and raised us. Now we can seek to serve and intentionally be present during their times of emotional or financial challenge or failing health. How do we balance everything else in our lives and still give ourselves to those who first loved us? To what extent do we prioritize our extended family when our values and beliefs are so different from each other?

YOUR RELATIONSHIP WITH YOUR AGING PARENTS

Are there general goals I should try for in relating to my parents in this life stage?

LYN: An important goal I've learned is to treat my parents how I want to be treated. Our children (and our grandchildren) are watching us. We are modeling behavior. Ancient wisdom says that we are to "honor" our mother and father and we will live a long, good, full life (Exodus 20:12).[1]

CAROL: It's helped me to make peace with the fact that nothing stays the same—there are many stages of aging, from infancy to old age. How you interact with your parents will need to evolve in the same way your interactions with your child evolved through infancy, childhood, adolescence, and beyond. Just when you have it figured out, loved ones enter a different stage and you need to figure it out again. As age weakens your parents physically, mentally, and emotionally, you may need to increasingly act as "the parent" in the relationship while also demonstrating deference and respect to preserve their dignity.

What does it mean to honor our parents in this last season of their lives?

CAROL: Yesterday I held my mom's hand in silence for a while. She's eighty-seven and is not able to speak much now. To honor is to be with them, to be present, and to see the precious worth our parents possess in this season. We show honor by giving them the gifts of our time, patience, and unconditional love.

LYN: The Oxford Dictionary describes *honor* as "highly respecting, greatly esteeming, giving much privilege and grace to another." We can do this in many ways.

Forgive them. They have done the best they could with the character and money they had at the time. It's best to forgive and move on. Again, the eyes of your clan are watching.

Speak well of them. I must be reminded of this, even though my parents have already passed on. When I find myself grumbling about their strictness or how many times we moved in my school experience, I realize I need a reminder to forgive again.

Focus on their strengths publicly and privately. As we watch them in their most vulnerable stage of life, getting irritated at things like their slowness or forgetfulness can be easy. I was impatient at times, and now I have great remorse. When we forget to be intentional, we may slip into treating elderly parents with disrespect and a rushed selfishness instead of loving honor.

Stay present when you are with them. Seek their wisdom and opinions. They've had lots of life experience, and it's important to glean what they have learned. I regret lost opportunities to interview my parents on various journey experiences. I now see them as separate people who were my close companions. I hope I treated them in a way that they felt cherished. Don't miss your opportunities.

Finally, support and provide for them. This season of life will end, and you will be free of having to take care of them. Do the assignment well and you will enjoy the blessing of knowing you honored and loved your parents well.

I'm sad thinking that one day my parents will be gone, and I won't know key things about their lives. What are some questions I can ask to get them talking—to get the conversations started?

MARY: My dad died when I was in my late twenties, and I'm so glad I had the presence of mind to ask him to record some key memories from his life. I suggested a few I knew about, and he took it from there. That recording is a treasure for me now. I also asked him to record himself reciting some humorous poems and sayings he used to share when my sister and I were growing up. I felt awkward asking him to make this recording, especially since we knew he was in his final months due to a terminal illness. But he gladly made the recording, and I think he felt very honored to do so. It was a cherished experience for us both.

LYN: Here are a few questions you might ask, and be sure to write, audio-record, or video their answers:

- What do they remember as they were growing up: early childhood, middle school, high school, and beyond?
- What was their first job? Second? Favorite?
- How did they meet your other parent?
- What scared them?
- What made them proud?
- Who were their close friends and why?
- What important lessons did they learn throughout life?

MARY: You can buy a storytelling service that will guide your parent to recall and write or record stories from their lives. The services will then put these in a book format. Here are a few to check out:

https://www.storii.com

https://welcome.storyworth.com

https://vitalifestory.com

CAROL: My brother did a series of recordings with our parents while he was single. He did it to learn more about our mom and dad, and because he realized that if he got married and had a family, this might be the only way his children could get to know their grandparents. Fortunately, that wasn't the case—he married and had kids before our parents died. But now we're so glad he has this record of their lives.

My husband has never gotten along with his parents—his upbringing included abuse. They want to be a part of our lives and I feel stuck in the middle. What can I do?

MARY: The type of abuse may dictate your response. Verbal, physical, or sexual abuse each require different considerations. Overall, it would be best to bring in an impartial third party to guide conversations—ideally a trained family therapist. This therapy can start based upon who is willing to attend. It might be your husband or you, or you both as a couple. It could start by you encouraging his parents to begin seeing a professional family counselor with the goal of eventually attending as a family. Any family member willing to seek therapy can receive help for their part in the journey and the road ahead.

PROBLEM-SOLVING REGARDING YOUR PARENTS

What if my aging parents have expectations of me that I find difficult to meet?

LYN: Even if we aren't going to do what they want, and even if they are ornery or demanding, conveying respect is important. This life stage may be full of fear and pain; showing respect with our tone, attitude, and actions will go far in supporting their hearts.

Also, in my experience, doing as much as we can—physically, mentally, and emotionally—will curb regrets later when they are gone.

MARY: Boundaries are important at every stage in our lives, and we have to protect our own emotional, mental, and physical resources. We must keep the oxygen mask on ourselves to be able to provide support for others without depleting what we need. Having said that, we may need to cut other things out of our lives to give ourselves time and space to be present and help our parents during this opportunity that will never come again. The balancing act requires our own careful consideration and prayer to know when we can meet their expectations and when we simply can't. Sometimes we can best meet their needs by connecting them with other resources, people, and groups.

CAROL: If you can go the extra mile to guide and care for your parents, even when it's not easy—as they did for you—you are following the example of Jesus. This is important, whether they did a good or bad job. My experience is that you will not regret this extra effort, even though it may be difficult.

My mother irritates me. How do I handle being around her when she's driving me crazy?

MARY: Be comforted by the fact that you're not alone in experiencing this. People of all ages can be frustrating and irritating, and parent/child relationships can be among the most challenging. Consider the following options.

Explore the underlying feelings causing your anger. Impatience or anger amidst the changes that come with aging can be normal. If you're personally involved in her care, you may feel frustrated with the way her needs interfere with your life. People also may feel guilty as their parent ages for a variety of reasons. Try to identify the root cause.

A parent's cognitive and physical decline can be hard to see. Make sure you have healthy relationships with people who can help you process what you're feeling. Find the humor in difficult situations or even envision them as scenes in a sitcom. This can be a healthy release for your emotions.

Identify possible solutions for situations that irritate you. Explore options with a friend or counselor.

Talk with your parent to arrive at solutions or improve your communication. Keep your words as calm and respectful as possible. Hear what your mom has to say. Rather than trying to win the argument, know that discussing an issue may allow you both to think things through and make improvements.

Find healthy outlets for your anger to prevent it from building up. Listen to music, exercise, write down your feelings and thoughts. Try deep breathing and mindfulness exercises.

Be gentle and compassionate toward yourself. This is a difficult time of life, so give yourself all the grace and kindness you would offer a dear friend going through the same thing.

My parents really need help because of their failing health but I'm not sure how to meet the need. Assisted living facilities are too expensive, and my apartment is too small for them.

CAROL: This is challenging, but there are options. Find out what kind of Medicaid or Medicare is available. Housing in a private home with caregiving and food provided may be more affordable. In this setting, seniors can be with others in the same stage of life.

MARY: Check out the resource section Section 4, Chapter 8 to find specific help for these things.

When is it right to have an elderly parent live with you?

CAROL: I think it's important to evaluate the needs, desires, and limitations of everyone involved and determine if this is the best fit. All parties already living in the home would need to agree for this to take place. If finances are an issue, inviting a parent to move in can be an affordable option. There also can be an evaluation period after a month to decide if the situation is working well for the long run. If not, you can look at other options.

In conjunction with your parent living with you, it's helpful to have other family members or a caregiver assist with transportation. Arrange for family and friends to help in every way that will make this work for the long haul.

My dad lives with us, and he spends a lot of time on his computer watching porn. I don't like it but what can I do?

MARY: Start by educating yourself about how to talk to someone about their porn use. You are right to be concerned, and help is available for you. Porn is a difficult area for someone to change, especially if it's become an addiction. Users are commonly in denial, even to themselves, about their porn behavior and its harm to themselves and others. However, you can have conversations and set boundaries to help yourself and your dad.

Your best bet is to seek out resources, experts, and support. We've listed some in Section 4, Chapter 5. One for you to consider is S-Anon International. This is an organization that specifically helps family and friends of those struggling with porn and addictive sexual behavior. Additionally, consider seeing a counselor or attending an online or in-person support group to help you navigate the situation.

When your dad is ready, Sex Addicts Anonymous is an organization that helps those involved with porn and addictive sexual behavior.

God bless you on your journey. He can be your guide to peace and even joy as you utilize these valuable resources.

CAROL: Remember, this is not what your dad was created for. It's interfering with his relationship with you and probably with other activities that would improve his quality of life: exercise, games, reading, conversation, or pursuing his faith journey. Depending upon his age and health status, some of these may be options you could encourage him toward. In the end, though, it's important to find ways to have peace whether he changes or not.

My dad is chronically ill and demands my mom's entire focus. She is exhausted and seems to feel trapped, but never admits it. What should I do?

LYN: I had the opportunity to walk this exact path. My mother took very seriously her vow of "in sickness and in health" and had great difficulty ever leaving my dad's side when she knew he wanted her there.

You and family members can offer to take shifts with your dad so she can go out with friends, shower peacefully, or do errands without having to rush home. You might organize a weekly schedule that includes family, friends, and church members. You may have to talk her into it, but having breaks is vital and prevents her from developing her own health problems due to exhaustion. Help your mother understand that this schedule can provide new memories for your dad with loved ones, which might convince her to allow others to assist.

In these tough circumstances, we can be a listening ear for the one serving this difficult assignment. Debriefing the anguish and frustration can help her regain strength and get back to the tasks at hand. Knowing that other people understand we are struggling helps make our loads a little lighter.

Grief after the death of a loved one is often less tormenting when we know we served a person as best we could with our time, energy and strength.

CAROL: Some of the following ideas may help:

- Encourage the caregiver to engage in a hobby or other healthy outlets, even if only for a brief time each day or week.
- A support group can be vital to their mental health.
- Take the caregiver out weekly for coffee or a meal. Arrange for someone to stay with the patient.
- Weekly attendance at a place of worship can lift their spirits and help them to engage with others.
- Depending upon his health and mental status, someone could chat with your dad about his tendency to be overbearing. The family could discuss his real needs: Is he scared? Is he angry? How might these needs be addressed?

MARY: Your mother definitely needs to find ways to "put the oxygen mask on herself" so she can continue to put the "oxygen mask" on your dad. If the family can afford it, you might hire a caregiver to come at times. You can also consult with a doctor to see if medication could help calm your dad's emotional state. Agitation toward the end of life due to illness is common, and anxiety-relieving medication can provide peace during this difficult time. Anger, fear, insecurity, and overbearing demands are signs that anxiety is making the patient miserable. You might also have a spiritual leader visit your loved one weekly to help discuss these things.

My elderly father has gotten romantically involved with a woman who is not good for him, but he won't listen to reason. I'm afraid she's trying to take his money. How can I help him?

MARY: This happens more and more, especially through scams, but it can also happen during the natural progression of a relationship. In either case, the issues are complex, but you can help in a variety of ways.

Since the relationship is already advancing, you might stage a type of intervention with several loved ones expressing their objective reasons for concern, along with possible solutions. This means you first need to get together with family members and friends who love your father to discuss exactly what you want to say in the intervention as well as your desired outcome. You might hire an intervention specialist to lead the discussion and help you formulate what to say in advance. Basically, you want to tell your dad the reasons you are concerned and lay out specific options that you want him to follow for his best interests. If he refuses to listen, you might lay out consequences, like no longer getting to spend time with specific loved ones or limiting his funds, if that's an option. The severity of the repercussions would depend upon the severity of what he is involved in. And of course, talk to your father with compassion and empathy.

Ideally, adult kids can help their aging parents either before or very early in a problematic romantic relationship. Warn your parents about possible problems, especially about online romance scammers, including those on dating websites. Caution your parents to never send money to someone they haven't met in person. Even when they've met someone and are spending time with them, warn your parents about red flags that might mean someone is interested in their money. Educate yourself about scams targeted at the elderly and talk to your parents about these. The American Association of Retired Persons (AARP), offers helpful information about this on its website (http://www.aarp.org), as well as a podcast about scams targeted at the elderly, called *The Perfect Scam*. Both are listed in Section 4, Chapter 8.

LYN: Spend some time with her. You may find that she is not as greedy or sneaky as you suspect. In addition, once you are more involved in their world, your father may be more open to your concerns if you still have them.

There's also the perspective that this may be how he wants to spend his last amounts of time and money. You may have seen this bumper sticker: "Spending my children's inheritance." In the end, you may have to accept the realities that come with your father's independent adult decisions, as unwise as they may seem.

SIBLINGS AND PARENT ISSUES

How do I handle decision-making regarding our elderly parents when all the adult siblings see life differently?

LYN: As our parents began to decline, my brother and I had to really listen to one another. Our goal was to find common ground to tackle the opportunities and challenges before us. Since I lived in the same area as our folks, it was only natural that I would be more of the day-to-day caregiver. He had many suggestions and ideas but often I felt I knew best. However, during many of the difficult sections of the road, his ideas ended up being exactly what my parents needed. Over time, my brother and I learned a lot about compromise during the journey; he would often say, "I know what they need . . . they are MY parents too." Good point brother, good point.

MARY: This is an opportunity for us as adult children to grow and change in positive ways. Compromise may be needed all around. Don't forget to bring in objective third parties along the way to help everyone navigate the difficulties in decisions and relationships: spiritual leaders, trusted friends, or family counselors.

How critical is it to have at least one sibling live near their elderly parents?

CAROL: It depends on the circumstances. If the parent is well enough to live independently—or to live in assisted living but advocate for their own care—it may not be important to have an adult child nearby. But if the parent has dementia or is not able to advocate for themselves or to report problems, it's essential that someone with their best interests at heart be close enough to provide or oversee the parent's care. That may mean relocating the parent to live with or near a sibling. Even if the parent will be living in a reputable facility, regular visits from family members can make the difference between feeling loved or feeling abandoned—and between good or bad care.

Our elderly parent has dementia. How do we as siblings deal with managing my parents' financial assets and contributing to their financial needs?

MARY: This is a complicated matter, possibly requiring experts to assist with legal and financial planning. The Alzheimer's Organization published an excellent article that may help: "Legal Plans—Considerations for Helping a Person Living with Dementia Plan for the Future (https://alz.org)."

LYN: Whenever possible, it's important to talk ahead of time with your parents and siblings about goals for the later years and what finances need to be set aside. We need to do this for ourselves, too, with our grown children. Having these conversations early can be immensely helpful when problems increase if their health declines. As Mary said, an attorney and/or financial planner may be crucial in this process.

When a parent's health declines, it's important to have scheduled family meetings in person or online with siblings and their spouses. These times allow for debriefing, sharing of goals, processing the grief of your parent's situation, and discussing concerns before they become huge issues. You need each other during this trial that may last for years.

If you need to contribute financially for your parent, following are some things I have found helpful.

Recognize, respect, and accept the fact that each sibling may be in a different stage of life and financial situation. Make plans accordingly with kindness and grace.

List your parent's current and potential costs and contributions from others toward their financial needs. Decide together what the long haul will require financially and how to practically manage this. Again, a professional financial planner can be of great assistance.

Figure out together a care-sharing strategy you can each commit to. Some siblings may be able to contribute more practical help than financial, and both are valuable.

Through this process, keep a loving and compassionate attitude. This will serve you well, because bitterness and resentment poison the container in which they are held. You don't want to grow into a bitter, sour old person.

Sometimes siblings can't agree or support their parents at all. In that case, find support and help elsewhere. Don't bad-mouth one another. Even if a sibling is no help at all, your parents need you to show up. Ask for help or advice from family members, cousins, spouses, church friends, support groups, and friends who have been caregivers themselves. They can provide guidance and a heartfelt listening ear.

This season of your life will not last forever. Let go and let God. Breathe and continue in love.

My father lives with my sister, and I think she's using his debit card and basically stealing money from him to buy things for herself. She denies this, but I have seen receipts. What can I do?

CAROL: Consider whether there might be a reasonable explanation for the receipts. For example, since your sister has opened her home to your father, perhaps she has needed to buy things for him in day-to-day life.

Even if your suspicions are correct, you have to consider carefully the pros and cons of your options moving forward. Even if your sister is using your father's debit card without his permission, would fighting that be worth ruining your relationship with your sister and maybe even with your father? Would involving law enforcement or the courts make the situation better or worse?

MARY: If your sister is doing what you suspect, you have to evaluate the benefits and costs of moving forward with your accusations. This would include benefits and costs for you emotionally; in your relationships with her and other family members; and use of your time and money. The stress and time alone may cause you to decide it's not worth major efforts on your part. At the very least, you could have a talk with her and your father. You might consult a lawyer, financial expert, or family counselor to explore your potential options.

LYN: Since your sister is caring for and responsible for your father 24/7, they may have made some agreements regarding "his share" of helping by allowing her the privilege to use his debit card as needed. Being roommates is a personal arrangement that looks different in each household. You could ask him outright about that, as part of a conversation, not as an attack on your sister or him.

Often unresolved sibling rivalry comes out when our parents become more dependent on family members. Problems might be rooted in past ordeals that the two of you have experienced but not finalized and forgiven. The offenses may be between you and your sister, you and your father, or both.

My parents designated me to be the executor of their estate. My siblings avoided any responsibility for our aging parents. Now that they have both died, my siblings want to come in and take all of the valuables and are asking how much money they get. There are ugly arguments between them and with me, and I am stuck in the middle. What should I do?

CAROL: The executor of a will has the legal mandate to carry out the wishes of the deceased person based upon the instructions spelled out in their will or trust documents. If a person did not leave a will, each state has laws regarding how the person's estate is to be distributed. You don't have any choice but to follow these legal requirements. You can explain this to your siblings and, if necessary, get an attorney to explain it to them. If discord continues, you might consider bringing in a mediator or family counselor to facilitate a discussion with everyone.

LYN: Being the executor of the estate is a huge responsibility and a huge privilege. You must be responsible for many tasks. Your parents chose you to carry out important decisions, and it's a privilege to know they trusted you. You can feel confident and secure in this awareness.

However, this privileged responsibility can be accompanied by various challenges. Treat your siblings with fairness, regardless of their behavior. Try to be as impartial and generous as the estate allows. You will never regret being kind and setting an example for your own children and grandchildren. Work to create positive memories that will leave a legacy.

MARY: When my parents died, my sister was the executor of their will. I became aware of what a huge task this was, involving over a year of her valuable time and ongoing efforts to handle everything. I told a lawyer friend that I felt bad about this, and he recommended having her pay herself a reasonable salary for the job she was doing. I did this, allowing her to choose the amount, because she was trustworthy. Our good relationship was more important than the amount of money I might lose because of this salary. I write this to remind you of the invaluable service you are giving to your parents and to your siblings, even though they may not currently acknowledge this.

In everything regarding our parents' will, it's important to try to maintain good family relationships. With that in mind, Carol's idea of bringing in a mediator or family counselor might help. If you suggest it and they decline, you have done your best and they are each responsible for their own attitudes.

As my siblings and I prepare for the funeral of our father, how can we best honor him?

CAROL: I attended a funeral several years ago where all the siblings shared favorite memories and character qualities of their father. They also had the grandchildren read a Scripture passage about loving people, a quality that he exemplified. The grandmother also felt honored as she mourned the loss of her husband of over sixty years. It was a joyful occasion and one to replicate.

MARY: Most funeral homes have resources to guide you in this process. My sister and her husband visited a funeral home a couple of years before he died in order to plan their funerals and make financial arrangements for everything. At that time they also made a written record of what they wanted to have said and done at their funerals. When her husband died a couple of years later, my sister found this to be immensely helpful; she also added some things to honor him at the service. Making plans and preparations beforehand greatly alleviates our loved ones when the time comes.

SIBLING RELATIONSHIPS

What's realistic to expect in my relationships with siblings now that we're grown? How high can I aim in hoping for closeness?

CAROL: I think we start by accepting that each sibling is allowed to aim for whatever level of closeness they desire. If I expect others to think like me, it leads to frustration; we each may march to the beat of a different drummer. If my sibling is different from me, it serves us both well for me to accept this. We can talk about our differences and try to clear away anything hindering our relationship. We might decide to go to counseling together. But in the end, sometimes we have to accept what we have and fill our relational needs with other friendships.

My brother has four young adult kids. I have always been attentive to them, but he does not try to communicate with mine at all. How do I approach the subject of his becoming a better uncle?

MARY: Start with a positive approach. Communicate that you'd love for your kids to have more interaction with him. You might state a couple of reasons without pressuring him or making him feel guilty. You might tell him you love him and want your kids to know him more, or that he's special to your kids. You might suggest a few ways he could connect, like occasional texts or emails, getting together, or even comments from him on their social media. You probably know which methods would work best for your brother. Ultimately, though, it's your brother's choice.

CAROL: Trying to get someone to be more like me only leads to frustration. The way each person approaches extended family is a personal choice. I wouldn't want a sibling to expect me to be a certain kind of aunt to my niece or nephew. Acceptance is a gracious choice in a situation like this. I want to freely love and care for my nieces and nephews from a sincere heart, not in response to any kind of pressure I might receive. It's a good reminder in all areas of life for me to accept and embrace people exactly as they are.

My sister has cut off communication with me because we differ in our opinions about religion. What should I do?

MARY: Learn to "live and let live," as recovery programs teach us. We can't control others and we will only be frustrated when we try to. This applies for both you and your sister. She might have internal issues that aren't about you at all, and you can't change her choices.

Also, you might review your part in this and ask yourself some hard questions. Have you come across to her in a way that has made her prefer distance? Without meaning to, sometimes we appear negative, judgmental, and even unloving as we state our views. No one wants to be around someone who comes across like this. If you feel this is true, you might apologize for things you've said or done that she experienced in a negative way. A gentle, humble attitude can open doors that were shut tight. You might ask her for a fresh start.

LYN: Does she know that you like her even though she differs from you in religion? Perhaps she knows that you "love" her, but does she know that you "like" her?

Some people, whether family or friends, just need time and space to think things over. Allow some time to pass.

MARY: This makes me think of the old admonition to be very careful about discussing religion and politics. This principle was expressed by everyone from Mark Twain to Charles Schulz in his Peanuts comic strip. We have to tread carefully in these topics, or avoid them altogether, because they are mine fields that can damage or destroy relationships.

My sister is very jealous of my husband and me. At every family event she makes snide comments that cause the whole room to cringe. I know she's hurting, but I don't know what to say back. Any suggestions?

MARY: Wow, that's hard and painful. You could try either an indirect or a direct approach.

An indirect approach might involve going out of your way to show love and kindness to her in words and actions. You could also examine your own words and ways to see if there are things you and your husband say or do that bring attention to your positive attributes and circumstances. I've learned the hard way that talking about something I'm doing or excited about can result in others having bad attitudes toward me. You might be adding to her jealousy without realizing.

A direct approach would involve privately, gently, and carefully talking with her about it. Instead of stating you think she's jealous, express that you want to have a good relationship with her but sometimes she hurts your feelings, even though she may be unaware of it. You could ask her if there's anything you've said or done that has bothered her. Proceed with an open and humble heart about what she might say, admitting your faults and shortcomings when appropriate.

CAROL: This is a difficult and tender circumstance. Can you gently discuss this tension with her? You could say, "I felt uncomfortable when you made the comment in front of the family about how we parent our youngest son. I was hurt, but it made me think maybe there's something you need to talk to me about. Have I offended you? If so, I want to hear your thoughts." At that point, you can ask, discuss, and seek understanding. If she continues to be jealous, there may be nothing more you can do about it. We do our part and then we must let it go. On a practical level, even during family gatherings we have the option to not hang out in the same vicinity as those who are difficult for us.

My brother is bipolar, and my parents are no longer living. His behavior is erratic and he's basically living on the streets. Is there anything I can do to help him?

LYN: We hear more about bipolar disorder than ever before. Your brother's situation is multilayered and complex, as you have experienced. It's obviously a case for professionals.

From what I have observed in others, it's important to have clear boundaries for yourself and your family members since your brother's behavior is so inconsistent. Consult with reliable resources and professionals to determine your plans and limits.

As we've mentioned before, you can call 211 in most states in the US. They will help you to find specific resources in your area.

You can also find information about housing options through HUD: Department of Housing and Urban Development, listed in Section 4, Chapter 9.

MARY: In addition, NAMI, the National Alliance on Mental Illness, is an organization that helps the families and loved ones of mentally ill individuals. Find it listed in the resources for this chapter.

TAKE ACTION

- o   What expectations do your parents have of you? Which of these are you able to meet? Which expectations are unrealistic?

- o   What conversations do you need to have with your parents that you will regret not having once they are gone?

- o   Is there a relationship with your parent or other relative that you'd like to improve? What next steps will you take?

- o   Did this chapter bring to light anything you're doing well in one of your family relationships? What is that and how might you celebrate or acknowledge it?

- o   Is there a problem you're experiencing that this chapter addressed, and what are some ways you can proceed?

Look through the resources in Section 4, Chapter 8. Write down any that would be helpful for you. Enter these resources on your calendar.

9

YOUR FRIENDSHIPS

In this phase of life we deeply need friendships—people with whom we can laugh, play, cry, and share the most painful parts of our lives.

TRUE FRIENDSHIPS

What does mature friendship look like during these years?

CAROL: A wise friend once told me, "A true friend is someone you can put your full weight upon and they are able to hold you." A seasoned friend embraces the good, the bad, and the ugly. To journey through this stage of life with true companions as we share the joys and pains of our daily lives is a precious gift. When we are accepted by one another, "warts and all," we feel safe. Safety draws us closer and allows us to be seen and valued for who we are. As a result, we mature in our relationships.

LYN: With friends whom I've known for a while, different relationship facets have blossomed as we've supported each other through good and bad circumstances. In my experience, each exciting or befuddling situation has demanded character qualities I need to work on and sometimes am blind to. My closest friends can point out the hard truths; we have developed a secure trust with one another, and they make me better. They also remind me of predicaments I solved in my past and cheer me on with promptings that encourage and strengthen me.

How can I deepen my most significant friendships?

MARY: Lyn and Carol have been great examples of this in my life. Carol deepens our friendship by consistently asking me questions about myself and listening intently. She initiates fun outings, including for my birthday. Lyn and I do improv comedy together. As we ride to events, we cover a broad range of what's happening in our lives. Lyn also initiates meeting and getting to know the close members of my family. The three of us text throughout our days about the high and low points in our lives. In these ways and many more, Carol and Lyn take the initiative to deepen our relationships, and I'm so thankful.

LYN: Carol and I consider Mary one of our favorite people. The deep friendships we share make us very rich indeed.

CAROL: In close relationships, grace plus truth plus time equals growth. Grace means I love my friends unconditionally as we authentically face the realities of life together over time. That friend becomes a refreshing and life-giving resting place. This brings great depth between us. My friendships are like delving into treasure chests full of precious gems.

Depth develops as we intentionally spend time together in various ways, conversing and enjoying one other. With my long-distance friends, we have traditions like annual visits to each other or to a fun location, where laughter and life can be shared away from daily responsibilities. I meet regularly with local friends for meals, coffee, or walking dates. Of course, phone calls and texts are part of this mix. We also grow to know each other's families and significant others, which adds to our relationship in other ways.

MARY: Doing projects together will deepen your relationships. Writing this book with Lyn and Carol has drawn us closer. You can garden together, work on hobbies or causes, host game nights—live and play together.

How much time should I spend with friends in my daily and ongoing schedule?

MARY: This is so different for each of us, based upon our priorities, needs, personalities, and health. I have been so busy at times with work or family that I barely had time to sleep. My problem throughout life has been that I stuff too much into my schedule. Wonderful friendships have happened along the way, but I want to nurture them with more intentionality. I've learned to stop and think through how much time to devote for my friendships to thrive, because I so desperately value and need these people. We are relational creatures who can't flourish without friends. This goes back to our first chapters about deciding on your goals and scheduling things accordingly.

LYN: There are only twenty-four hours in a day. I want to be at every event, with every person, and to come through for all. But we are only human. Where we are in each phase of life often drives the amount of time we can give to friends. It helps me to think that a friend may come to me for a reason, a season, or maybe a lifetime. Each is appropriate and valuable in its own way.

CAROL: It's been said that spending time with friends not only increases your life expectancy but also decreases your stress and depression. Time with friends also can have a wonderful impact on your health—sign me up! I schedule time with one of my friends at least once a week. A friend of mine makes Friday her social day. With a flexible work schedule, she purposefully makes Friday a lighter day so she can schedule a lunch or outing with someone. What a fun end-of-the-week treat to anticipate!

Is my priority to have many friends, a few close friends, or a combination?

CAROL: We have to be wise in this area. Being with too many people requires energy and can end up wearing you out. However, if we pace ourselves and have a close inner circle of friends and family, we can enjoy an outer circle of others periodically. There can be a number of friends in this outer circle, but our inner circle will be very small.

Another take on this comes from an Israeli proverb: "The man of *too many* friends [chosen indiscriminately] will be broken in pieces *and* come to ruin, But there is a [true, loving] friend who [is reliable and] sticks closer than a brother" (Proverbs 18:24; The Amplified Bible). The quantity of our friends is less important than the quality of each individual.

LYN: I have to consider the amount of time and energy I'm able to give. Deep connections require investments of my heart, energy, time, and even money as we do things together. These factors help us decide how many people we can give ourselves to.

MARY: I need a variety of friends. Different relationships meet different needs. It's kind of like needing a variety of foods to meet our nutritional needs.

We need that safe friend who is deep and can engage about our most personal problems. We need another friend who likes to do fun things and be spontaneous. They might not be quite as deep, but we enjoy them. We need friends going through the same things as we are to talk about specific challenges. We might have a friend who shares one of our specific interests or talents. We must proactively cultivate and nurture these friendships—they usually don't "just happen." But as Carol and Lyn have said, we have to balance our energy and priorities.

How do I determine if a friendship is worth pursuing with all my other priorities?

LYN: After fifty, we may find ourselves still heavily involved in a career, so that will drive our available time. Others may have a more flexible schedule. Whatever the situation, if a person brings out the best in us and leaves us feeling hopeful and respected, the friendship is one to be pursued.

MARY: Does the person give me joy and encouragement? Do they bring comfort and peace? If our health is failing, or we're in a slower pace of life, or even when our schedules are busy, simple qualities like these are important.

CAROL: When I'm in the midst of a full schedule, it's been helpful to think through the following:

○ Do I have the time and ability to invest in this friendship and what will they expect of me? Phone calls and texts? Coffee or meals together? What is the rhythm I will establish with this friend?

○ How will I help meet the needs of this relationship? When difficulties come up in this person's life, will I be able to be involved proactively?

○ Friendship manifests differently depending on personality. Your style might be to show love in practical ways. I have a friend who organized all the files in my office so I could use them efficiently. Maybe you are a person who gives love through verbal encouragement and deep conversations. Everyone is unique and we can do what means the most to our individual friends, but we have to make sure we have the time and energy to do that.

I love to share life with my girlfriends. What are some inexpensive things we can do so that we don't spend all of our retirement money?

MARY: It's always fun to go for coffee in a variety of places. You could set up a regular "date" and go to a different spot each time. Do an internet search for something like, "fun cheap dates for friends," and try adding your city. My own search returned these suggestions:

○ A day at the museum
○ A potluck dinner

- Attend a local event
- Spend time together at a bookstore
- Explore your city
- Gather clothes and donate them to charity
- Hit a garage sale
- Play tourists for the day
- Break out your board games
- Do crafts together
- Go to a trivia night
- Attend a band performance
- Take a long walk
- Go fishing
- Visit an art gallery
- Volunteer
- Write a friendship bucket list together

CAROL: Going for walks or biking in pretty spots are great ways to get healthy and spend time together. Having lunch in each other's homes brings good conversation, laughter, and closeness. We just have to make time and do it.

What's your advice about telling my best friends about difficulties in my marriage or about my adult kids?

MARY: You're wise to be cautious about this. Our family members need to feel safe with us, meaning we won't unnecessarily tell others negative things about them. However, every person needs friends they can vent with and explore ways to improve what's going on. We need those few with whom we can totally be ourselves, which includes talking about the hard things involving family members. Verbally processing with someone else helps us solve our problems. When we talk to a close, safe friend, we are actually working toward a solution.

The caveat is that we need to carefully choose the friends in whom we confide. These need to be safe people who will keep what we say confidential. Also, it's ideal if they won't judge our family members, but try to help us work toward solving things in an objective way. At the very least, they shouldn't add fuel to our fire by heaping on negativism about our family, which will only make things harder for us. It's good to discuss all of these aspects with your close friend.

When you need to simply verbally process, you can say, "For now, I just want to talk and not get any advice. I need to get my feelings and thoughts out." Then, at other times, you can be open to their input. Both of these approaches are helpful toward improving things and soothing your soul.

CAROL: It's easier to be real about hurts and deep concerns with a friend who shares the same struggles that I have in marriage or with adult kids. When we can both can relate, it's comforting to know they "get it." Most women at our stage of life are not surprised or judgmental because they too have gone through deep trials by this point in life. Choose and share wisely but know that we need each other.

Even though I'm sixty-five, I long for an older woman in my life to mentor me. How do I go about finding someone?

MARY: Mentors cause our lives to blossom and flourish, and we usually have to seek them out intentionally. I think of a mentor as someone who is a few steps ahead of me, whose wisdom and experience I can draw upon for various challenges in my life. We need both "peer mentors" and "spot mentors." Peer mentors are those who are at our same stage of life. We draw upon one another for various challenges. We might also decide to keep each other accountable to reach our goals. We can meet regularly to talk about how things are going in our lives and to plan and evaluate our priorities and plans.

A "spot mentor" is someone I seek out for help in a specific area of life because I can benefit from what they've learned and the example they've set in what I'm struggling with. For example, when I've needed advice about something with my kids, I've observed those who seem to be doing well in this area and asked the parents for specific ideas and input. We can find a spot mentor for anything in which we're trying to improve.

Finally, you might find someone older than you to be your mentor. Sometimes we just have to look around and not wait to find perfection. With any mentor, I advise agreeing to a certain amount of time—maybe six to twelve months—that you'll both commit to this relationship. As the end of the time period approaches, you can both evaluate at that point whether you want to continue. This will avoid awkwardness if you reach the time when you're ready to move on without that person as a mentor. Both of you might change in your availability and desire, and this gives you the natural opportunity to do so.

CAROL: Wow, Mary. What if I am covered with "spots?" I guess some of us need more spot mentors than others! Yes, I agree we need to seek out mentors even as we age. We can always learn from those who have more life experience than we do. Older women have already gone through my present reality, so they can guide me to helpful ways of navigating the issues.

As a new grandmother, I asked for and received some valuable advice from my seasoned grandma friends. A common bit of advice has been to "zip" my mouth in responding to grown kids and helping with grandkids. Learning from wise people makes us wise. We can look for these treasured older women in groups or gatherings where our values are expressed.

FRIENDSHIP PROBLEMS

I have trouble making friends. How can I do a better job of making friends at this age?

CAROL: Find a group that does things you enjoy. I heard the story of a business-woman who retired and was looking for places to plug in. She was invited to a "women in the afternoon of life" meeting. A need arose for a cookie-maker for their monthly meetings. She met that need and it helped her to integrate into the group. She's become a friend to many and anticipates those monthly meetings and social connections.

What comes naturally to you? Exercise groups? Quilting? Book clubs? Do what fits you or take the challenge of growing in a new area with others who are doing the same.

MARY: Yes, begin activities where you can meet new people. Take classes. Volunteer in your place of worship or for causes that are meaningful to you. Look through meetup.com in your area. Interact on a neighborhood app from a source like nextdoor.com and attend gatherings that are listed. If you are physically limited or home-bound, look for online groups or start your own. Invite people to interact in a safe way through your contacts or social media. You might invite people that you know to your home to start a group or class.

We all need to periodically look at ourselves objectively and see if anything holds us back from friendships. Do I talk too much? Am I a good listener? Am I negative, or do I talk about controversial areas so that others avoid me? If I'm having trouble making friends, there may be areas where I need to grow and improve.

CAROL: That makes me think of the old adage: "To have a friend we must be a friend." Each of us needs to check to make sure we're not inadvertently hindering ourselves in relationships.

Now that I'm older, many of my friends have died. It's hard to start up fresh with new people.

MARY: Starting fresh with new people can feel challenging, so begin by taking baby steps. Most areas have senior centers, or you could visit retirement residences and engage in their activities.

I was very ill when I was in my fifties and couldn't leave my house for many months. A dear elderly woman, Margaret, heard about my situation and called from another state to check on me. She was housebound due to failing health. I hardly knew her, but we sparked a friendship, and she called me every day to talk for a while. Margaret was always loving, positive, and humorous at times. She passed on many years ago, but I will always treasure the relationship that came about because she reached out to me. Even in dire and limited circumstances, we can create life-changing friendships across many miles.

CAROL: Go to the places you enjoy and prayerfully keep your radar out for those relationships where you have a connection. Regular phone calls and video chats can be life-giving as well. Sometimes we need to simply take the first step.

I'm an introvert. I really like being alone—why do I need friends?

LYN: Introverts sometimes prefer seclusion, but being with others provides benefits we can't get any other way. As a species, humans are social and need interaction to thrive. Introverts usually don't need a wide circle, but building deep connection with one or two friends will enrich our lives.

CAROL: We grow and flourish in the context of relationships. Introverts can alternate times of social interaction with times to pull back and refuel. Alone time is peaceful and necessary but we can balance that with healthy and growing connections with others.

I love the ancient proverb reminding us that "two people together are better off than one, for they can help each other succeed (Ecclesiasters 4:0, 10, NLT)." We were created to need each other. Another says, "As iron sharpens iron, so one person sharpens another (Proverbs 287:17)." By interacting with good friends, we become better people.

When is it right to lovingly address an issue causing a friendship to be difficult?

MARY: This is a tough one because it's hard for most of us to hear negative things about ourselves. I'd love to say, "Yes, talk to her, and it will greatly improve things." But a lifetime of experience tells me that talking with her may change your relationship, and it might be difficult to continue in the way you have up to this point. You also might be hurt from things she will say. Ask yourself several questions:

- ○ Are you able to overlook her difficulties and continue with your relationship without bringing up the issue? Can you forgive and overlook her flaws, knowing all of us are imperfect?

- ○ Are you willing to take the chance that this conversation may permanently hurt your friendship? She might feel unsafe with you after this, even if you are loving and kind in your discussion.

- ○ How important to you is this issue?

- ○ If you feel that a discussion like this might permanently damage your friendship, would you rather simply back away and spend less time with her? In other words, reduce your amount of time and closeness so that her issues don't bother you as much.

CAROL: Recently, I had a difficult conversation with a dear friend. I was nervous and did not want to bring up the issue—but after getting wise counsel, praying, and writing out my thoughts, I got together with her and shared my hurt. She was extremely apologetic and humbly acknowledged her fault. The experience drew us closer and heightened my respect for her as a result.

One of my good friends has begun to gossip about everyone we know. It's gotten so bad that I worry she is telling others about things I've shared with her. What should I do?

MARY: Your friend may not be aware of her habit. First, lovingly let her know what her behavior is like for you and probably for others. What she is doing is not serving her well. When you tell her these things, express that you love her and want the best for her and your relationship. Then watch and wait to see if she chooses to change. In the meantime, you probably want to avoid telling her anything you don't want to be public knowledge.

King Solomon addressed this problem in ancient times: "Better is open rebuke than hidden love. Wounds from a friend can be trusted, but an enemy multiplies kisses (Proverbs 27:5–6)." Letting her know she's harming herself and others with her behavior shows how much you care.

My husband and I have been friends for years with a couple, but recently there are things he dislikes about the other husband and doesn't want to spend time with them anymore. I miss the camaraderie we used to have. Is there anything I can do?

LYN: You might try letting some time go by. This will allow your husband to process things, and he might grow to miss the couple and want to try again. Whether this happens or not, you could still enjoy the wife's friendship. Initiate coffee or lunch together. Stay away from the topic of your husbands and develop your own friendship around things you both are interested in.

CAROL: Also, gently communicate with your husband from time to time about your friendship with the woman and how it's going.

It can be a rare thing to find couples that you both like and enjoy. Sit with your spouse and brainstorm about couples you want to focus on in the upcoming months. This might be five couples or fewer. Reach out and put them in your calendar. There are seasons for friendships and not all of them are long-term.

TAKE ACTION

○ Look back through this chapter: what's one point of action you want to take regarding friendships?

○ Is there anything missing in your group of friends: someone fun, meaningful, deep, safe? What might you do to look for a person to meet this need?

○ How will you deepen your most significant friendships?

○ Are there friends with whom you want to reconnect, but you haven't had time in the busier seasons of life? List their names below.

○ As you look deeply into yourself, is anything holding you back from being a good friend to others? What can you do to improve this?

Look through the resources in Section 4, Chapter 9. Write down any that would be helpful for you. Make a plan to use the resources and add them to your calendar.

SPOTLIGHT STORY

KARLA DOWNING

Licensed Marriage and Family Therapist
Founder of ChangeMyRelationship.com

Karla Downing helps others by drawing from a deep well of difficulties she has experienced in her own life. She is a speaker, author, teacher, and licensed counselor. Karla is also the founding director of Change-MyRelationship.com, an outstanding website that connects people to her books, articles, videos, podcasts, and group studies. Her resources are devoted to helping people with difficulties in their relationships. She wrote the award-winning book, *10 Lifesaving Principles for Women in Difficult Marriages*. Her second book, *When Love Hurts: 10 Principles to Transform Difficult Relationships*, applies the same principles to all family members. Her third book, *The Truth in the Mirror: A Guide to Healthy Self-Image*, offers a unique and effective approach to looking at self-image. Her fourth book, *Change My Relationships: 365 Daily Devotions for Christians in Difficult Relationships*, offers understanding, validation, comfort, and practical advice. Karla is the author of several ebooks and hundreds of articles on relationship issues, including LifeWay International articles focused on training female leaders to help other women struggling in difficult relationships.

Karla grew up in a dysfunctional family and then found herself struggling for years with codependency in her own difficult marriage. Through her personal challenges, Karla discovered the practical principles that she now imparts to others. Her passion is to see individuals, marriages, and families set free from the chains of dysfunction, misunderstanding, and emotional pain. She also trains other counselors and leaders to help people in difficult relationships.

Karla lives in southern California, has been married for over forty years, and has three adult daughters and two grandchildren. She continues to navigate and learn on the complex journey of diverse relationships in this season of life. She communicates with refreshing candor and vulnerability.

The chapters in Section 2 covered a lot of territory: significant others, adult kids, grandkids, aging parents, and other relatives. We love Karla's honesty in the following pages as she explores her own struggles and experiences in the relationships we've discussed in this section.

What has most helped your relationship with your significant other during this season of life after the kids are grown?

This season for us has been busy and stressful. Together, we've run our company, taken care of elderly parents, helped adult children, spent time with grandchildren, and dealt with many crises. We are committed to each other through it all. We see vacations, spending time with friends and family, or participating in charities as opportunities to nurture our relationship. While taking time to separately pursue our passions may seem antithetical, this has also helped us. My husband is an avid bow hunter and fisherman, and I love to swim, ski, counsel, write, and speak. We give each other space to independently enjoy these things.

Even in good marriages, there are times we wish our spouse would change in an area but that doesn't seem possible. Have you experienced this, and how did you handle it?

My husband and I have had a difficult 44-year marriage. We both came into the marriage with dysfunctional backgrounds. One problem was the hurtful, habitual responses that he had learned from his family of origin and thought was normal. During much of our marriage, I tried to force change by lecturing, explaining, threatening, arguing, and appeasing. In the end, the only thing that worked was setting boundaries. I had to reach the point where I wasn't willing to live with hurtful behaviors. Even now, I stay vigilant to maintain healthy boundaries. He has grown to respect my zero-tolerance policy regarding harmful words or actions, and I appreciate that so much. I've worked hard on myself and my marriage. This turned into my work of helping others in difficult relationships.

Both of us have accepted certain things about each other after many years of trying to force change. We express support and love by accepting one another for who we are and giving each other grace to be ourselves.

How do you continue to nurture your relationship after many years together? How do you keep growing as a couple?

We are getting ready to retire after working hard throughout our marriage. We haven't figured out all the details yet, and we have some issues to resolve. He prefers not to live in California, and I prefer to stay. He wants to be free to travel and I want to continue my work. We will have to let go of some things to give each other the freedom to pursue our passions while we figure out ways to do things together to stay connected. We also need to leave the past behind and not let negative or hurtful memories rob us of the opportunity to repair and build a mutually respectful relationship. These are normal and common challenges couples face in this phase of life, and we seek to resolve them with integrity and love.

When we are opposites in so many areas, how can we continue to grow when we don't seem to like the same things?

My husband and I are opposites in many areas, but we also have things in common. We each pursue passions and interests separately. As I wrote previously, he hunts and I ski. I love the beach and swimming more than he does, but he goes to Hawaii with me. We watch different TV shows and YouTube channels. We have similar political views, like the same charitable causes, and share the same faith. Most importantly, we share our history and want to invest in the lives of our children and grandchildren. We both also value finishing strong together. We can focus on the things we share and support each other in the things we don't.

What has helped you to keep the bonds close with your kids, their spouses, and your grandkids?

We frequently stay in touch with our daughters to be involved in their lives. We were busy building our business when they were children, and we want to ensure they know, as adults, that we value them. I adapt my interaction style with each of them, not because I need to change who I am, but because I want the best relationship possible. I listen to them when they tell me I have crossed a line or caused hurt. I work to be the person I wish I had been when they were growing up. That's how I make amends, along with talking openly about their dysfunctional upbringing.

My husband has worked incredibly long and hard to provide for our family by building a business. He wanted to help them get a house and fulfill their dreams. We are generous with our kids as long as they are responsible and work hard. We want to see them enjoy some of their inheritance now.

One of our daughters has many physical and mental health problems. She depends on us for help with many things, including finances. Managing that with the rest of life takes wisdom and boundaries because overwhelming demands can easily push everyone and everything else out of the way. Rather than put her needs first, I prioritize maintaining my own health and life, which ultimately benefits the whole family. Because I have a better understanding of her complex needs, my husband and I have agreed that I am the parent responsible for making decisions on her behalf.

In the end, these types of factors work together to keep our family bonds healthy and strong.

What advice would you give for maintaining a good relationship with your son or daughter-in-law, especially if your personalities don't blend well?

The most important thing I have learned is to accept them for who they are. They might not be the individuals we would have chosen for our children, but they are the ones our children chose. I consider it my responsibility to make the relationship with them work as much as possible.

What is your best advice for grandparenting?

My life has been incredibly busy, but I have prioritized spending as much time as possible with my grandkids even though they live out of state. I have driven 700 miles in a day many times to bring them to my house to stay and then returned them a week later. I add their school breaks and events to my calendar a year in advance. My husband and I recently started flying to watch their sporting events. We have made it a tradition to take them to Hawaii with us every summer and they love it as much as we do. Most importantly, we have been their spiritual grandparents and have instilled the love of God into their hearts. I want my grandkids to talk to me about anything and everything. For them to feel close enough to do that, there must be a strong bond with memories of love and safety.

How did you handle any difficulties that came up as your parents got older? What practical advice would you give to those who are struggling in this area?

Just recently, my husband and I had three parents in their middle nineties. His father lived out of state alone and my parents lived near us. My father had dementia and my ninety-four-year-old mother took care of him until he passed away at ninety-six. Sometimes I worried about her and urged her to get more help, but it wasn't what she wanted. I supported her decision and helped her assist him until the end.

Now that my mom is released from my dad's care, I want to help her take better care of herself. We took her to visit my out-of-state daughters, to see her great-grandson play soccer, and to visit her granddaughter in New York. I treasure the memory of my 94-year-old mom walking around New York City and the vision of her with the Statue of Liberty behind her on Ellis Island, where her father arrived from Sweden as a young man.

I maintained boundaries as my parents got older. I was incredibly busy working in our business in addition to my work of counseling, writing, and speaking. On top of these things, I cared for my adult children's needs.

There were times I told my mom to call one of my siblings when she asked me for help and times I called them myself. There were also times I told my mom she had to get outside help. I did more than my siblings because I was the oldest and lived closer. I didn't compare how much I did to how much they did because I did what was right for me. My mom had cataract surgery in both eyes, which required eighteen doctor visits. Someone suggested that it was too much for me and that I could set up a driver, but there was no way I was going to let her think she didn't deserve my time when she needed me. She took care of us selflessly her whole life and then took care of our father.

I had to do some difficult things with my parents, such as removing control of the money from my mom when she fell victim to manipulative scammers. I had to take away my father's driver's license and might have to do the same for her.

We handle these tough but necessary decisions because we love our parents and want the best for them.

How have significant friendships been important in your decades after fifty?

Wise friends who've experienced troubles—especially those who've lived through circumstances similar to mine—have been my rock through difficult times. No matter what happens, I can be honest about my confusion, sadness, anger, and fears. They listen without judgment but are honest with their opinions. I know I will never be without the support I desperately need, and neither will they.

What specific and practical choices have helped you experience meaningful relationships through your decades after fifty?

I have been intentional about spending time with friends by planning girls' nights. This has grown my friend circle as well as allowed me to maintain the friendships I have. The best decision I made regarding friendships was to intentionally stay involved with my college friend Lori, even though we don't live near each other. We've been through college, marriage, marriage problems, pregnancy, raising children with problems, and now getting older. Since we both turned 50, we've set a goal to spend one week together every year doing something fun. We don't always make it, but the goal caused us to do a lot more together than we would have without that definite intent.

I've worked hard and accomplished many goals, but as I move into this later stage of life, my most important goal is to have the best relationships I can. Even though I've made mistakes and will continue to make them, I hope to journey through this chapter with the grace and wisdom I've learned throughout my previous years of life.

SECTION 3

YOU:
INSIDE
AND OUT

In this phase of life, awareness of your attitudes and thought processes is more important than ever. People can be proactive mentally, emotionally, spiritually, and practically to experience these years as positive and vibrant. How will you manage the realities of this final chapter?

10

YOUR MIND
AND EMOTIONS

In the years after fifty, maintaining and reinforcing positive mental and emotional health is necessary to flourish during this time. Your physical brain changes, bringing psychological patterns and pitfalls for the fifty-plus years. Let's talk about various approaches and resources to stay mentally and emotionally happy and healthy.

WHAT'S HAPPENING WITH MY BRAIN?

What natural changes happen in my brain in the years after I turn fifty?

MARY: The National Institute on Aging website notes a number of potential changes:

- As a person gets older, changes occur in all parts of the body, including the brain.
- Certain parts of the brain shrink, especially those important to learning and other complex mental activities.
- In certain brain regions, communication between nerve cells may not be as effective.
- Blood flow in the brain may decrease.
- Inflammation, which occurs when the body responds to an injury or disease, may increase.

These changes in the brain can affect mental function, even in healthy older people. For example, some older adults may find they don't do as well as younger individuals on complex memory or learning tests. However, given enough time to learn a new task, older individuals usually perform just as well as younger counterparts. Needing extra time is normal as we age. Growing evidence shows the brain maintains the ability to change and adapt so that people can manage new challenges and tasks as they age. Maintaining your physical health may benefit your cognitive health, too.[1]

CAROL: We can use this knowledge to do things to help ourselves thrive. Also, we need to give ourselves lots of grace during the natural process as our bodies get older.

These are scary aspects of an aging brain. How can I be proactive to help myself?

MARY: The National Institute on Aging (NIA) recommends specific things you can do in the following areas to keep your brain healthy:

- Take care of your physical health
- Manage high blood pressure
- Eat healthy foods
- Be physically active
- Keep your mind active
- Stay connected with social activities
- Manage stress
- Reduce risks to cognitive health

According to the NIA, a combination of these healthy lifestyle choices may reduce your risk for Alzheimer's disease.[2]

CAROL: Putting a priority on good sleep and hydration can help. I once asked an older mentor if she had advice for me as I aged, and she said "hydration." I didn't understand it then, but I do now. According to the National Council on Aging (NCOA), dehydration can lead to urinary tract infections (UTIs), which can cause us to appear to have dementia when what we actually need is an antibiotic. The

[1]How the Aging Brain Affects Thinking. National Institute on Aging (NIA). Content last reviewed October 19, 2020. Content accessed June 5, 2023. https://www.nia.nih.gov/health/how-aging-brain-affects-thinking

[2]Cognitive Health and Older Adults. https://www.nia.nih.gov/health/cognitive-health-and-older-adults

NCOA also reports that dehydration can lead to heart problems, kidney failure, blood clot complications, and heatstroke. Since dehydration affects the health of your cells, it can also lower your body's ability to ward off infections and heal from injury or illness. Let's all drink lots of water for our brains and overall health.[3] We also need some kind of brain activity: reading, crosswords, games—anything that gives us a challenge. Having good social interactions stimulates our brains as well.

LYN: We have choices and possibilities and, as always, we reap what we sow. Now we must lean on wisdom gained from life experience and ask ourselves how we want to use our energy to keep our brains strong. Maintaining a healthy brain is well worth our time and effort.

How can I help my memory stay strong? I forget little things more than I used to.

CAROL: Noticing our memory slips can make us feel insecure. A friend told me that when she is parking at the grocery store, she looks at the parking lot row number before she enters the store and says it out loud—this helps her to remember it. By slowing down and focusing, we develop new habits, like always parking in the same row at the grocery store, that will help us avoid confusion in the future.

I've been studying short-term memory for a while and learned that focused attention is necessary to remember something or learn something new. Our minds tend to get distracted easily, but we can be intentional in what we need to remember.

LYN: When I'm multitasking, I'm less able to remember little things like where I put my keys or why I entered a room. I intentionally slow my movements (which also prevents falls) to remain aware of where I am setting papers or who I am about to call.

Before our fifties, we were able to do many, many things at one time well. Now, I'm finding that I can still do a lot of work, but I must do it more carefully and slowly. It's made me happier because I'm truly focused instead of living on autopilot.

MARY: We can find apps and websites with mental games and exercises to keep memory and other aspects of brain function stronger. One of my favorites is Lumosity. My daughter, in her thirties, enjoyed playing their games on my phone so much that she got it for herself. You can find Lumosity in your phone app store.[4]

---

[3] https://www.ncoa.org/article/how-to-stay-hydrated-for-better-health
[4] https://www.lumosity.com

How can I prepare my adult children for what is in our future regarding my shortcomings?

LYN: We can prepare them as they see how we are helping and loving our aging parents and other loved ones as they decline in their abilities. As my parents grew weaker and less capable, my kids saw me care for them. We teach by example as we serve our parents. We can talk to our kids about how one day this may be their situation with us and process what that might be like.

Sometimes the aging process is sudden, and that is hard. Sometimes the process is slower, which is also hard. Each stage of our lives brings challenges and opportunities to love one another with an unconditional love that leaves no regrets.

If it turns out that our children must serve us in later years, let's point out how well they are helping so that when we die, there are memories in their hearts of having done well in this regard. This will truly help them in their own grieving process and growth as individuals.

MARY: Yes, it's good to normalize talking about possible mental and physical decline in case it happens. You might discuss positive and negative situations you and your kids have seen, and what you glean from these examples for your own future. Of course, if you're already experiencing difficulties, open discussion and planning are very important.

PSYCHOLOGICAL PHASES, PATTERNS, AND PITFALLS

Are there certain phases people usually go through during our fifties, sixties, seventies and beyond?

LYN: One of my favorite reference resources for understanding this is Gail Sheehy's book, *Passages* (Dutton, 2013). She divides the decades in this way:

Fearless Fifties

Influential Sixties

Age of Integrity: Seventies, Eighties and Beyond

Let's dare to confront each of life's phases with hope, expectation, and solid goals.

CAROL: The decades after fifty can be the most significant years of our lives. By this time, we know more about who we are and the strengths we have. We usually have more disposable time and may not be so squeezed for finances. We've learned many life lessons and can help others by telling stories from our wealth of experience.

MARY: Psychologist Erik Erikson developed a respected approach known as Erikson's Stages of Psychosocial Development. He found that humans go through eight predictable stages of life from birth until death. The last two stages pertain to those of us who are over fifty.

In Stage Seven, from 30 to 64 years old, Erikson found that a person's biggest goals are to contribute to society and be part of a family. He found that people who do well in this stage have a healthy concern for their family and society in general. Success with these goals brings a sense of usefulness and accomplishment. On the other hand, people don't do well in this stage if they only have concern for themselves and their own well-being and prosperity, while maintaining a shallow involvement in the world. These things lead to feelings of unfulfillment and emptiness, according to Erikson's research.

In Stage Eight, from ages 65 onward, Erikson found that our main goals are to assess our lives and make sense of them, and to assess the meaning of our personal contributions in life. People do well in this stage if they come through it with a sense of integrity, fulfillment, and willingness to face death. In these things, they will have feelings of contentment and wisdom. People who don't do well in this stage have dissatisfaction with life and despair over prospects of their own death. They feel regret, bitterness, and despair. To read more about Erikson's approach to the stages of life, check out https://positivepsychology.com/erikson-stages

What are some negative psychological patterns and pitfalls that are common as people get older?

MARY: Here are a few:

Attitude: Simple changes like choosing joy or limiting our exposure to the news can help us avoid becoming grouchy, negative, and judgmental.

Poor Self-esteem: This can come from no longer having a job or career, our culture's negative view of seniors, or loss of productivity or health.

Family Issues: Problems with our grown children, grandchildren, and others need to be addressed with wisdom, grace, and healthy boundaries for all. Otherwise, they pull us down.

Grief: Assuming we outlive them, experiencing the death of beloved relatives and close friends is inevitable. We can address our loss in healthy ways while nurturing relationships with friends and family.

Isolation: Memory problems, reduced mobility, and health difficulties can prevent seniors from connecting with others. Creative interventions are needed.

Becoming Inactive: A sedentary lifestyle, particularly one involving too much screen time, can foster negativity and unhealthy self-focus, leading to depression and anxiety.

Substance Abuse: Unfortunately, many seniors develop addictions to alcohol, medications, and illicit drugs. We can proactively address these in the same ways younger people do, including recovery programs like Alcoholics Anonymous.

Anxiety and Depression: All the aforementioned tendencies can lead to anxiety and depression in varying degrees. We need to utilize counseling through every stage of life. We're blessed to live at a time when it's available both in person and online.

CAROL: We make daily choices, like deciding between being mean and selfish versus kind and patient. The filters can come off as we age, so we must choose our words wisely. Knowing our energy limitations can ensure we have the needed inner strength to make positive choices amidst challenges. Otherwise, we may fall prey to the things Mary mentioned.

LYN: My mother-in-law was just never happy. She was mean some days and nice on others. Family members often wondered aloud, "Who will she be today?" Sometimes I would try to rescue her reputation. One day she was speaking to me with a hateful tone and words when another person came into the room. She switched quickly into the presentation of a well-cultured, loving older woman. After the person left, I asked her about it. She giggled and smiled, like she was happy to be fooling people.

She had an awful reputation with her sons, grandchildren, and both daughters-in-law. This has motivated me to remember that we are always working on our family's memory of us, and our eulogies. Let's purposefully leave a rich heritage for them to follow.

How can I avoid the psychological pitfalls of aging?

CAROL: I recently heard a ninety-year-old woman share three secrets for aging: move your body well, feed your body well, and rest your body well. She said the third was most important. Caring for ourselves physically has a huge impact on our psychological well-being. When asked what she would pass on to the next generation, this lady replied, "Never quit, have a bucket list, and make your life interesting." She lived her own advice. At sixty years old, she was offered her dream job in Europe. She moved to make that dream come true.

MARY: That's a great example of how our mental health is boosted by living for our dreams.

STAY EMOTIONALLY STRONG

How can I stay happy and emotionally strong throughout this season?

CAROL: I think it's important to establish 5 consistent daily practices and life rhythms to grow and thrive. Regular exercise, good nutrition, daily sunshine, spiritual growth habits, community, fellowship with others as a way of life, date nights with significant others, reading, writing, music and enjoying creation can all contribute to mental health. Dr. Curt Thompson, MD, talks about keeping yourself on a path of "oncoming beauty," whether that beauty is something creative, an art form, or some other soul-nourishing source.[5] These things can be part of keeping our minds and souls healthy. Of course, life happens. We cannot control certain hardships that come our way. And yet, we must do our part to make the best of things and to live our lives well.

LYN: Part of staying emotionally healthy and strong involves remembering my motivation for doing so. I'm inspired when I think of the legacy and influence I want to have. In today's social media world, everyone is concerned about being an "influencer." Influencing means having an effect on the character, development, and behavior of someone. We must be good role models.

I have a friend whose mother was rude and unwise in all of her dealings with her adult children and her grandchildren. When this woman died, no one was really sad; instead, they were all relieved.

I have another friend whose mother was a beacon of light in the way she lived with good judgment. She was careful and wise when relating to her adult children and grandchildren. The result was a legacy of love, strength, and motivation within her clan to be able to live with integrity, joy, and wisdom.

Which of these life results would you choose? Living for the influence I can have on others fills me with joy and strength during this season of life.

---

[5]https://curtthompsonmd.com/beauty-will-save-the-world

MARY: I couldn't keep going without my personal, intimate interactions with God throughout each day. This starts each morning as I spend time talking with God about what weighs on my heart. I learn from the Bible. The strongest, most joyful older people I've known through the years have done these things. None of us should miss out on experiencing God.

There seems to be a lot of information about the negative emotional aspects of senior adulthood. Are there any positive aspects?

CAROL: Big question. You are generally more philosophical. On a humorous note, you can wear the same clothes for three days and not take as many showers.

MARY: Oh Carol, I love how you always look on the bright side of things! As we advance in years, don't forget about the following:

o We now have a wealth of life experience to draw upon for everything we encounter. We've learned so much.

o People generally have more free time to devote to the things that matter most to them.

o Grandchildren.

o More time for loved ones.

o Opportunities to pursue your dreams and interests.

o Participation in civics and volunteering.

o Better social skills and more empathy—our failures and successes have taught us things.

o Medicare and Social Security.

o Senior discounts.

o A sense of accomplishment.

LYN: There are so many positive aspects to aging and, if you are a person of faith, you can find joy in being much closer to meeting your Creator.

What can I do to stay positive through negative experiences like friends dying, health problems, or feeling devalued by my culture?

CAROL: I think this goes back to a spiritual answer. Positivity comes through pursuing a relationship with God, trusting him, and letting go of expectations.

MARY: Take firm control of what you put into your mind. Don't simply fill it with whatever the media or internet dishes out. A wealth of uplifting and nourishing reading material, spiritual wisdom, and relational gold is available to be mined. Your entire well-being is controlled by what you allow into your brain and body. Feed them wisely.

LYN: Social media can be negative but can also be very inspiring. Find some folks who post positive and exciting things. Be transported into a realm of ideas, positive outlets, and ways of thinking you may not have ever considered. Review the resources in Section 4 for some excellent content and places to join.

Are there some authors or role models I can follow regarding my emotional health in this season?

CAROL: Look for people who have been influential in your own life who set positive examples. You can emulate their character qualities and life choices.

MARY: I think of my dear friend Jo who, at 90, lived with positivity and joy as she devoted her time for the good of others in her retirement home. Queen Elizabeth, Nelson Mandela, and Mother Teresa were selfless and emotionally strong until late in life. Read biographies of people like these to glean information and inspiration to be vital and resilient. Our own Judy Douglass is a role model for me. In addition to her many books, she has a weekly podcast, continually meets with people, and travels to enrich the lives of others.

I'm anxious about my family and the world. Is this just part of getting older?

MARY: Our spiritual habits are crucial. Phrases like "Let go and let God" and "Be still and know that I am God" are not just sayings; they must become a way of life. Habits of spending time with God, talking to him about what's going on in my life, and finding verses that bring peace—these continually infuse tranquility into my soul.

Also, the practices and principles of mindfulness can drastically reduce anxiety. Mindfulness trains your brain to be calm through relaxation and visualization exercises. Many people start their journey in this approach with mindfulness apps. My book, *Rest for Your Soul*, provides mindfulness exercises for those coming from a faith perspective.

CAROL: The changes that occur in aging can make us more anxious. Many things are moving out of our control, and I think our nervous system becomes agitated more easily. We have to remember it is not our job to "fix" our loved ones. Our goal is to stay in relationship, love them, and trust God.

MARY: Physiological changes and needs can also cause anxiety, so we need to have our doctors check our hormones, blood sugar, iron, and thyroid to help us address any problems. Also, caffeine, sugar, and chocolate can be anxiety-causing culprits. Finally, stress and biological change in our bodies can affect our biochemicals, increasing anxiety and depression. Antidepressants address these, so consult your doctor to find out if medication might help.

A lot of people get judgmental as they age. How can I avoid this?

LYN: Judging others might come from a sense of pride—when we have success in areas of life, we sometimes self-appoint ourselves as experts. We think we know what behaviors or habits are best. Also, we can set ourselves up as watchmen over others who break "the rules," judging others from our set of rules and not theirs.

CAROL: I've found it helpful to keep my mind on very positive things. This ancient wisdom is powerful: "Whatever is true, whatever is noble, whatever is right, whatever is pure, whatever is lovely, whatever is admirable—if anything is excellent or praiseworthy—think about such things (Philippians 4:8)." Our thinking and ultimately our hearts will determine whether we choose kindness and love over having a critical spirit and mouth.

MARY: I think being judgmental can come from being negative. The good news is that you can train your brain to be more positive. I've had to fight this in my own life and wrote a book with little creative activities that helped me. *Retrain Your Brain for Joy: 31 Mini-Adventures* (Westbow Press, 2014) has thirty-one simple daily activities to help you develop a consistently positive outlook, which counteracts judgmentalism. You can actually have fun while retraining your brain.

I'm a very adaptable person, but my husband is closed-minded and irritable. How can I help him?

LYN: There have been people in my life who were so skeptical and fearful it's almost funny—but it is also draining and miserable. Each of us has a certain disposition and bent toward processing the world around us, which can include negative aspects.

Sometimes it's beneficial to let them vent, truly listening to the fear or concern they're expressing. This can earn their trust and make them feel heard and loved.

At that point, they might be willing to learn from your example or careful input. In the midst of this though, it's important that you don't let someone else's negativity steal your joy as you continue to be adaptable and positive. Those qualities are part of your legacy.

CAROL: Be as patient as possible. We can't fix other people. I was a very slow learner in this area. Let him be himself as you hold on to your own perspective and decide what boundaries you need to stay healthy.

MARY: Karla Downing's website (https://www.changemyrelationship.com.) has excellent resources for this. Also, it's never too late to seek counseling to get ideas for yourself. Your spouse may eventually come with you.

STAY INVOLVED WITH PEOPLE

How can social isolation and loneliness affect my mental health and what can I do about it?

MARY: Being isolated and lonely leads to depression and anxiety, which can result in health problems, insomnia, addiction, and other issues. In short, it can make us miserable. Health challenges and lack of employment contribute to isolation as we get older.

Whatever your situation, you can add meaningful relationships into your life. Start with family and friends, setting up times to call or get together. You might begin reaching out more through social media, commenting on their posts. To meet new people, explore activities that involve things you enjoy, like classes or a book club. See what's going on in your place of worship or senior community center. You might ask a relative to help you or accompany you to get yourself started.

Also, check out the following two phone numbers. Both are available 24 hours a day, 7 days a week, for no charge.

Institute on Aging Friendship Line: 1-800-971-0016

This phone service is designed to support people 60 and older and adults living with disabilities. Their trained volunteers specialize in active listening and friendly conversation with older adults. They provide emotional support, well-being checks, grief support, suicide intervention, resources and referrals for isolated adults. They can also help report elder abuse.

The Samaritans HelpLine: 1-877-870-4673

You can call or text this number. They provide compassionate support to anyone who is feeling anxious, depressed or isolated. This service also offers online chats for those who prefer to use digital tools.

Is there such a thing as too many people at this stage of life? Where does rest fit in?

LYN: I think this goes back to whether you are an introvert or an extrovert. Introverts are energized by spending time alone. Extroverts are energized by spending time with people.

Some people are a combination of both, getting energized by people to a point, then requiring time alone to refuel. This determines how many people you will want to be involved with.

Both extroverts and introverts need rest. We must all be aware of our inner gauges and learn what will best satisfy the need to replenish ourselves. We need to proactively manage our schedules in order to ensure we have enough rest. I am an "extrovert's extrovert" in that I love to be with people and am energized by them. I have found, though, that I have to mentally check to see if I'm growing tired. This has helped me to realize when I need downtime. I now know that I shouldn't schedule back-to-back events day after day. Now that I'm older, I too need alone time, even as an extrovert. Who knew?

CAROL: Having a lot of acquaintances is not negative, but interacting with a lot of people over time will diminish even an extrovert's energy. We must decide with whom to invest our energy. I've found it necessary to establish habits of rest and replenishment, even as an extrovert myself. A weekly "day off" or Sabbath day allows me to stop working, relax, and be refreshed. It's also important to have a consistent sleep schedule in order to bolster inner resources. In addition, rest is not always passive. Sometimes rest is just doing enjoyable things.

Since my husband retired, he watches TV a lot and wants to stay home all the time. I think he's getting depressed, but he resists my efforts to get him out more. What can I do?

LYN: I can be, and have been, very opinionated about my husband and how he should be living. I am neither his boss nor his mother. I can only control myself.

Opposites attract. What you see in the use of TV and solitude may be an example of that. Our significant others often have positions that are diametrically different from what we would do. Longevity in marriage, peace in the home, and kindness modeled are values that help us to live and let live.

Let go of him. Let God do the changing if there needs to be a change.

CAROL: Also, make sure you are still connected with others and go out with friends yourself. Encourage him to join you where appropriate, and if he says no, accept that graciously.

MARY: You might communicate with him about this in the right time and way. You could start a list together of enjoyable activities to try as a couple. Start slowly and discover things together.

How can I stay socially involved now that I'm bedridden and housebound due to permanent illness?

CAROL: Develop the habit of initiating phone calls with others. Avoid spending much time talking about your illnesses—focus on other things, especially topics that are uplifting and positive. You could read a book together and talk about it or find a friend or two to pray with over the phone on a weekly basis.

MARY: When I was very sick and housebound for a long time in my forties and fifties, my dear friend Sally helped set up regular socialization opportunities for me. She scheduled times for church people to visit, call, or drive me to medical appointments. Many places of worship have specific ministries to assist people in difficult times, so look into one of the larger churches in your area through their website or a phone call.

The internet has opened many possibilities for those who are physically limited or housebound. You can be involved with others through all types of video calling. You can make new friends through online groups like book clubs, spiritual discussions, game-playing where you socialize, or involvement in whatever topic interests you. Find these by searching social media sites, your local library website, or online searches. If needed, have a younger relative or friend help you with this.

Your faith community or social group might be willing to set up their regular meetings at your home. Be open to this and have someone assist you in getting your living space ready. You need people, so do whatever is necessary to keep this life-giving component in your regular schedule.

Caregiving for my wife's chronic illness prevents me from being involved with other people. Social involvement just isn't realistic for me.

CAROL: It is a challenging balance to be available for your wife and also to have meaningful relationships with others. I know this is difficult. Can your family be more involved? Medicare covers programs for in-home care. Not having social involvement can destroy your own health.

LYN: Be careful to not develop a savior complex or a martyr mindset. These are recognized patterns, marked by self-sacrifice and service to others, but at your own expense. It's thinking that only you know how to best serve your wife, but it can create a codependent, unhealthy relationship. These behavior patterns can become toxic for you, your wife, and those around you. You might feel that you can't take responsibility for your own well-being because you are trapped there to serve, and you cannot have any social involvement. This results in burnout and stress in our relationships—with our spouse and/or others who are trying to reach out and help.

Others may like an opportunity to come through for their mother, relative, or friend. Also, qualified professional caregivers are ready to serve. You are not alone.

Get some help and become socially involved. You will serve your wife better with your rejuvenated energy and perspective. Of course, voluntarily sacrificing your time and energy to serve your wife is of utmost honor and value. But recognizing and addressing these other tendencies are best for everyone in the long run.

HELP OTHERS TO HELP YOURSELF

For individuals in their seventies, eighties, and nineties, there seem to be fewer options for helping other people. Do you have any suggestions?

MARY: Look for opportunities in your community centers, your place of worship, and with others who are elderly. There are foster grandparent programs, needs in the foster care system, animal shelters, food delivery needs, reading to others, or volunteering at the library. Also, check out Americorps, an organization that specifically guides people in finding ways to help others (https://americorps.gov). Once on their website, click on the tab at the top that says "Serve," then scroll down to "Americorps Seniors" to find opportunities in your exact area. If you don't find what you want, the site provides ideas to seek on your own.

CAROL: In these years, it's still important to deepen relationships we already have or to develop new ones. We can be interested in whatever our friends are going through, give to younger people in their personal lives or service endeavors, join a book club, and get to know our neighbors. We can ask people about how we can pray for them, then follow up by asking how things are going in the things we prayed for.

LYN: Having more free time in our later years is a beautiful opportunity. Use this time to study your spiritual beliefs and help people using that perspective. You can make an impact that will be remembered long after you are gone. Your spiritual life will allow you to maintain a peaceful essence and help those who come into your realm. If you are a person of faith, ask God to increase your love, joy, and faith, remembering that love is the most important calling ever.

My doctor told me to help my depression by getting involved in something that helps others. How can I do this when I'm always tired and unmotivated?

CAROL: Get help with this from a therapist who can guide you. Start with baby steps and increase these over time.

MARY: Carol is right, and your motivation may grow as you take those first steps.

I have lived a rich and rewarding life and I long to be a mentor for younger people. Does anyone in the younger generations want that? If so, how do I go about this?

LYN: Being a mentor has happened organically as I've continued to participate in exercise classes, support groups for my issues, or having my grown children and their friends over for dinners and gatherings. As I talk to young adults, the conversations evolve into mentoring opportunities. I hear that the younger person is struggling with something I've learned because I have personally gone through it or studied it and realize I could help them. I might invite them to go out to breakfast or lunch and then listen to them. The rest evolves naturally.

Mentoring involves providing support, guidance, and feedback. We help others by being a good role model, teacher, advisor, sponsor, advocate, or ally. We can provide them with tools they need to become a better version of themselves. There is someone out there waiting for you, perhaps right under your nose.

CAROL: There are definitely younger people who would love to have a mentor. Are you involved with communities that include younger generations? Look for programs that match a mentor with someone less experienced. Show a personal interest in those you naturally connect with. I've found it works best and attracts others when I don't give advice, but instead listen and encourage.

I really enjoy children and young adults, but I don't have any grandchildren. Where could I be of service?

CAROL: You could nurture relationships with children and young adults around you: people in your neighborhood, family, or place of worship. Some community programs match volunteer grandparents with children who either don't have grandparents or live far from them.

LYN: I've come to realize that all young families need babysitters or someone to take the children on errands or to activities. Young married couples need to continue to date, but often can't afford the date and a babysitter. This is where your calling comes in. Remember though, that you must earn parents' trust before you extend the offer.

If you are a person of faith, worship community programs for kids and young adults are always looking for help in a variety of ways. These can be fun and rewarding—and they need your services. As you develop friendships within these contexts, they may evolve into relationships outside of the programs.

CELEBRATE YOUR SUCCESSES AND RESOLVE YOUR REGRETS

I like thinking about my successes in life, but I don't see the benefit of dwelling on mistakes or failures. The past is past—why dwell on it?

LYN: As we've entered our fifties and beyond, we have a wealth of experience behind us. I agree that it can be unhealthy to dwell too long on the past, but it is oh-so-helpful to learn and glean from our experiences. We've had the privilege of gaining life lessons through mistakes and failures so that we can truly relate to others and empathize with them. The circumstances I've endured have provided me with many opportunities to speak into others' lives, whether they are younger or comrades who are my age, because I know what I'm talking about.

MARY: Our past affects us whether we're aware of it or not. Negative thinking and self-talk are often present in those who least suspect it, stealing happiness from them and those around them. The point is not to dwell on the past, but to be aware of it, process it, and get free of its negative effects on you and others. You might start by asking a close loved one to help you think through your life successes and missteps. Ask them to be honest with you if they suspect anything from your past is holding you back.

If you like to journal, you might title a page, "Things I wish were different from my past." Then write whatever comes to your mind. What do you do next? Keep reading for ideas that can help.

There are things I regret but what can I do?

MARY: If we're honest, we all have regrets because none of us has had a perfect life. I use these five steps.

1. Recognize my regrets.
2. Grieve the losses involved.
3. Forgive myself when needed.
4. Discover the lessons I've learned.
5. Think about how my experiences have made me stronger, better, and more able to help others.

You might start by writing down the personal regrets you carry. You could then process these using the five steps by continuing to write or talking through them with a friend.

For example, one of my regrets is that I've had a chronic illness, fibromyalgia, since I was in my forties. No one knows what causes this condition, but it was made worse by poor nutritional choices in my first few decades, along with living a stressful lifestyle. I've grieved the many limitations it's caused along the way, forgiven myself for things that made it worse, and journaled about the lessons it's taught me. I've been able to help others because of my experiences with it. If I had not done these things, I think it would have weakened me emotionally and mentally.

CAROL: I would also ask myself if the things I regret are affecting important relationships. If so, it may be beneficial to talk through my regrets with those people, listen well to their responses without being defensive, then decide together how to proceed more effectively.

What do I do with my hurt feelings from past relationships and interactions?

MARY: For me, it comes down to three factors.

1. I work through my feelings and thoughts on my own, thinking objectively and/or processing them confidentially with others.
2. I forgive the other person and/or myself.
3. I talk through it with the person in order to reach a state of peace. Each situation is different, and if the first and second options don't bring resolution for me, adding the third may be what is needed.

CAROL: I ask myself, "Are these hurt feelings realistic?" In other words, did I over-react to or misunderstand what was said or done? An honest and discerning friend may be able to give frank feedback.

Feelings are of great importance in processing where we are in life and what triggers us or brings us joy. But we don't want to let our feelings pull us along without evaluating and processing them in healthy ways. I heard this train illus-tration years ago: Picture the diagram of a train showing the engine attached to a caboose. The engine represents the FACT of what happened or was said to you. The caboose is filled with your FEELINGS about what happened. We don't want to be pulled around by our FEELINGS, but by correctly perceiving the FACTS of what happened, just as an engine pulls a caboose. When the caboose tries to pull the engine, it doesn't go well. As we do our due diligence to correctly perceive and understand the FACTS, our FEELINGS can follow in a peaceful way.

What plan can I follow to think through my successes and failures in a satisfactory and positive way?

LYN: At the beginning of this book, we discussed and created our life mission statements and personal goals inventories. Refer to your entries to determine whether you are succeeding or failing at meeting some of them. Satisfaction and peace arrive when we know we have tackled the things we proposed to do and given our best in these areas.

MARY: And of course we'll fall short. Sometimes we don't achieve all we'd hoped, and we utterly fail at times. This is normal human experience, and we can learn to accept our shortcomings, forgive ourselves, and resolve our regrets. I focus on the part of the glass that is half full or even a quarter full in my life, not the empty part. We're all together in being imperfect. Joy comes from focusing on what we have instead of on what we lack.

You might try listing all the things you view as successes in your life. Spend time reflecting on these. Celebrate achieved goals in your own way: talk about them with a friend, have a special dinner, or do something creative.

My parenting mistakes are my main regrets. I would parent differently now. How can I live with myself?

CAROL: There is no perfect parent. Each of us will have regrets. You and your child have both learned from your mistakes. I've found peace and comfort in real-izing I was a "good enough" parent. At the right times, my husband and I discussed negative family patterns and made apologies. Now I get to live as a more experienced and aware person with our grandchildren.

LYN: Regrets are heavy as they make us sad and disappointed because of perceived missed opportunities. The truth is that even in parenting missteps, our children can still glean from our mistakes by not repeating history with their children. I've realized this from my own launched children. You may be surprised at how your regrets can turn into new behaviors going forward for you and your grandchildren.

By the way, remember that we all must look back and grieve for some areas where we fell short, especially now that we are older and know more than we did then. I mourned my past parenting behavior to a very good friend, and he said, "It seems like you expect yourself to be perfect." I countered with, "I do, especially regarding my parenting." He was kind as he reminded me that only God is perfect; the rest of us are fallible. When we accept that no human is perfect, it helps us live with ourselves.

When should I try to talk to a loved one about how they have hurt me, and when is it better to just leave it alone? I regret not bringing this up years ago, but maybe now it's too late.

CAROL: This might be something to talk over with a therapist, or with safe people in your life who will keep it confidential. Harboring bitterness in our hearts is not the way we were designed to live. If you decide to move forward and talk with the other person, do so with caution, wisdom, and careful navigation. I've learned that many words lead to mistakes, and I ask God to guide me.

LYN: Care and wisdom are needed when bringing up past issues that can make someone defensive or angry. Sometimes our loved ones or friends don't have the capacity to hear what we want to say. Timing is more than just important; it is crucial. Be sure the person has slept well, has eaten, and is not walking out the door to go to work or do something important. Sensitive people may need a warning before any discussions can take place. Just a simple, "May we carve out some time to talk about something that has been on my heart for a while now?" will go a long way, allowing the other to prepare inwardly rather than being blindsided by a seeming accusation.

Allowing time to pass instead of speaking up at the moment of an offense has helped me get my thoughts in order. If you decide to talk about it, set your goal to be loving and to reconcile with the person, and you may win a friend.

MARY: More than once, I've learned why there is a saying: "It's better to let a sleeping dog lie." Weigh the pros and cons carefully before bringing up a past hurt. I've tried it at times and come away even more hurt, with nothing resolved. God bless your road ahead!

THOUGHTS AND FEELINGS
ABOUT YOUR CHANGING APPEARANCE

Is it wrong to try to look young for as long as possible?

MARY: It's not so much about right or wrong, but what will make you happiest in the long run? We can try to look our best at every stage of life, but we have to balance that with focusing on higher, more meaningful mental focuses and pursuits. It's frustrating and even depressing when we don't learn to accept and value who we are at any stage of life. We're happiest when we value exactly who we are and focus on higher life goals, like loving God and other people.

LYN: We can try to look our best at every age, and it's exciting to tie that goal to a higher one, like loving and connecting with people. Let me explain what I mean. I've found that clothes are a very personal tool we can use to express ourselves. Each generation had a look that expressed that time frame. Remember the Sixties? Seventies? Eighties? Nineties? The new millennium? Now it seems anything goes.

I have a game I play each day: I think about my schedule and ask God, "Who will I see today and what do You want me to look like? What will help me to connect with this person?"

If I am mentoring a younger person, I try to choose something "edgy."

If I am going to be in a professional or conservative arena, I choose classic styles.

If I am going to be with my children, I often copy a thing or two they wear to show them that I not only approve of their choices, I like them.

And if I am with my husband, I try to be a bit sexy (but not vulgar to the rest of the world) and wear the styles he has expressed that he likes.

Looking "young" can come from your attitude and mindset. It's not wrong to look your best: it can be a fun way to love and connect with those you're with each day. Be you.

I'm getting wrinkles and saggy skin. Is it possible to not get dragged down emotionally by this?

CAROL: As we age, it's difficult to see ourselves looking different than when we were younger. We can still try to look our best, but we have to come to peace with the changes in our appearance. Why do some women embrace their gray hair but others don't? Every woman navigates aging in her own way. Sometimes the acceptance comes gradually over time. I can be hard on myself when my thoughts are in the wrong place, especially about changes in my body. Reminding myself that I like the person I am now helps me stay positive.

MARY: I'll admit that it's taken time for me to accept my wrinkles and aging skin—and I'm still in the process. I was horrified when I first saw the skin on my arms and neck begin to wrinkle, and I bought all kinds of anti-aging creams that didn't work. Over time, though, I've come to accept my aging appearance. Here are some things that have helped me cope:

○ Grieve the aspects of your appearance that you don't like.

○ Develop and use your strengths, giftings, and service for other people. This takes your mind off yourself and enhances healthy self-esteem.

○ Feed your mind with input that emphasizes and establishes your inner values and de-emphasizes external appearance. Think about this in terms of what you're reading, listening to, and watching.

○ Do you spend a lot of time with people who highly value outer appearance and follow the thinking of a youth-idolizing culture? If so, add new friends who don't.

○ Work on accepting your aging appearance. There are good online articles, and also books like *Face It: What Women Really Feel as Their Looks Change,* by Vivian Diller and Jill Muir-Sukenick (Hayhouse, 2010). Be intentional and devote time to accepting and valuing yourself just as you are.

○ If you are a person of faith, focus upon what God says about your inner beauty and his great love for you.

How can grieving help me be at peace with my declining appearance?

MARY: Grieving helps us accept what we have lost, which includes our physical characteristics from earlier years. Allow yourself to explore and feel the losses of your changing physicality. What most people don't realize is that if you take the time to truly feel and process emotions, you'll feel better faster. A technique called

D-A-Y-S-A will help you to do that, and it involves simply noticing, expressing, and accepting the emotions of grieving (Denial, Anger, Yearning, and Sadness) until you come to a place of Acceptance. As you notice things you don't like about your appearance, think about which of these emotions you're feeling. Express them out loud to a friend, to God, or when you're alone. You could journal about them. After expressing the feelings of D, A, Y, and S, you will slowly find yourself Accepting the lost aspects of your youthful appearance. Peaceful acceptance is a natural result of grieving well.

Everybody says, "Focus on being beautiful inside" as I see my outside getting old. I've tried, but is it really possible?

LYN: My mother always said, "Pretty is as pretty does." As a child, teenager, and young adult, I wasn't quite sure what she meant. Now that I have age on my side, I've come to understand that it's not only possible to be pretty on the inside, but it is also critical. Our insides are where our hearts and consciences live. Our hearts are made up of our thoughts, wills, and emotions. We cannot escape these, nor our consciences, as we interact with our parents, children, friends, neighbors, and workmates. When you focus on how to bring honor to a situation, you will find that you are beautiful on the inside. As we know so well, our outsides continue to grow older day by day. The inside is where we can continue to grow fresh and richly add to our beauty, whatever age we are.

MARY: We become what we focus upon. Make a concerted effort to focus upon your inner beauty every day. I love this quote: "Whatever is true, whatever is noble, whatever is right, whatever is pure, whatever is lovely, whatever is admirable—if anything is excellent or praiseworthy—think about such things (Philippians 4:8)."

CAROL: A lot of life has happened to us and maybe, just maybe, we are more beautiful now than ever.

How can I be content with an older and heavier body? Is it realistic or even wise to get down to my college weight? What is the best perspective on this tension?

LYN: The fact that we are having to consider this topic shows the century we live in. In past centuries, being heavy-set was the goal—it showed privilege and health!

With each of my pregnancies, I gained about ten pounds and have not been able to lose them. I've come to accept that I do not need to be at my college weight; I'm in my sixties.

If we are too thin, we look unhealthy. If we are too heavy, our joints, backs, and knees suffer. My goal is to continue to be active, stretch, eat wisely, and leave the worry of weight behind.

CAROL: Remembering that my ultimate goal is contentment, whether with much or little, in loss and in gain (pun intended) helps with this challenging area. Aiming for a 20-something body will probably lead to frustration, not contentment. I've found that the weight journey is a combination of discipline, freedom, professional input, and lots of grace along the way.

My husband and kids have started teasing me about my body. What should I do?

MARY: My husband and sons love to tease each other and me about many things, but at times I've had to tell them to stop. In sincerity and humility, I've let them know that this kind of teasing hurts my feelings. When they forget and lapse back into it, I gently remind them of my feelings, or quietly leave the room for a while. I don't "punish" them or get irritable. I simply draw a boundary and reinforce it.

CAROL: I just tell them that there is more of me to love now. Honestly, I love what Mary shared. I agree and desire to respond as she described. I have been too easily offended in the past by criticism or even honest observations.

There are many attitudes and perspectives about having cosmetic surgery. What are the pros and cons of cosmetic surgery? How do I know what's right for me?

MARY: An obvious benefit is that you should feel better about the part of your body that you improved. You may be more self-assured and confident about your appearance. For some people who are in the public eye, this may help their professional success. Possible cons are health risks, costs, dissatisfaction with the results, and the reality that you may still be discontent even when the surgical results are good.

LYN: Growing up, I was so thin that people called me "Olive Oyl" (Popeye's girlfriend). Thinking of myself like this tormented me throughout high school and college. As soon as I moved to Los Angeles and had enough money, I found a cosmetic surgeon known for safe procedures. I got breast implants and loved having them for ten years. After I had two children, I did not want to jeopardize my health by keeping the implants, so I had them removed and don't miss them now.

Cosmetic surgery is a very individual decision for each person. As in all things, caution and wisdom must be our guides as we weigh the pros and cons.

What are some spiritual, emotional, or mental techniques to help me accept my aging appearance?

CAROL: Spiritually, I love to remember that even though my outer body declines, my inner person can be renewed day by day. Spending time in silence and reflection is a healing balm to my soul and to my countenance. While I have my morning coffee, I often light a candle and watch the flame. I do this to quiet my spirit before I enter a time of prayer and reading.

Emotionally, I process aging situations with my husband and close friends. Recently, I've been repeating in prayer the statement "I am free." This underscores the reality that I am free to be who I was created to be in body, soul, and spirit—including my weaknesses and imperfections. This spiritual and mental exercise reinforces right thinking. I become the inwardly beautiful woman God designed me to be by choosing to exercise spiritually, emotionally, and mentally.

MARY: We can read books or articles about accepting our aging appearance and retrain our brain's inner self-talk. If we catch ourselves thinking negative thoughts about aging, we can substitute them with positive, realistic thoughts.

We can grow closer to God to have inner peace about many issues. As you experience his great love and value for you, you love and value yourself more. I memorize and meditate on specific Bible passages, like Psalm 139 and Psalm 1. Your emotions will be more positive as you grow spiritually. Additionally, your emotions can be helped by mindfulness techniques.

LYN: It's so important to guard what we allow ourselves to see. TV shows, movies, social media, and magazines feature young bodies. Women shown in media often have not had any children yet, or they devote a lot of time, money, and energy to maintaining their physical appearance. Their habits may not be healthy emotionally or spiritually, so they aren't role models I want to emulate.

I have had three children, am in my sixties, and need to eat regular meals. I have grown to love myself and give myself grace in the following ways:

- Exercise.
- Eat right.
- Get eight to nine hours of sleep.
- Don't let the sun go down on my anger or fears.
- Keep close to friends and family.
- And breathe.

SPECIFIC EMOTIONAL
CHALLENGES IN THIS SEASON

I lost my job because I was replaced by someone much younger. I can live on my savings, but how do I keep from feeling worthless and "put out to pasture" for my remaining years?

CAROL: A number of federal laws protect workers in the U.S. from various types of employment discrimination. The Age Discrimination in Employment Act of 1967, or ADEA, specifically protects you from being discriminated against on the basis of age in the workplace. If you are qualified as an older employee, you can still keep or secure employment if desired. However, if you can live on your savings, you may want to think through what you most value at this time of life. Retirement allows us to do what we most want to do if we keep those priorities before us and intentionally pursue them. Now is a great opportunity to pour yourself into what you really enjoy.

LYN: Companies often want to hire younger employees because they expect less pay, not because they are better qualified. You can hold your head up because you brought experience and knowledge to the job.

This can be a great time to focus on something equally or even more valuable. Don't focus on your past. Focus on the interests you have always wanted to follow, including your family and friends. A new adventure waits for you.

Sometimes I feel very lonely. I'm surrounded by my loving husband, great adult children, and tremendous grandchildren. What's wrong with me?

MARY: Loneliness can be a sign of depression, so consider whether you need to seek help for this. Also, ask yourself what is missing in your life relationally. Do you need a deeper quality of vulnerability and communication in your relationships? Maybe you need to find a really good friend or two—our relationships with those outside our families are fulfilling in different ways. Are you missing a personal connection with God? As you answer these questions, you'll know where to focus your attention in meeting these needs.

LYN: Friend, there is nothing wrong with you. We all feel lonely at times. I love being with people, and yet I sometimes feel a deep sense of loneliness. What Mary said helps us go deeper if loneliness just won't leave us alone.

CAROL: Feeling lonely is a difficult and sad place to be. As a normally positive person, I have learned that sadness is actually a mature emotion. I can sit in that feeling and know that I live in an imperfect world and will feel lonely at times. My favorite illustration is that of a winding path with trees by a brook. If I am to build a beautiful path to walk down, I must put things on it that make me healthy and reduce my loneliness. Some examples of those things might be intentional, regular time with family and close friends; sunshine and exercise; and reading about others who have learned important lessons in life and make me feel less alone.

French philosopher and mathematician Blaise Pascal once said, "There is a God-shaped vacuum in the heart of each man which cannot be satisfied by any created thing, but only by God." If we are growing in our relationship with God, we can know we're valuable and seen even when those feelings escape us. We can know that we are never alone.

As I grow older, I feel so out of touch and archaic, which is depressing. How important is it to keep up with recent trends like fashion, social media, music, current events, and general cultural news?

LYN: As we age, it's important to continue to be curious and intentional learners. There are always new things to discover and explore, keeping our minds active and our hearts renewed. Don't let "not knowing" depress you. In this Age of Technology, all of us feel out of touch in some areas because there is constantly so much new information. You are in great company.

Take note of topics that make you feel out of touch and study them. You might ask one of your family members or a younger friend to teach you about the subject or direct you to where you can learn about it.

MARY: Also, we have to ask ourselves how keeping up will serve us and our higher goals. This will vary for each person. For some, it will be important in order to relate well with loved ones or in our work. For others, it will be less important in these areas. But we all need to be aware of the tendency as we get older to be out of touch and unrelatable to other people, which won't allow us to achieve what we want in terms of our legacies and personal happiness.

I'm getting more afraid to go out on errands, even to the grocery store. I don't like living this way, but I'm not sure what to do about it.

MARY: I've been hounded by fear in various areas throughout my life, so I decided when I was young to never let fear be my reason for not doing something—I didn't want to miss out on life. If we become obedient to fear, it grows into a slave driver, taking over our lives. If you find you can't pull away from its grasp, please talk this over with a trusted person in your life, a spiritual advisor, or a counselor.

CAROL: Could you help yourself by creating scheduled times to have a grown child take you out for some errands? This could alleviate your fears while allowing you to run errands and have quality time with a loved one. Triple win.

LYN: You could utilize delivery companies to do errands for you or bring items straight to your door. Most grocery stores have delivery services as well. My daughter works for several of these services and it's a win-win as she makes money and helps her clients.

I have been in several car accidents, and my adult children say I should stop driving. I don't want to give up my freedom and have to depend on them. How can I get them to understand?

CAROL: I know a dear elderly woman who literally accelerated through the wall of a Walgreens store. Fortunately, no one was hurt, but she learned that she could no longer drive (she also learned she shouldn't wear flip flops as a driver, which contributed to the accident). That is an extreme example but there is clearly a time when it is wise to stop driving. All of us need to know our limitations in life. Our adult children love and care about us. They want our best and are protective of our safety.

LYN: None of us wants to give up freedoms we have had since we were young. They were rites of passage for us as we became independent. However, as we age, there will be areas we won't physically be able to continue without some help. We must grieve this reality because it's hard to face. I've realized in my late sixties that I am not as strong as I used to be. It's frustrating—and often mind-boggling—to have to ask for help and then wait for my children to have time and willingness to get something done.

We have to accept that our cognitive functions may slow as we age. The accidents you have had are warnings to you. Wisdom says to stop while you are still in one piece, you have not killed or maimed anyone, and you might provide your vehicle to someone who needs it. There are ride-booking services, taxis, friends, and family to chauffeur you around. It's a new season for you to learn to embrace. Aging is just not easy.

MARY: A natural progression of getting older can be that our eyesight gets worse, making us a danger to ourselves and to others when driving. We have to place the well-being of others over ourselves. Grieving the loss of abilities like eyesight and driving will help us to gain peace about these losses. I don't think any of us want to be that stubborn old person who values independence over the safety of others and ourselves. I hope to be loving, gracious, and caring, even amidst the challenges of aging.

When should I seek counseling for emotional issues as I get older? And how can I afford it on a very limited budget?

MARY: It's normal to need counseling at various times in our lives. Here are a few signals that you need to seek some help:

- Ongoing anxious thoughts
- Hopelessness
- Ongoing relationship problems, negative patterns, and tensions
- Disproportionate rage, anger, or resentment
- Alcohol, substance, or porn issues
- Extreme overuse of screen devices
- Significant changes or disruptions in sleep or appetite
- Ongoing difficulty adjusting to a new job, role, location, or situation
- Feeling incredibly overwhelmed
- Avoiding social situations
- Inability to control your emotions
- A pattern of just not caring
- Significant work issues
- Depression
- Attention Deficit Hyperactivity Disorder (ADHD)
- Trauma
- Grief

CAROL: I've utilized lay counseling at transitional times in my life. This is a type of psychological support provided by staff or volunteers who do not have a formal degree in counseling. You might find a lay counselor in your place of worship or in a community organization. In addition, it can be helpful to converse with older friends who might have gone down the road you're struggling with. Places of worship also offer free programs such as GriefShare. Programs like these bring great help and healing as we experience pain and prolonged emotional issues in our lives. Help is available. As we seek, we will find it.

In my culture we don't get counseling, but my grandmother really needs it. How can I help her?

LYN: Perhaps she would go if you find a counselor, maybe from your culture, and go with her to the sessions. The counselor will know how to move the conversation where it needs to go.

Some cultures frown on counseling because they don't understand it. They feel that counseling is for weak or uniquely flawed individuals, and it carries a sense of shame. Those who have participated in counseling know its tremendous value; my husband, children, and I can personally attest to this from personal experience. We've seen counseling set the participants free from areas of hurt, abuse and loneliness. It's a great act of love to help your grandmother in this way.

CAROL: I wonder if your grandmother could be helped by a wise and loving friend. That could be a starting point—someone who can hear her struggles and wisely interject questions as your grandmother formulates her own conclusions. They might meet weekly for coffee and set reachable goals together in an atmosphere of grace and love. Baby steps can lead to bigger steps.

MARY: You could meet with a counselor to discuss ways to help your grandmother. You could tell your grandmother you're doing this and invite her to join you after a time or two. You wouldn't be going as a codependent, trying to fix her. Instead, you would be joining with your grandmother to work toward her improvement.

TAKE ACTION

o   What would you like to do to keep your mental faculties as strong and healthy as possible? Glance back at the early questions in this chapter for ideas.

o   Do you notice yourself developing any negative psychological patterns or problems? What steps will you take to change this?

o   Are there ways you'd like to be more involved in helping others? How can you move in this direction?

o   Write down at least three successes from your life and at least two regrets: things you wish were different from your past. How will you celebrate and honor your successes? How will you grieve and process your regrets? Write the lessons you learned or the good that resulted from your regrets.

Look through the resources in Section 4, Chapter 10. Which ones do you want to explore? Make a plan to use the resources and add them to your calendar.

11

FINISHING WELL– PREPARE TO LEAVE THIS PLANET

We will all leave this world. Accepting this blessing in disguise allows us to prepare and plan with intentionality. How can we arrive at a place of peace about our own mortality? How do we effectively manage the practical realities that come with our inevitable departure from planet Earth?

POSITIVE PREPARATIONS

I really don't want to think about dying. What's wrong with simply living in this moment and letting things unfold one day at a time?

MARY: How about doing both? We all benefit by living in this moment and by preparing for the fact that one day we will die, because both are realities. We suffer when we live in denial of reality—as do our loved ones. Things like preparing my will or planning for potential medical costs will be immensely helpful to me and others when the time comes. I try to keep my sense of humor. As I drive around our area with my husband, I point out cemeteries and say, "So what do you think about that as the place we will one day reside?" It helps me to ease myself into the idea.

CAROL: Hahaha! Mary, how can I reserve a plot near you? I love the saying, "Reality is the most secure place on earth to be." I am realistic about my aging and where I am in life presently. I know I am in the encore of my performance, taking the stage as the culmination of all I've done before. That is not a morbid thought but a motivation for me to live to the fullest every day, whether I have ten, twenty, or thirty more years on this planet. This propels me to leave an intentional legacy behind that can impact the world and even eternity.

LYN: Being intentional about our legacy is so important. And as Mary said, it's absolutely critical that we are deliberate in helping those who will be left grieving our departure from this earthly body.

I had the privilege of being my mother's guardian at the end of her life and then the executor of her estate. My parents prepared me for their deaths, not only verbally, but also by having all their documents in order. When they died, I knew exactly what to do and with what document. As I continued to grieve their absence, I was extremely grateful for their preparation, the clear documentation, and our discussions ahead of time. As I prepared for their funerals, others around me noticed how calm I was.

Each one of us will die, and our denial of this burdens those who have to handle our affairs after we leave this earth. Let's show them love even after we have departed.

What do you mean by "prepare to leave this planet?" How can I prepare myself?

MARY: I think one of the first preparations is to accept the fact that one day we will die. For much of my life, I avoided thinking about this. When I was little, a neighbor boy realized I was afraid of dying, so he would say "DEATH" in an ominous tone just to rattle me (in the way that schoolboys liked to tease girls.) Experiencing the deaths of loved ones, especially those who had peace with God, has helped me accept the inevitable fact that I will die. I think the questions and answers in this chapter will help you in this process of preparation and acceptance.

I want people to remember me positively when I'm gone, but what can I do about it?

CAROL: I remember a professor saying, "If you want to know what kind of person someone is, ask them, 'Where are your women or men?'" In other words, where are those you have influenced for good? We can all multiply our lives and influence the world through those who come after us. This takes focus, passing on our passions, and purposeful living. We can hand off the baton by modeling, training, and teaching others. We might even catch a glimpse of the positive and lasting influence we have created as they run ahead of us and impact the world.

MARY: It's what we've been talking about: knowing and living our values, and investing these in the lives of others. For a practical exercise, title a page "How I want to be remembered," then write a list of things you want to be remembered for. Make your list a reasonable length so you can accomplish it. Then live your days making that list come true.

LYN: My list includes certain character qualities that I want to be true of me. For example, I want to be remembered as a good listener. I love to process out loud and with that exuberance comes interrupting, unfortunately. When people think of me, I want them to know that I listened and really wanted to know them, instead of only talking about my own issues. I also want to be remembered as a faithful friend, which comes from both listening and celebrating the good things in the lives of others.

They say "leave the world a better place" after you're gone. I don't have a lot of money, and I definitely haven't lived a perfect life. What can I do at this stage to make my life count for something?

CAROL: Evaluate what you most value in life and make your moments count by living out your passions and priorities. This doesn't require money or perfection. A friend told me recently, "Retirement is great because I can do exactly what I value." I love that.

LYN: Through technology we can now be involved globally, nationally, and locally. Making a significant impact within our own families is equally important—we are their world, and that calling has far-reaching implications. We don't need money to love and encourage the people around us. However we use our lives, we want to use our energy to make others' lives better so we won't have any regrets on that inevitable deathbed. No one dying ever said, "I wish I spent more time at the office."

What can I do to leave a positive legacy for my kids and grandchildren emotionally, spiritually, and physically?

MARY: This goes back to our very first few chapters: what are your vision and goals for this time of life? The answer leads to practical things you can do for your kids and grandkids to accomplish this.

Here are a few ideas to get you started:

o Make a photo album of your life, or of their lives, and include sayings, poems, or comments that express the values you want to impart.

○ Write an endearing letter to each adult child and grandchild, expressing your love for them and things you want to say to each one personally. You might frame these and give them as Christmas gifts.

○ Decide upon one or several of your items to leave to each person. Include a note that expresses your feelings about that person and important values you want to bequeath to them.

CAROL: One of the most impactful funerals I have ever attended was for a woman named Liz who died in her sixties. During the service, her three children each stood up and shared about the profound impact their mother had made on their lives. One fact they shared was that she had written letters to each of her grandchildren as she was confined to her bed. She even wrote letters to those not yet born.

We've already pointed out the principle that "more is caught than taught." That is the saying that comes to mind when I think of Liz. If I truly desire to leave a positive legacy, I must ask myself, "What model am I conveying in my life emotionally, spiritually, and physically?" Of course, we have weaknesses as well as strengths and will never be perfect. That is to be human. And yet, am I a lifetime learner in crucial areas of my personal development? Do younger generations see me taking steps to grow in emotional wholeness through seeking counsel and working on key relationships in my life? Do I pursue my spiritual life and live as God's creation designed to do good for others? Am I aware of my physical health and doing things to make necessary changes? Integrity involves living our beliefs in our actions and words. What greater impact could we have than to be examples of what we believe?

People talk about a "Bucket List." What do they mean? Is it important?

MARY: This idea was made famous by *The Bucket List*, a movie from 2007 starring Morgan Freeman and Jack Nicholson. A bucket list is a number of experiences or achievements that you hope to accomplish during your lifetime. Creating a bucket list can be a good way to focus your thoughts and intentions for the rest of your life and may include things like travel destinations, enjoyable activities, and meaningful pursuits. It helps you to accomplish what you'd like before you leave this planet, and to be at peace with the fact that one day you will die.

When I was very sick in my forties and fifties, there were times when I was in a wheelchair and could barely feed myself or brush my teeth. Even in that state, I read, listened to audio books and speakers, prayed for others, adventured through my computer, and talked by phone to friends and loved ones. I still fulfilled bucket list items in the capacity I had, so no one is excluded from this.

LYN: As you go through your years, you can always add or change items—you may get new ideas along the way, even into your eighties and nineties. Happy Bucketing!

PRACTICAL PREPARATIONS

I'm fifty-two and hopefully have a long life ahead. What practical things should I consider now for my later years?

MARY: One of the best things my husband and I did very early was to consult a financial advisor to plan, budget and save for the rest of our lifetime. I encourage everyone to do this. For less expensive ways to find advice, check with your community resources or call 211 to get ideas and information.

Here are a few more things to think about:

○ Evaluate your best housing options for the coming decades. You might consider downsizing, moving closer to loved ones, saving money through less expensive housing, or a mature living community.

○ Over the years, most people find it helpful to slowly get rid of unnecessary furniture, decorative items, and stored things. My friend in her seventies recently moved to a retirement home and wished she'd gotten rid of things sooner.

○ Set up your legal will.

○ Decide to whom you want to bequeath your various belongings and maybe start giving them to those people.

○ Make legal decisions now for the types of medical care you want if you're ever too sick, confused, or injured to voice your wishes. These are called advance care directives and include things like a living will, a durable power of attorney for health care, a living revocable trust, and a health care proxy. Every adult should have these documents.

○ Decide upon your burial or cremation plans and how to finance them.

○ If you have end-of-life fears and concerns, talk to a spiritual leader, counselor, or good friend. You also might look for helpful reading on this topic, including Chapter 12 of this book. Explore and process your thoughts and feelings until you come to a place of peace.

I'm fifty-five and comfortable with all my stuff. People say I should get rid of things, but why should I at this stage of life?

MARY: I've known family and friends who were greatly burdened by having to go through their loved one's stuff after they die. I don't want to leave that heavy work for someone else. Plus, there are things I'd like to personally give to certain individuals or donate to organizations. Also, you might have items, letters, or journals you'd be embarrassed for someone else to see—I know I do. Finally, it just feels good to live more simply and with less clutter. All of these reasons have motivated me to get rid of things little by little through the years.

LYN: I had the burden of sifting through belongings after my mother-in-law and my parents passed. Things they valued didn't mean so much to the loved ones left behind. Each generation has different preferences, priorities, and needs in what they've accumulated.

I agree wholeheartedly that while we are still alive, we should give select items to family, friends, and others. Alleviating the burden after you are gone is itself a great gift.

As you eliminate possessions, prepare for a very personal journey through your own life. It might even help you to make some changes in your current life choices. Purging stuff, like pruning our plants, is beneficial for our growth and health.

Is there an organized or prescribed way to go about getting rid of things and assigning items to certain people? How would you suggest I proceed?

CAROL: I find it helpful to have a plan. On the internet you'll find many articles by searching for "steps to help me get rid of my stuff," or you can use this as your guide:

Decide to declutter one room per week.

- For each room, make three piles: keep, throw out, donate. If you can't decide, make a fourth "maybe" pile and decide in a week which of the other three piles you will place it in.

Get rid of duplicates and extra items that are not used or needed.

- Kitchen: Extra mugs, forks, knives, spoons, plates, cookware
- Desk: Scissors, stationery, pens, pencils, erasers, notebooks
- Closet: Shoes, bags, purses, hats, t-shirts, clothes
- Bathroom: Towels, washcloths, soaps
- Miscellaneous: Sewing kits, sunscreen bottles, bookends

Get rid of hazardous or unusable items.

- ○ Old rugs
- ○ Items on the floor
- ○ Old or broken chairs/couches/furniture
- ○ Unnecessary or unused decorations
- ○ Old medications
- ○ Old or expired food items
- ○ Damaged glass, pots, and bags
- ○ Broken/unused items, electronics, or tools

Ask someone to help you or coordinate with a friend so that you're both taking the same steps each week. Check in and encourage one another.

MARY: My friend went through her house and put a little sticker on the back of certain items: pictures, furniture, candle sticks, jewelry, dish sets, etc. She thought about various family members and friends; if she wanted to give an item to a certain individual, she wrote the person's name on the sticker. She also wrote the timing of when she wanted to give it to them—now or after her death—and made a note in her will for those who would receive items when she died. My friend wasn't wealthy but wanted to give her things to specific people as an expression of love and meaning.

CAROL: There's also the Japanese method of decluttering (KonMari) where you hold every object that you own and if it does not bring you joy, you throw it away. So far, I have thrown out all the vegetables, my bra, the electric bill, the scale, a mirror, and my treadmill.

I love my belongings and it's hard to think about giving things away, even my old clothes. I can get rid of some things, but not others. Why is this?

MARY: I have a vest that is completely out of style, and I'll never wear it again, but I can't part with it because a dear friend gave it to me at a difficult time in my life. We have emotional attachments surrounding some items, and there can be other psychological reasons that have nothing to do with the item itself. I don't want things to control me, so I'll get rid of that vest someday...maybe!

CAROL: I take a photo of the item with names, dates, and special places written on it so I can keep the memory but let go of the item. You might write why it is meaningful to you. Also, giving items to relatives or friends who understand their value (monetary or emotional) can make letting go more bearable. If you're moving to a smaller place, consider donating or selling old furniture and buying items to fit the new space.

MARY: If an item contains fabric, you can use a small bit of it to make a Christmas ornament or a quilt. That way, you can remember the item's significance even when you no longer have it.

HOUSING CONSIDERATIONS

I see people moving to "fifty-plus communities." What are the pros and cons of these, versus living in my home until I need something more?

CAROL: Here are some pros of moving to a fifty-plus community:

- You have a community with others in your same stage of life.
- You can live independently.
- You have a built-in social life.
- They have greater security: sometimes they're gated or have security staff.
- These tend to be quieter neighborhoods.

And here are some cons:

- They sometimes have lots of rules.
- The neighborhood includes no children or people in younger stages of life.
- You usually need to be in good enough health to live independently. There are no healthcare facilities provided. Therefore, this may involve another eventual move to an assisted-living situation.

A fifty-plus community may not be what you want if your current home is in a vibrant, social neighborhood. However, as people get older, they may not realize they're becoming more socially isolated, which affects their quality of life along with their mental and physical health. This is why a fifty-plus community can be beneficial.

Is a "continuing care retirement community" something I should consider? What exactly is it?

MARY: My family and friends who have chosen this option really like it. A continuing care retirement community is a long-term residence option for older people who want to live in the same place through different phases of their aging process. They're also known as CCRCs or life plan communities. In these communities, people can live in a house or apartment and then, as needed, can move into an assisted-living or nursing home in that community.

CCRCs provide a wide range of services, activities, and care in one place, and you know the same people living in your community throughout the later phases of your life. This gives residents a sense of stability and familiarity as their abilities or health conditions change. It's important to remember, though, that all of this comes at a cost, so you'd want to look at the expenses closely.

CAROL: My elderly parents moved from living in their longtime home to an elderly community. They progressed through the stages of "Independent Living," "Assisted Living," and "Memory Care" in the same facility. It worked really well and eased them through their aging process.

I'm a huge fan of continuing care communities. You can live independently, but as you age, they will help you with your physical needs. As a resident, you can drive but they often provide a ride service. I watched my father, mother, and other relatives flourish in this type of community. Knowing loved ones are not living alone and isolated gives family members peace of mind. My parents had lots of friends, were much more relaxed, had less fear of dying, and felt valued. Finding a place close to family members is ideal.

It's best for people to move to a CCRC before their health declines so they can make friends and feel supported by the community. Having support from caring staff prevents the healthy spouse from overworking and compromising their health by trying to care for the declining spouse alone. Stuart and I are planning to move to one of these communities and hope our friends will join us.

My daughter and son-in-law want me to live with them now that my husband has passed on. I'm not so sure that's a good idea. What should I consider when thinking about living with a family member?

LYN: This can work if everyone gives each other space and kindness.

My mother lived in a CCRC in San Antonio, then moved in with my husband, me, and our three kids. After my father died, she financed building an addition to our home, a separate place for her when she came to visit. At first she stayed for holidays and some weeks in the summer; then it became months at a time. Her CCRC was an hour-and-a half drive from us, so it was a bit inconvenient. Her solution, to create a private place for herself in our home, was perfect. She had a place to go if she was tired of the family energy or just wanted time alone. It allowed me to know that she was safe and sound and had all her needs covered. She ate her meals with us but also could have snacks or coffee in her area.

If you decide to not live with your family, you could live nearby and have your own place. I would write down the pros and cons of each. Think through your own physical and emotional needs and possible negative things that would come up. Think about your values and ways of thinking and living, and how these might cause problems. Discuss your thoughts with your family to help you decide and to navigate your relationship wherever you live. "Doing life" with your grown kids is a great privilege, whether living with them or in your own place.

CAROL: Living with family depends on the dynamics of your relationships, financial needs, and other factors. Discuss the specific expectations of all involved family members. Explore what is available if you live near them versus with them. The fantasy of living with family is not always the reality.

YOUR MEDICAL CARE

People say there are certain legal decisions I should make ahead of time about medical care at the end of my life. What's involved in this?

MARY: A living will, an advanced care directive, a durable power of attorney , and a "do not resusitate order" are important to set up. Here are some things to consider.

A *living will* is a written, legal document which spells out medical treatments you would or would not want to be used to keep you alive. It includes your preferences for other medical decisions, such as pain management or organ donation.

An *advanced care directive* is a written document stating how you want medical decisions to be made if you lose the ability to make them for yourself.

A *durable power of attorney* designates a person who will make decisions for you if you are incapacitated to the point you can't make your own decisions.

A ***do not resuscitate order (DNR)*** is a legal request by a person to not take extreme measures to save their life. It's used when a person would have low quality of life, or a long time before death, if they were resuscitated. It can detail how much medical intervention a person wants before death. This needs to be discussed with and written by a healthcare provider.

You can also put in writing your decisions about remaining at home for your final days and whether you'd want an autopsy.

The National Institute on Aging has more information on this, along with help in finding legal forms and instructions for setting these up. You'll find this webpage in Section 4, Chapter 11.

LYN: Making decisions before they are needed is helpful for everyone involved. Discuss your choices with your loved ones so they are fully aware, and then put your desires in writing.

This is a way to honor, serve, and love your children and family. Don't leave them with the burden of wondering what you would want or what they should do next. We can love and take care of those dear to us until the end.

What do people mean when they talk about "end-of-life" care?

CAROL: End-of-life care describes the treatment plan used by medical professionals when a person is in the last stage of a critical illness. This is a time when it would be important to have already set up your living will and other legal decisions that Mary covered in the previous question.

End-of-life care includes active curative medical treatment for illness, easing physical symptoms, and providing emotional and spiritual support. Unlike hospice care, which is provided for patients whose remaining time is expected to be limited, life expectancy is not a factor for end-of-life care.

These are stages of end-of-life care:

Stage 1—When a person is stable in their illness, the medical team develops and implements a care plan.

Stage 2—When a person becomes unstable in their condition, the medical team adjusts the care plan and prepares the patient and their loved ones for what might come next.

Stage 3—As the person deteriorates, the medical team adjusts to manage physical symptoms and pain management.

Stage 4—In the terminal stage, the medical team makes final adjustments for the patient's medical and emotional care before death.[1]

MARY: These are hard to think about, but it's important to be aware so that we can think ahead for ourselves and our loved ones.

LYN: It's important to accept that this process is coming one day so that we can get our affairs in order. It is tough to think about, but it would really be hard on others if we fail to prepare and plan.

FINANCIAL WISDOM OR FINANCIAL WORRIES?

What areas do I need to consider for financial preparation and peace during this time of life?

CAROL: You always need to know where you stand financially. This requires a net worth statement, which shows how much you own and how much you owe. You might want to update this frequently, maybe quarterly. Track how much you earn and how much you spend. Budgeting has not been my personal strength, but I'm working on it. A budget helps you monitor how much you spend monthly and yearly on your needs (housing, utilities, auto, insurance, food, savings) and your wants (entertainment, eating out, gifts, charity). This awareness will keep you both prepared and peaceful as you wisely handle your finances.

LYN: We previously mentioned the resources provided by Dave Ramsey, a financial expert, author, and speaker. He created Financial Peace University, a program available online or in person. Dave presents a step-by-step process to analyze where you are in your finances and then address these with tangible tools and strategies, even if you are in extreme debt. Using this program, thousands of people have worked their way out of tremendous monetary difficulties into a stable financial life. Find his information in Section 4, Chapter 11. Go to https://www .ramseysolutions.com and click on "Products" for more information.

---

[1]The 5 Stages of Palliative Care," Nurse Next Door website, https://www.nursenextdoor.com.au

What are the biggest financial mistakes people make after fifty so I can avoid them?

MARY: Carrying too much credit card debt; expecting to work past retirement age (unexpected health problems come up); taking on college debt; not planning ahead financially for medical problems; not having enough health insurance; and overspending on luxury items like vacations or home renovations.

CAROL: Another common mistake is not having an emergency fund for things like auto repair, a utility breakdown, or other unexpected expenses. Most Americans live paycheck to paycheck. Plan for unforeseen needs.

LYN: For many of us "recovering enablers," a big mistake is choosing to pay our grown children's bills. Our adult kids must learn character lessons through their own failures. It's easy to take on their financial responsibilities in the effort to help them get on their feet or bail them out of problems. My husband and I have done this and stolen our kids' opportunities to learn by making mistakes. Humans learn life's wisdom from being uncomfortable—or even miserable—at times.

I live on a low income, so the future scares me as I get older. I barely have enough money to get by each month; how can I save for the future?

CAROL: Here are a few ideas:

○ Start small and work to pay down your debt and increase your savings.

○ Focus on your financial needs, not wants.

○ Live and die by a budget.

○ If your health permits, either get a job or change jobs to something that pays better. Search for these online and check out our Resources for more information.

○ Ask for raises at appropriate times.

○ You might go to night school or get additional training to improve your income prospects.

○ Consider a second job if you are physically able.

○ If your company provides a 401k or other matching plan, participate.

MARY: If you are in poor health, need-based government programs like Medicare and Medicaid can be helpful. As you probably know, Medicare covers many medical expenses for individuals over the age of 65, and Medicaid can provide coverage for eligible low-income seniors.

Elderly individuals who are unable to turn to family for financial support and have no money can become a ward of the state. This may be the case if the senior develops a health emergency and is no longer able to live alone. However, becoming a ward of the state is far from ideal and should be a last resort.

Contact your local Area Agency on Aging for more information. These agencies are organizations designated by the state to address the needs and concerns of older persons at the regional and local levels. "Area Agency on Aging" (AAA) is a generic term—specific names of local AAAs may vary. To find one in your area, simply do an internet search for "Area Agencies on Aging" in your city or zip code.

I have just been let go because my employer is "going in another direction." What do I do now, at my age?

LYN: Guard against despair. Life often gives us things that startle or shock us at first glance. But as we sit with the news, we may realize our new situation is the best thing for us. Seek other employment opportunities that will serve you well in this season. Rest as much as you can. Get your exercise regime back on point. Look at that bucket list you made.

CAROL: It's best to not make quick, rash decisions. Be careful with your money until you have a plan. Discuss your situation with trusted friends and family members. Be sure to take stock of where you are with your net worth statement and your budget. Living conservatively will certainly bear fruit.

MARY: Don't forget the previous question that has good information for you, including job-search ideas.

My spouse recently died, who always took care of the money. I'm not good with finances—what should I do?

LYN: This is a very hard time for you, and I'm so sorry. Beginning to address your finances can feel overwhelming, so be patient with yourself. Don't forget to seek assistance from either a financially savvy friend or a financial expert. Here are a few things that may help:

o Find all of the financial documents in your husband's file cabinets and computer folders. Sort through these to find information like your bank account details, savings, stocks, investments, and insurance policies. Find out what you need to do to receive any insurance money.

○ If you haven't already, go to the bank and ask an account representative to help you figure out where you actually stand with your account balances.

○ Know that many financial institutions will need a certified copy of your husband's death certificate, along with proof of his will and documentation that you are the executor—if that is the case. They will let you know what they require as you proceed.

○ An estate attorney can help you with all of this.

○ Give yourself a full year to have all the pieces finalized. It may not take that long but knowing it will take time can help you be less frustrated or discouraged as the months go by and entities ask you for more information. You will process through many grieving stages in the midst of this, so be kind and loving toward yourself. Be sure to ask for help from knowledgeable friends and experts along the way.

MARY: My friend lost her husband when she discovered that he was cheating. In addition to going through a divorce and huge emotional crisis, she didn't know what to do regarding her finances. Years later she said it's worth the work to learn about the details of your finances and how to manage them before a crisis comes. Your question is helpful for all of us to prepare as best we can.

Scams seem to be in the news a lot, preying on even intelligent people. They seem to get sneakier and more sophisticated. How can I avoid getting taken in?

MARY: Scams are increasing in number and older people are a prime target. I've learned a lot by listening to a podcast designed to keep us informed about scams: The Perfect Scam Podcast, produced by The American Association of Retired Persons and narrated by Bob Sullivan. Staying informed about current scams is one way to protect yourself. Here are a few others:

○ Don't buy services or items from telemarketers. If you do, research well before doing so.

○ If you're really interested in a product or service, go to their website and check them out directly and thoroughly.

○ Guard your medical information carefully. Health insurance fraud is a common scam affecting seniors.

○ Be very selective about revealing your personal information on social media.

○ Research and ask for references to avoid home repair or contractor fraud.

- Verify the person's credentials before giving out confidential information.
- Don't let anyone rush you.
- Talk with someone you trust if you're unsure whether it's a scam.
- Join the free AARP Fraud Watch Network. It's designed to help you spot scams and get guidance from their fraud specialists (https://www.aarp.org/money/scams-fraud/about-fraud-watch-network).

CAROL: I heard the sad story of two adoring grandparents who were scammed. They were told that their beloved grandson had been in a wreck due to drinking and was being held in jail. To bail him out, they wired thousands of dollars to the person who called them. In the end, the whole thing was a farce, and they lost their money. These grandparents learned the hard way not to send money or personal information to anyone you don't know and trust.

YOUR WILL

I don't like thinking about setting up a will, but I know it's important. What should I do?

LYN: None of us loves the idea of preparing for death. However, most of us do want to save our loved ones from stress and potential arguments over money, property, and items we have acquired. Putting your desires in writing allows your family to honor you by fulfilling your wishes and ensures they receive exactly what you intend. Without a will, your loved ones' relationships may be strained or ruined, which can be avoided by simply creating your will.

CAROL: Yes, wills and trusts are investments in peace of mind for you and for your family. Once again, seek competent information and guidance from people you know and trust.

How do I decide on a good lawyer to set up my will?

MARY: Reliable people in your life can point you in the right direction. Ask for referrals from family, friends, or people at your place of worship. Writing a will can be intimidating and it's a good idea to get the help of someone you trust.

LYN: While dealing with my mother's estate, I found I needed a trustworthy, patient, and thorough person who was willing to explain and re-explain to me until I fully understood.

One guy was irritated and condescending when I didn't understand what was needed. I changed lawyers and the replacement was tremendously rewarding and helpful. Don't accept disrespectful treatment. They work for you.

I don't have enough money to pay a lawyer to write my will. Is there an alternative?

MARY: You are not alone—many people are faced with this dilemma. You can find great low-income resources online at https://www.211.org or by calling 211. If you find it challenging to contact 211 by phone or their website, have a loved one help you.

FUNERAL CONSIDERATIONS

This seems so morbid, but how do I go about setting up my funeral and grave plot?

CAROL: One of my best friends passed away recently after a long illness. I asked his wife about this question. Here is Annette's response:

> My husband of 46 years passed on after an extended hospital stay of 15 months. I thought I understood his desires for a funeral service, but I found many of my questions unanswered when the time came.
>
> Think about your desires for your end-of-life memorial or celebration before your loved ones need to know and make plans. Write down your desires, put them with your will, and tell your loved ones where they can find them.
>
> Ask yourself what you would like to have emphasized in your service. Would it be your accomplishments in life, your family, your spiritual beliefs, or a personal account of God's goodness to you? Who would you like to preside, speak, or share remembrances? Do you have any favorite songs? Would you prefer a burial (open or closed casket) or cremation?

Cremation was the one preference my husband always stated long before his passing. He said, "When I go to be with Jesus, I want to be cremated. I'll be getting a new body anyway, and I don't want you to have the extra expense." I'm so glad he said that clearly, because I had a hard time imagining cremation as an option I would have picked. Cremation gave me time to plan a service when much of the family could be present. If you prefer burial, make sure you purchase a plot ahead of time and have money set aside for the additional expenses.

If you would like to direct gifts to a charity in lieu of flowers, write that down as well. During the week that you pass, your loved ones may have lots of company and little time or emotional capacity to plan a memorial service. Therefore, the more ideas you can leave with your loved ones, the easier it will be for them to plan a service that reflects your personality and spiritual values.

LYN: When we were young, we often felt invincible. As we got older, we realized we were not. We know that we will depart this earth one day. We are born; we will die. The dash in between the years of your birth and death is what your family and friends will honor and celebrate at your funeral service.

Planning your funeral can be a very special spiritual experience for you. It's important to realize that each person is worthy of being recognized. You have made an impact on the lives of others. You are important to people.

There are specialized companies that will work with you ahead of time, usually through funeral homes, giving you information and resources for planning your service. Research the funeral homes and cemeteries in your area, choose one, set up your details, and then pay for as much as you can before you die. This will make the experience more peaceful for your family as they go through one of humanity's most vulnerable times of life.

MARY: Also, your place of worship might guide you in thinking through and setting up arrangements for this. They may have resources and information since they're usually involved in funerals as part of their service to others.

I want to be cremated to save the money, instead of buried in a casket and plot. What are the pros and cons of these alternatives?

MARY: My husband wants to be cremated and I want to be buried, so I understand and respect both sides of this issue. It's a very personal decision, with varying considerations for each person. Burial is often considered to be more traditional, and some people prefer to think of themselves or their loved ones this way in the final resting place for their bodies. However, burial is generally much more expensive than cremation. Also, traditional burials are not considered to be environmentally friendly.

Cremation is usually a much cheaper alternative than burial. It's considered to be more environmentally friendly and there are more options for where cremated remains can be kept, scattered, or buried. The remains can also be transported easily. However, some people have difficulty thinking about themselves or their loved ones going through the cremation process and becoming ashes.

LYN: I had very positive experiences with cremation for both my father and mother, eight years apart. Both parents were clear that this is what they wanted and hired people to help me through each step. They used an organization called Neptune Society (https://neptunesociety.com). I knew exactly what to do and when.

You can be buried in a cemetery whether you choose a casket or cremation. With cremation, you can designate a place, like the ocean or forest, where your remaining family can distribute your ashes. Both choices can be significant and beautiful.

I want specific songs and readings at my funeral. Do I tell my kids now?

CAROL: One approach is to write things down and let the kids know where the information can be found. You can include preferences for your funeral including special music, readings, and other important details. If this does not happen, the family members can find songs that fit their loved one who has passed. My father tried hard to not have enemies, so we chose the song "No Hard Feelings" by the Avett Brothers for his service. It's a special process to think through these things.

LYN: Every time I go to a funeral, I think about what I want to express through my funeral to others left behind.

I've shared with my daughter several songs that are a must. We laugh about how many there are and that the event might end up being hours long. Obviously that can't happen, but there is so much we can choose for our funerals to leave a mark of love on those who attend. I'm even considering producing a film they can play at the event. Please don't tell my children—I want to surprise them.

TAKE ACTION

o   What practical things do you want to accomplish now to
    get ready for your later years? Think of things like finances,
    material items, housing, your will, health concerns, and
    funeral arrangements. List the first two steps you will take to
    accomplish each item you wrote down.

o   Who can you openly talk with about end-of-life thoughts,
    concerns, and fears you may have?

o   Ask yourself the questions, "How do I want to be remembered
    by people?" and "What do I want my loved ones to say at my
    funeral?" Write these things down. Do you need to make any
    changes in your life to be remembered in that way?

o   List specific items you want to give to your children or family
    members. Which ones do you want to give now, and which
    will you designate in your will? Do you want to include a note
    with any item, and if so, what will it say?

Look through the resources in Section 4, Chapter 11. Which ones do you
want to investigate further? Make a plan to use the resources and add
them to your calendar.

12

YOUR SPIRITUAL LIFE

We can follow a variety of spiritual pathways that will either enhance or hinder our quality of life after fifty. People contemplate life after death more than ever during this life stage. Let's explore spirituality and reinforce perspectives that bring positivity and peace.

THE IMPORTANCE OF SPIRITUALITY, ESPECIALLY NOW

I don't like to think about the end of my life. The word "death" scares me when I think about this life phase. What can I do?

LYN: In my life, when I've avoided facing a truth and tried to deny reality, it made matters worse. In fact, I often lost my chance for important growth or decisions. We can't escape or shun the inevitable. Instead, we can stare our fears straight in the eye, work through them, and learn something significant in the process.

CAROL: You could begin meeting with a spiritual leader, minister, or other spiritual friend with whom you can talk about this question. Paying attention to the reality that we will die can help us live with more intentionality and wisdom today.

MARY: When I was young, I couldn't stand the word "death." I cringed and got away when anyone mentioned it. Finding peace with God has made death something totally different: it's the entrance into eternal life. I encourage you to pursue the path to spiritual peace.

Can I just "eat, drink, and be merry" until I die?

MARY: I'm a big believer in both enjoying this life to the fullest and finding peace with death and the afterlife. Why not have it all?

CAROL: I love that we have so many things to enjoy in this life, which includes the joy of generosity and sharing with others. It also includes finding security and assurance for our afterlife.

LYN: Living the "eat, drink, and be merry" lifestyle with no thought of the future can cause us to neglect the benefits of having deeper spirituality and meaningful involvement with others. If I just continue to eat and drink with no thought of my future, will I miss opportunities? Will this lifestyle lead to poor health or even addiction? Will it reap negative spiritual consequences? I know I sound negative, but it's important to consider these things. Life is indeed short. Before we know it, our time will be up. We don't want to miss the abundance that comes when we include things that are spiritual.

I've never been religious or spiritual, so why should I start now?

MARY: Because you're missing out. (If I can be so blunt, now that we know each other after all these chapters!) Spirituality enhances your life in so many ways. Do you want to have more joy, love, and peace of mind? These are the results of flourishing in the spiritual part of your life.

You don't need to be religious—that word can carry the idea of a lot of rules and regulations. But "spirituality" addresses the part of you that is deep inside. We have already shared Blaise Pascal's profound words, but they bear repeating. Pascal was a noteworthy French scientist, philosopher, mathematician, inventor, and theologian in the 1600's. He wrote, "There is a God-shaped vacuum in the heart of every man which cannot be filled by any created thing, but only by God, the Creator, made known through Jesus Christ." This relationship with God brings peace, joy, and love to the soul.

CAROL: When you stop growing you start dying. What will it hurt to explore the spiritual part of life in a way that you haven't previously? You may learn things that will change your life for the better.

LYN: It's said that humans are made up of three parts: body, soul, and spirit. Our bodies are the physical part of us. Our souls house our minds, wills, and emotions. Our spirits contain our intuition, our conscience, and our abilities to commune with humans and with God.

As we go through this life, if we never become aware of our spiritual abilities, we will operate strictly out of our souls and bodies. This is where we can get in trouble with physical and mental health problems, and also miss out on deeper, richer things in life. Our spirits thrive with connection to something greater than ourselves.

HELPFUL PRACTICES FOR SPIRITUAL VITALITY

What can I do to enhance my spiritual life during this season?

CAROL: I shared in Chapter 10 the importance of putting ourselves in a "path of oncoming beauty" (Dr. Curt Thompson). Our spiritual life is enhanced by building a beautiful path in this season. To create your own life of "oncoming beauty," draw a path and write your specific "beautiful" areas along the path. Put it where you can see it on a regular basis. What beautiful things will you include? What gives you vitality and nourishes you? What builds your relationship with God and others?

My always-evolving beautiful path includes daily devotional reading and prayer; time with my husband; time with our adult children and grandchildren; family holidays; sunshine; reading; my ministry and job; relationships with close friends and neighbors; nutrition; exercise; and small support groups with other women.

LYN: Carol, this is spot on. I would like to add that for me, spiritual music about God is always a space where I find my bearings. It nourishes my spirit in a way that nothing else does, through the words and melodies that the musician creates. I listen to a song over and over until I know the words by heart. Then, when I'm going about my day, living my life with others, those attitudes and phrases come out in my language and mindset.

Another part of my beautiful path is the Bible. As I read it and meditate on specific verses, I memorize them. This helps me know who I am and that I am deeply loved by God. The Bible has become God's conversation with me, and it never fails that when I am going through something confusing or a crisis, I can always find what I need in the Bible—God's loving words to us all.

MARY: This is a time of life when we can slow down and "smell the roses" on our path. I literally do this when I'm on a walk in my neighborhood, and I've been surprised that those beautiful flowers I have rushed past in life abound in delights for the senses. How have they been there all along and I haven't stopped to drink them in? That's how all of life can be as we slow down and savor everything Lyn and Carol have mentioned, along with the plethora of other pleasures that can draw our hearts to God if we ponder him while enjoying them. I'm thinking of things like sunsets, forests, deserts, grandchildren's faces, pets, and artistic expression of all kinds. Savoring each of these can enhance my spiritual life when I experience them through a sacred mindset.

I hear people say that the Bible enriches them and makes their lives so much better, but to me it seems like merely words on a page or nice stories. Are there methods or practices people use to experience this vitality from a book?

LYN: This is a great question because the answer involves getting to know God and not just knowing about Him. I once heard that the Bible is "shallow enough for a child to wade into and deep enough so that an elephant can happily swim." I've found that wherever a person is, the Bible will meet them when approached with the mindset of knowing God.

There are many lifegiving methods and practices that guide us in this pursuit, including online or in-person studies of the Bible, teaching podcasts, and commentaries on each of the sixty-six books of the Bible. Some of these are listed in Section 4: Chapter 12.

Here's a method that enriches me: when a specific verse draws my attention, I read not only that verse, but also the verses before and after it—sometimes the entire section. It's important to know the context. Then I will study the verse and think about how it applies to me personally. The Life Application Study Bible (Tyndale House Publishers, 2024) is a good book to guide you in this process.

In any endeavor, it's helpful to have a mentor. See if you can find someone you respect who has a life-giving relationship with God and the Bible. Together you might read line by line through a portion of the Bible and discuss it. The book of John is a good place to start.

Welcome to this adventure that is truly like no other.

What is helpful in the topic of "prayer" for this season of life?

MARY: It helps me to remember that prayer is simply talking to God. We don't need to be formal or use awkward language, but to have conversations with him.

God wants a friendship with us. Talk to him as you go through your day, because he is always present and he loves you!

CAROL: I use the acronym A–C–T–S as a helpful method of prayer.

A-doration: When we first start a time of prayer, we take time to acknowledge God for who he is, praising his character and attributes. The book of Psalms in the Bible is a great place to see God's character.

C-onfession: There is a New Testament verse that explains that if we confess (agree with God about) our shortcomings, then God will cleanse us (1 John 1:8, 9). It's like when a pipe becomes clogged and needs to be cleared in order to let water flow through freely. We remove barriers that hinder our relationship with God by simply admitting that we know we've done wrong.

T-hanksgiving: We can give thanks in everything, knowing that God is in control. That sounds crazy, especially when things are hard, but we become more joyful, positive people when we acknowledge our specific blessings every day. A dear friend of mine keeps a gratitude journal that now has over four thousand entries. That is a lot of gratitude and there will be more to come. No wonder my friend is so outward-focused and finds joy in the small things of life.

S-upplication: This means that we can ask, seek, and find in prayer. We can request things about everything and everyone in our lives and God hears us. We can be very specific in our requests. Prayer unleashes God's power in our lives. He answers in three ways: yes, no, or later. We don't usually like the last two, but they are answers given by God in his love and wisdom.

This A–C–T–S format can be used when you go out for a brief walk or jog a mile. It can be used when you are falling asleep, waking up, or waiting at the dentist.

LYN: There is also "The Lord's Prayer," found in the Bible in Matthew 6:9–13 and Luke 11:2–4:

> Our Father in heaven, hallowed be your name.
> your kingdom come, your will be done on earth as it is in heaven.
> Give us today our daily bread;
> And forgive us our debts as we also have forgiven our debtors.
> And do not lead us not into temptation, but deliver us from the evil one.

MARY: That's a good example, Lyn, because that prayer was Jesus's response when people asked him to teach them how to pray. One idea is to take each line of that prayer, then study and ponder what it means. You might write down each line, then write your thoughts about it to God as your own prayer to him.

Is there anything about church that is especially beneficial as I get older? I like to commune with God alone, especially in nature, and I don't get that much out of church.

MARY: I love to commune with God alone and in nature, but I miss out on significant benefits if I only do that. Church gives me strength and encouragement through a community of people, along with the opportunity to learn from others who have studied more than I have and who bring their unique spiritual perspectives. In this group of people, I'm able to use my own strengths and gifts to help others. Church also brings beautiful music into my life, and the melodies and lyrics often linger in my mind throughout the week, uplifting me. Finally, churches help their people when we are going through difficult times. When I was seriously ill in my forties, I could not have survived without my church driving me to medical appointments, bringing me meals, helping me financially, and visiting me to provide cheer and comfort. These benefits are too valuable for people to miss out on.

LYN: These benefits are true for me as well. An additional positive is that members in a church can collectively serve the community, and even the world, as a unit. We are only one person or one family, but when we belong to a church, we can pool our resources together. We become God's hands and feet to those who are hurting or lost. This includes people in prison, the poor, the sick, and orphans, to name a few. There are also opportunities for churches to come alongside government relief efforts or other groups who help those in need, providing both volunteers and finances.

What else can I do to improve my spiritual life during this season? What exercises, practices, or perspectives do you find helpful?

CAROL: Two resources that have been valuable to me are Adele Calhoun's *The Handbook of Spiritual Disciplines* (IVP, 2015) and our very own Mary Henderson's *Rest for Your Soul.* Various guided practices have propelled me forward spiritually in this season.

I'm also in the process of learning the value of rest, both physically and spiritually. I like to light a candle and sip my coffee in the quiet of the morning. As I gaze at the candle, my thoughts settle like particles in a shaken snow globe, allowing me to see everything more clearly. I can then respond with greater effectiveness to my life and to the day that awaits me.

LYN: It helps me to intentionally stay present in my current moment of life, asking God to speak to me about something specific in that moment—and he does. The more we seek him, the more we begin to know his voice, different from all the other "voices" rolling around in our heads. Obviously, knowing what God says in the Bible helps us to discern his spiritual voice. It's always one of comfort not cruelty, counsel not confusion, conviction not condemnation, bringing a real desire to follow God and experience more and more of him. All this takes time and practice, but you will find guidance and support as you sincerely search for God.

MARY: The Significance Project[1] website has resources to help you grow spiritually, live out your purpose in life, and help others to do the same. These materials have enriched the lives of many, and the website provides tools and guidance for group studies.

HELPING OTHERS SPIRITUALLY

What are some ideas for helping others in their spiritual lives?

CAROL: Frederick Buechner wrote, "The place God calls you to is the place where your deep gladness and the world's deep hunger meet."[2] Where has God gifted and called you? People need what you have to offer.

MARY: This is where your involvement in a place of worship is important; there are many opportunities for a great variety of giftings. Whether your strength is financial expertise, childcare, practical help, teaching, or administration, all of these are spiritually helpful for a worship center to function.

One night I was longing to help others spiritually in new ways, so I looked on my church's website. I was surprised and delighted to find many opportunities listed to help my church, our city, and even internationally. I did a little research and became involved in a prison ministry, which is one of the most fulfilling things that I do to this day.

---

[1]https://thesignificanceproject.org.
[2]Buechner, F. (1993). *Wishful Thinking.* San Francisco, HarperOne.

How do I live out my spirituality with my family, friends, and the world around me at this stage of life?

MARY: When I'm getting ready to spend time with family or friends, I ask God to utilize me to accomplish his purposes for those who will be present. I ask him to guide my thoughts, words, and actions, with a goal of helping others to know and love him. I try to tune in to God throughout the event so that I don't get carried off by my own agendas and reactions. I've made many, many mistakes in this, and like a toddler learning to walk, there have been many failures along the way. We can all pray like St. Francis of Assisi in our relationships with others:

> Lord, make me an instrument of your peace:
> where there is hatred, let me sow love;
> where there is injury, pardon;
> where there is doubt, faith;
> where there is despair, hope;
> where there is darkness, light;
> where there is sadness, joy.
> O divine Master, grant that I may not so much seek
> to be consoled as to console,
> to be understood as to understand,
> to be loved as to love.
> For it is in giving that we receive,
> it is in pardoning that we are pardoned,
> and it is in dying that we are born to eternal life.

LYN: Every moment is an opportunity to bring God's presence and peace to people around us.

Because we are older, the wisdom we have gained through hard lessons can guide us to know what is really important and what is not. With age comes discernment.

I've learned that God is concerned about everyone in a situation, rather than just my agendas. There are subtle issues going on beneath conversations that hopefully we are learning to navigate. I try to stop my own thoughts long enough to ask God what he wants me to do or not do, say or not say.

I hope I can live out my relationship with God among others, especially my family and friends, in a way that points them to him.

During various holidays, I want to make an impact on those who are celebrating. How can I make a difference?

CAROL: Holidays are a great time to do something special for those around us. Since people are already celebrating and festive, I always want to add to the party and bring spiritual and relational meaning with me.

On Halloween one year, our family offered hot chocolate and cider for parents and kids on a cold Halloween night. We wanted to meet our neighbors, and it slowed down the coming and going to a more friendly pace.

We have also coordinated Christmas cookie exchanges to meet and build relationships with neighbors. You can have an afternoon party, inviting neighbors to bring a dozen of their favorite Christmas, Hanukkah, or other seasonal cookies. At the end of the party, they can take home the same number they brought, ending up with an assortment of different cookies. You can include guided group conversation questions, music, or even a children's nativity play as people enjoy the drinks and treats you provide.

Easter is often an overlooked holiday for many. However, throughout the years, we've sent Easter cards to our aunts, uncles, cousins, grandparents, and in-laws with a short Easter devotional inside. You could include a note explaining that this reading was meaningful to you and hope that it will be for them as well.

Have fun, be creative, and reach out to others, and you will have an impact. You can develop relationships that lead to conversations that lead to life.

MARY: This reminds me of a time when I did something risky with relatives and friends at our holiday meal. There were one or two attending who I didn't know very well. That morning, I had read a spiritual article that I thought might be winsome and helpful for those who weren't spiritually minded. I prayed about it, and after the meal, I said that I wanted to read something I'd found interesting that morning. It was short, and I invited anyone to comment or ask a question after my reading. The people I least expected to respond talked about deep, meaningful thoughts, affecting others profoundly. It reminded me that we can do simple things that make quite an impact.

SPIRITUAL QUANDARIES

In our family, my siblings have different faiths and it's hard to enjoy our holidays together. Do you have any suggestions for us all to keep the peace?

CAROL: Be curious about how they celebrate and why. Be willing to put aside your own preferences and embrace theirs. Talk together about how you can celebrate as a family. Different beliefs do not have to disturb the peace; they might provide opportunities to learn and grow in your relationships with others, which could open doors for future meaningful conversations.

MARY: At holiday events, it helps me to stay away from controversial subjects or topics where I know we disagree. When these come up, I gently change the subject. We're coming together for a pleasant experience and hopefully to pave the way for future times together. Disagreement and controversy will only disrupt those goals. If we build our relationships during holiday activities, there may be other opportunities to discuss important topics where we see things differently.

I've gone to church in my denomination all my life, but lately I'm curious to try something different. I'm not sure this is wise.

LYN: Our culture has changed through the decades and sticking with one denomination is not as common as it was years ago. Many churches have dropped the denomination from their names because it gives people preconceived ideas and they stay away. If you are curious about another place of worship, I encourage you to go and observe. God often works by stimulating our interests. He may also send special friends to introduce us to other ways to worship and learn of God.

My sister is so enthusiastic about Christianity, but I've never believed in the Bible or Jesus. I'll admit I'm curious, but why try something different?

MARY: It's never too late to try something new. I remind myself of this as I get older and am tempted to get stuck in my ways, missing out on the zest that comes from exploring and experimenting. Colonel Sanders established the Kentucky Fried Chicken restaurant chain at age 65; Laura Ingalls Wilder began writing *Little House on the Prairie* at age 65; Grandma Moses didn't begin painting until she was 78; and Mickey Rooney embraced Christianity at 60. It sounds like something is drawing you to explore Christianity. Go for it!

WHAT ABOUT LIFE AFTER DEATH?

There are so many views of life after death. How can anyone know what is true?

MARY: I struggled with this in my earlier years to the point that I did a lot of investigation and research. I read numerous books, including one by Josh McDowell called *Evidence that Demands a Verdict* (Thomas Nelson, 2017). McDowell was an intellectual who set out to disprove Christianity, but as he waded through all the religions and beliefs, he came to the conclusion that people can know they have eternal life as they understand the teachings of Jesus Christ. As I weighed the evidence myself, I came to the same conclusion.

I urge you to look at the fascinating research yourself on websites like https://www.josh.org and https://www.everyperson.com. You might also read the updated and expanded edition of *Evidence That Demands a Verdict* by Josh McDowell and his son Sean McDowell, as well as *77 FAQs About God and the Bible: Your Toughest Questions Answered* (Harvest House Publishers, 2012) by the same authors. Finally, you could explore the story of how C.S. Lewis came to settle this question in his book *Surprised by Joy*. You may know C.S. Lewis as the author of the children's series, *The Chronicles of Narnia*. A professor in England at the University of Oxford and then at Cambridge, he became a prolific writer of inspirational and philosophical books, as well as novels. *Suprised by Joy* is his autobiography, written at the age of 56.

I've gone to church off and on all my life, so why do I still feel unsettled about what will happen after I die?

LYN: When I was in my teens and twenties, I went to church because my parents wanted me to go. I knew about God, but I didn't understand much until I studied more. Perhaps your unsettled feeling will disappear when you learn more about the Bible's teachings on eternal life, which erased my uncertainty.

MARY: Yes, I was in the same boat, going to church but unsettled about life after death. I was so relieved when I studied the historical evidence about people closest to Jesus. They had lived life with him, seen his resurrected body, and then boldly spoke about eternal life, sometimes to the point of being killed for their unwavering belief that they would spend eternity with God. They were eyewitnesses to things that they simply couldn't deny.

The apostle John expressed their belief like this: "God has given us eternal life, and this life is in his Son. Whoever has the Son has life; whoever does not have the Son of God does not have life. I write these things to you who believe in the name of the Son of God so that you may know that you have eternal life (John 5:11–13)." John wrote that we can know with certainty—not merely hope—that we have eternal life and that this comes from having the Son (Jesus) in your life. I encourage you to study this more and to use the resources mentioned in the previous question.

Does a relationship with God help you more during these decades than previously, and how?

CAROL: Experiencing God's loving presence and goodness brings great peace amidst the challenges of aging. He helps us to be content with what is instead of always needing something else to bring satisfaction. Living with a settled certainty about who God is and who you are is a great blessing in this life phase, when many people are filled with negativity and gloom. You can bring light and life to others who are aging, giving you purpose and fulfillment.

MARY: The Apostle Paul wrote in the later years of his life, "Therefore we do not lose heart. Though outwardly we are wasting away, yet inwardly we are being renewed day by day. For our light and momentary troubles are achieving for us an eternal glory that far outweighs them all. So we fix our eyes not on what is seen, but on what is unseen, since what is seen is temporary, but what is unseen is eternal (Corinthians 4:16–18)."

TAKE ACTION

o   Carol wrote about creating your own path of "oncoming
    beauty." Using pen, paper, or artistic supplies, draw a path
    and then depict your specific "beautiful" areas along the path.
    What gives you vitality and nourishes you? What do you love
    doing, seeing, or experiencing? What brings beauty to your
    life? What builds your relationship with God and others? When
    you're finished, put this where you can see it on a regular basis.

o   Describe a meaningful spiritual experience from your past.
    What did you learn from it? Is there a way you'd like to
    replicate or build upon it now?

o   Find an idea from this chapter that you would like to
    implement for your spiritual growth. What are you hoping it
    will bring to your life? When will you fit it into your schedule?

o   What do you currently believe about your existence after you
    die? Is there anything you want to investigate in this area, and
    how will you go about it?

Look through the resources in Section 4, Chapter 12 and Appendix 1.
Which ones do you want to explore further? Make a plan to use the
resources and add them to your calendar.

SPOTLIGHT STORY

JUDY DOUGLASS

Global Director of Women's Resources, Cru
Author, Blogger, Podcaster

Judy Douglass is a role model for thousands of people worldwide. She has a weekly podcast and blog, has written many books, and travels worldwide to speak and meet with people. As the global director of Women's Resources for Cru, a multinational nonprofit organization, she is esteemed for her leadership, wisdom, authenticity, and inspiration to others. At 80 years of age, Judy is remarkable for her stamina and ability to connect with people of all generations and nationalities.

In former years, Judy partnered with her husband, Steve, to lead Cru globally. She has served as editor-in-chief of two national publications, *Collegiate Challenge* and *Worldwide Challenge*. She is the author of six books; *Single and Complete, Secrets of Success, He Loves Me, What Can a Mother Do?, Shaped by God,* and *When You Love a Prodigal.* She has had articles published in numerous magazines.

Judy is the mother of three adult children and has ten grandchildren. Her dear husband Steve passed in recent years. She currently resides in Orlando, Florida.

As her co-authors, we cherish our friendship with Judy and are delighted for you to hear from her. Judy is a very insightful encourager. She is a bright light to so many, and we're excited for you to benefit from her wisdom and life experience.

Find more about Judy at www.judydouglass.com. Her podcast, *When You Love a Prodigal,* is available on all platforms. She is on Facebook at https://www.facebook.com/JeedooDouglass and on X as @Jeedoo417.

How have you kept yourself emotionally and mentally healthy during this season of life?

Over the years, doing things I love has strengthened both my mental and emotional health, and this has helped to compensate for needing to do things that I don't love. I have learned what I do well—what seems natural and fulfilling to me.

As I have gotten older, I've had more freedom to choose what I do. I have increasingly chosen to focus on those things I do well, that give me joy, and especially that give a sense of contributing to others' lives and needs.

What practices and principles have you implemented to help your mental health?

I try to stay healthy physically, because that greatly impacts mental health, and have sought to eliminate or limit foods that can weaken my mind and body. I take supplements for areas of concern, such as asthma, which I've had all my life.

I've sought to be more physically active, as I was in my younger days. I taught horseback riding in my 20s, played football in my 30s, and coached soccer in my 40s. Recently my daughter, who is a personal trainer, suggested that I should move more, so I walk.

Since I am still working as a writer and speaker, keeping my mind sharp has been a priority. I read a lot, especially as I go to bed. And I play about an hour of online word games.

I seek to get at least seven hours of sleep each night, but my mind often doesn't shut down, so I take a natural sleep aid. Rest is one of the most important keys to good mental and emotional health.

Finally, one of my favorite ways to maintain my health is to be engaged with people. Even though I am an introvert, I love people and good conversation with friends, co-workers, people from church, my sisters, and my kids.

And my favorite: my ten grandchildren! They energize me even as they wear me out. Two young ones live an hour from me, and playing with them is wonderful. My three teen grandsons and I have special relationships; I text with them often. When I visit my Montana family, my ten-year-old grandgirl gives me her bed when I come. Also, I pray for them. This helps me to not worry about my loved ones as I entrust their care to God.

Was there a challenge you faced emotionally in this season of life, and how did you handle it?

For most of the last twenty years, my husband was president of our organization. We traveled the world to consult and speak with our global team members. And we did a great deal of entertaining. Thankfully, I had help to handle all the details of travel and hosting. I got spoiled.

Then my husband stepped aside from his position, and I mostly lost my helpers. Suddenly, I felt helpless—I didn't know how to do what needed to be done—and was almost panicked sometimes. I asked for help and enlisted people with experience to guide me. I am still not good or comfortable with those details, but I no longer panic.

Could you share a story that captures the importance of this area of our lives as we desire to be emotionally mature adults?

My husband's mother and I became close friends. She retired early to move near us and help with our two girls. When we moved from California to Florida, she came along and bought a house close to us. She kept the children when we traveled, and we spent lots of time together.

Then she began a slow decline mentally, and we made room for her in our home. As her mind weakened, our relationship was stressed. She resented that she couldn't drive or even be left by herself. In her eyes, her son was perfect, and everything she didn't like was my fault.

Eventually she went to a nursing home, but for several years I had to keep loving her, helping her, and being kind to her, even as she accused me of all sorts of things. Gratefully, God gave me compassion and strength.

What has been your experience with belongings and possessions during this stage of life? Has it been frustrating or difficult and how have you dealt with it?

It's been both frustrating and difficult.

First, a confession. I am incompetent when it comes to bringing order regarding things. My strength area is words. I can play with them and bring order for writing and speaking. My husband was very orderly, but he kept almost everything. So I have a great deal of well-organized stuff.

Plus, I am from the generation that inherited dishes and silver, which we used. But our children have no interest in these things. They won't even take the pictures from their former bedrooms in my house.

For a while, I had helpers who were good at bringing order, so it stayed contained. But then my husband had cancer and died from a reaction to his treatment. It was totally unexpected. Fortunately my kids, friends, coworkers, and neighbors have helped me with organizing our physical belongings. But there is still so much to do.

I have a large house and will keep it for now so my grandchildren will come visit. I have already given away a lot, and plan to continue giving. Giving to others to meet their needs and spark their happiness brings great joy to me.

What challenges or helps have you found in the planning and financial realms?

My strengths in the financial realm are shopping and giving. My husband handled saving and managing.

So now, I have all these responsibilities. My husband and I had put everything into a Revocable Living Trust, which relieved me of a lot of financial issues. I highly recommend it. And my sweet husband paid off the mortgage before he passed. However, I recently had to put a new roof on the house, which was challenging in many ways.

My son-in-law introduced me to a wonderful financial advisor, who has helped me with many decisions. I'm motivated to be wise with my finances because I don't want to leave my children with burdens, and I'd love to help my grands with some of their college expenses.

What would be your advice to someone desiring to truly finish well?

To me, finishing well means a number of things:

- Living out my values.
- Leaving this world with treasured relationships with my family and others who matter to me.
- Knowing what I want to be remembered for and having worked toward that.
- Recognizing what I have to offer this world—and doing it.
- Letting go of regrets—offenses done to me, that I have done, and things still unfinished.
- Assurance of a right relationship with God.

How has your spiritual life helped you as you've grown older?

My relationship with God has been the bedrock for me in these senior years. God encourages me to tell him my needs and to ask him my questions. He has consistently provided guidance, purpose, comfort, wisdom, forgiveness—and much more.

In the two years since my husband passed, God has welcomed my tears, assured me of his presence and care, guided me to people who could help, enabled me to make decisions I'd never had to make, walked with me as I've missed Steve, and helped me continue to live a meaningful, productive life.

What exercises or practices have improved your spiritual life?

The writer in me is always seeking to capture attitudes or practices that strengthen and sustain me, no matter what happens in my life.

Here are three of them:

- *Talk to God about anything and everything.* I tell him how I feel, what I wish he would do, and how confused or afraid I am. I ask him anything. Answers come in different ways, at different times. But he is there.
- *Look for the good.* When situations and events seem bad, painful, scary, or impossible, we see everything that is negative. When I look for the good, I get glimpses of possibilities, I focus on solutions, and I begin to believe that it is not hopeless.
- *Live in awe.* Yes, there is so much pain, fear, and horror in our world. But our world is also full of so much wonder. The beauty takes our breath away. The people in our lives can fill us with joy, hope, courage, and love. We have opportunities to touch lives, help others, use our gifts, and make a difference. There is so much to be in awe of.

In what ways have you found it helpful to be part of a spiritual community?

I love the small church I belong to. We are very close, we pray for each other, we step in when there is a need, we provide food, and we encourage each other. In the months since my husband left this world, my church has done all of that for me. It is a place of giving and receiving.

Have you experienced the fear of death, and if so, what has helped you?

Fear of death? Not really, at least not since I entrusted my life to God. I have the confidence of knowing God and the promises Jesus made. I believe in Heaven, and that I have lots of friends, family, and my husband there. But there's a great deal I don't know about, so I wait with hope and anticipation.

This stage of life has provided many opportunities to grow mentally, emotionally, and spiritually. I've tried to strengthen myself in all these areas, and it's made my years so much richer.

SECTION 4

RESOURCES

RESOURCES FOR SECTION 1: YOUR LIFE

We've listed multiple resources to help with your vision, goals, purposes, passions, strengths, jobs, careers, and commitments. Enjoy!

Chapter 1: An Exciting Vision for These Years

Books

- *From Strength to Strength*, Arthur Brooks
- *Half Time*, Bob Buford
- *How Full Is Your Bucket? Positive Strategies for Work and Life*, Tom Rath and Donald O. Clifton
- *How People Grow*, Henry Cloud
- *Procrastinate on Purpose: 5 Permissions to Multiply Your Time*, Rory Vaden
- *The Purpose Driven Life: What on Earth Am I Here for?* Rick Warren
- *The Wonder Years*, Leslie Leyland Fields

Podcasts

- "I'm Middle-aged and Miserable," *Dr. Laura: Call of the Day Podcast*.
  - https://www.drlaura.com/call-of-the-day-podcast-im-middle-aged-and-miserable

Chapter 2: Rediscover Your Passions and Strengths

Assessments

- The *Authentic Happiness* website*, from the University of Pennsylvania, provides numerous free resources so that people can learn about themselves in a variety of ways in order to thrive. Their goal is to help people lead fulfilling lives and utilize their strengths in work, relationships, and recreation. You first need to register to access their resources, but there is no charge.
  - https://www.authentichappiness.sas.upenn.edu/testcenter

- The *CliftonStrengths Assessment* (StrengthsFinder)* is an online test you take to identify and understand your unique strengths and how you can use them in your career, goals, and relationships.
  - For overall information: https://www.gallup.com/cliftonstrengths
  - To take the test: https://store.gallup.com/p/en-us/10003/cliftonstrengths-34

- The *DISC Profile** assessment is a personality and behavioral assessment to help you understand yourself and others, including strengths and weaknesses.
  - https://www.discprofile.com

- *The Meyers-Briggs Type Indicator** is an assessment that helps you understand yourself and others. It covers various aspects of your behavior, preferences and thought processes.
  - https://www.mbtionline.com

- The *S.H.A.P.E. Personality Test* by David S. Chang helps people discover their own strengths, talents, and interests for ministry.
  - https://artofthinkingsmart.com/shape-personality-test/

- The *Spiritual Gifts Discovery* test helps people to discover their gifts for helping others.
  - https://austinridge.org/uploads/files/Women/spiritual-gifts-assessment updated-1639500276.pdf

Books

- *At-A-Glance Calendars*, AT-A-GLANCE®, a division of ACCO Brands.
- *Network Participant's Guide: The Right People, in the Right Places, for the Right Reasons, at the Right Time*, Bruce L. Bugbee, Don Cousins, and Wendy Seidman

Videos

- "Rocks, Pebbles and Sand: Prioritizing Your Life," Carla Tantila Philibert
  - https://www.youtube.com/watch?v=cPgMeKfQFq8

Chapter 3: Define Your Purposes and Goals

Books

- *Courageous World Changers,* Shirley Raye Redmond
- *Financial Peace Revisited,* Dave Ramsey
- *The Purpose Driven Life: What on Earth Am I Here For?* Rick Warren
- *Shaped by God: Words for Life,* Judy Douglass
- *The Significant Woman,* Susan Heckman, Gail Porter, and Diann Feldman
- *Your Heritage: How to Be Intentional about The Legacy You Leave,* Kurt Bruner and Otis J. Ledbetter

Podcasts

- *The Incrementalist, A Productivity Podcast on Making Big Changes in Small Steps,* Dyan Williams
  - https://theincrementalist.transistor.fm/

Websites and Web Pages

- Dyan Williams' goal is to help you achieve your top priorities while living a meaningful life. Her website offers a blog, podcast, coaching, videos, and other resources.
  - https://www.dyanwilliams.com

- "How to Set Goals and Achieve Them: 7 Simple Strategies for Success," Amy Schlinger, *Reader's Digest* website.
  - https://www.rd.com/article/how-to-set-goals/

Chapter 4: Your Job, Career and Commitments

Books

- *Anxious For Nothing, Finding Calm in a Chaotic World,* Max Lucado
- *Boundaries for Leaders: Results, Relationships, and Being Ridiculously in Charge,* Henry Cloud
- *How to Achieve Your Potential and Enjoy Life,* Steve Douglass

- *How to Stop Worrying and Start Living: Time Tested Methods for Conquering Worry,* Dale Carnegie
- *The Leader In You: How To Win Friends, Influence People and Succeed In A Completely Changing World,* Dale Carnegie and Associates, Inc.
- *Learn How To DeClutter Your Life: Begin Your Journey to Living A Simple Life,* Rebecca Greig
- *The Power of Understanding People,* David Mitchell
- *The 7 Habits of Highly Effective People,* Stephen Covey

Organizations

- *American Job Centers (AJCs).* Provides free help to job seekers for a variety of career and employment-related needs. Nearly 2,500 AJCs, funded by the U.S. Department of Labor's Employment and Training Administration, are located throughout the United States. American Job Centers provide access to career guidance, employment and training opportunities for all Americans.
  - https://www.careeronestop.org/LocalHelp/AmericanJobCenters/find-american-job-centers.aspx

- The *Senior Community Service Employment Program (SCSEP)* helps older Americans to find and train for jobs.
  - For more information on SCSEP programs in your area, call the toll-free help line at 1-877-US2-JOBS (1-877-872-5627, or use CareerOneStop's Older Worker Program Finder at https://www.careeronestop.org/

Podcasts
- *Christian Woman Business Podcast,* Esther Littlefield
  - https://estherlittlefield.com/podcasts

Websites and Web Pages
- The "Careers" page on the AARP website is full of helpful articles for careers and job-seeking after fifty.
  - https://www.aarp.org/work/careers

- "The Guide to Finding a Job Over 60 (With Tips)," Indeed Editorial Team, *Indeed* website.
  - https://www.indeed.com/career-advice/finding-a-job/finding-a-job-over-60
- *JobFinder.com* helps people find rewarding jobs and careers.
  - www.jobfinder.com

RESOURCES FOR SECTION 2: YOUR RELATIONSHIPS

Here's a goldmine of help for your relationships with adult children, partners, grandkids, parents, relatives, and friends. Dive in!

Chapter 5: Your Significant Someone

Books

- *Aging and Loving: Christian Faith and Sexuality in Later Life,* James M. Childs
- *A Celebration of Sex After 50,* Douglas Rosenau, Jim Childerston, and Carolyn Childerston
- David English has written a variety of books and materials addressing various stages in the lives of men, which are applicable for women as well.
  - https://davidaenglish.com/shop
- *52 Ways to Have Fun, Fantastic Sex—A Guidebook for Married Couples,* Clifford Penner and Joyce Penner
- *The Five Love Languages: The Secret to Love that Lasts,* Gary Chapman
- *The Great Sex Rescue: The Lies You've Been Taught and How to Rescue What God Intended,* Sheila Wray Gregoire, Rebecca Gregoire Lindenbach, and Joanna Sawatsky
- *How We Love, Expanded Edition,* Milan and Kay Yerkovich
- *Intended for Pleasure: Sex Technique & Sexual Fulfillment in a Christian Marriage,* Ed and Gaye Wheat
- *The Intimate Connection: Secrets to a Lifelong Romance,* Kevin Leman

- *Intimate Issues: Twenty-One Questions Christian Women ask about Sex,* Linda Dillow and Lorraine Pintus
- *Making Marriage Beautiful: Lifelong Love, Joy and Intimacy Start with You,* Dorothy Littell Greco, Christopher Greco, and Gary Chapman
- *Marriage in the Middle: Embracing Midlife's Surprises, Challenges and Joys,* Dorothy Littell Greco
- *Passionate Marriage,* David Snarch
- *Sacred Marriage,* Gary Thomas
- *Sex Begins in the Kitchen: Because Love Is an All-Day Affair,* Kevin Leman
- *10 Lifesaving Principles for Women in Difficult Marriages: Revised and Updated,* Karla Downing
- *Why Am I Afraid to Tell You Who I Am?* John Powell

Organizations

- *Al-Anon.* Al-Anon is for any loved one or friend of someone with a drinking problem. This organization offers articles, books, meetings, and coaching—both online and in person. Follow the links on their website to find a full list of resources and meetings in your area.
  - https://al-anon.org/

- *Alcoholics Anonymous.* This organization is highly effective for anyone with a drinking problem, or who suspects that they might have one. Follow the links on their website to find a full list of resources and meetings in your area.
  - https://www.aa.org/

- *Twelve Questions Only You Can Answer* is a self-assessment for drinking offered by Alcoholics Anonymous
  - https://www.aa.org/self-assessment

- *S-Anon International.* S-Anon International helps family and friends of those struggling with porn and addictive sexual behavior.
  - https://sanon.org

- *Sex Addicts Anonymous.* This organization helps those struggling with porn and addictive sexual behavior.
  - https://saa-recovery.org

Podcasts

- *Small Things Often* podcast: Dr. John Gottman and Dr. Julie Gottman are renowned leaders in the field of marriage counseling. This podcast and many other resources are available through their website.
  - https://www.gottman.com/podcast/

Websites and Web Pages

- *211.* If you need assistance finding physical and mental health resources, food, paying housing bills, or other essential services, 211 can help. Available in most states, 211 provides a shortcut through what can be a bewildering maze of health and human service agency phone numbers. By simply dialing 211, those in need of assistance can be referred, and sometimes connected, to appropriate agencies and community organizations.
  - https://www.211.org online or by phone at 211.

- *DivorceCare* offers support groups to help people on the path of recovery after separation or divorce, providing comfort, hope, and guidance.
  - https://www.divorcecare.org

- *FamilyLife* provides conferences, podcasts, books, and other resources for all aspects of family life.
  - https://www.familylife.com

- *Focus on the Family* is a global Christian ministry dedicated to helping individuals, couples, and families thrive. They provide timely, relevant information, resources, and advice on marriage, parenting, faith, entertainment, life challenges, and social issues, all from a Christian perspective.
  - https://www.focusonthefamily.com/

- *Focus on the Family Counseling Network* provides counseling consultations and can help you find a counselor in your area. They also offer marriage counseling "intensives" to help couples on the brink of divorce.
  - https://www.focusonthefamily.com/get-help/counseling-services-and-referrals
  - Phone: 1-855-771-HELP (4357).

- *The Gottman Institute.* Dr. John Gottman and Dr. Julie Gottman are renowned leaders in the field of marriage counseling. Their many resources for couples and families are available through their website.
  - https://www.gottman.com

- *GriefShare.* This community gives help and support to anyone mourning a loss. It provides safety and understanding for the difficult emotions of grief.
  - https://www.griefshare.org/

- *How We Love.* This website by Milan and Kay Yerkovich offers outstanding resources for marriage and family relationships. Take their free online test to determine your attachment style and enter a whole new world of wisdom, understanding, and relationship satisfaction.
  - https://howwelove.com

- *Karla Downing* is a licensed marriage and family therapist, speaker, and author, and an expert on relationships. You can find her books, videos, and other resources through her website.
  - https://www.changemyrelationship.com

- *Meetup* website and app. People use Meetup to meet people, make friends, explore their interests, or find support. You can even start your own local group for these purposes using this platform.
  - https://www.meetup.com

- *New Life Ministries* offers a variety of resources for individuals and marriages. They also have a list of licensed counselors throughout the United States to help people with a wide variety of issues.
  - https://newlife.com
  - Phone: 1-800-639-5433
  - https://newlife.com/counselors

- "6 Strategies to Deal with Emotional Abuse in a Relationship," Jessica Ortiz, Marriage.com.
  - https://www.marriage.com/advice/domestic-violence-and-abuse/strategies-to-deal-with-emotional-abuse-in-a-relationship/

Chapter 6: Your Kids

Books

- *The Anxiety Cure*, Archibald D. Hart
- *Character Matters: Raising Kids with Values that Matter*, John Yates and SusanYates
- *Codependent No More*, Melody Beattie
- *Doing Life with Your Adult Children: Keep Your Mouth Shut and the Welcome Mat Out*, Jim Burns
- *Spiritual Seeds:How to Cultivate Spiritual Wealth Within Your Future Children*, Jon and Pam Strain
- *When You Love a Prodigal: 90 Days of Grace for the Wilderness*, Judy Douglass
- *You Are Not Alone: Hope for Hurting Parents of Troubled Kids*, Dena Yohe

Podcasts

- *When You Love a Prodigal Podcast*, Judy Douglass
  - https://judydouglass.com/podcast

Websites and Webpages

- *Ever Thine Home* is a blog with resources designed to mentor women in their relationships with God, husband, children, extended family and friends. Its author is Barbara Rainey, co-founder of Family Life.
  - https://everthinehome.com

- *Hope for Hurting Parents* is a website with multiple resources for parents needing help with destructive behaviors or choices of their teen to adult children.
  - https://hopeforhurtingparents.com

- *Judy Douglass*. Judy provides many resources for parents and loved ones of troubled teens and young adults.
  - https://judydouglass.com

- *Ramsey* is an excellent website for learning to manage finances or getting out of debt. It's helpful for all ages of launching adults and their parents. Dave Ramsey, its creator, is a highly respected financial expert, author, and syndicated radio host.
  - https://www.ramseysolutions.com

- "10 Ways Your Adult Children Need Your Encouragement," Karen Whiting, Crosswalk.com.
  - https://www.crosswalk.com/slideshows/10-ways-your-adult-children-need-your-encouragement.html

Video

- "Boundaries with In-Laws," Henry Cloud
  - https://www.boundaries.me/boundaries-with-in-laws

Chapter 7: Your Grandkids

Books

- *How to Get Better Grades and Have More Fun,* Steve Douglass
- *Suicide Prevention: Hope When Life Seems Hopeless,* June Hunt
- *The Mindful Grandparent: The Art of Loving Our Children's Children,* Marilyn McEntyre and Shirley Showalter
- *Cousin Camp: A Grandparent's Guide to Creating Fun, Faith, and Memories That Last,* Susan Yates

Websites and Webpages

- "Creative Ideas and Tips for New Grandparents," Edie Melson, Focus on the Family website.
  - https://www.focusonthefamily.com/parenting/creative-ideas-and-tips-for-new-grandparents

- "Frequent Video Chats Help Grandparents Bond with Their Young Grandchildren," Brittne Kakulla; Rachel Barr; Jennifer Zosh; Gabrielle Strouse; Lauren Myers; Georgene Troseth; and Elisabeth McClure, AARP website.
  - https://www.aarp.org/research/topics/technology/info-2021/video-chat-grandparents-grandchildren-pandemic.html

- *Legacy Coalition* is a Christian organization that helps grandparents through their resources and events.
  - https://legacycoalition.com

Chapter 8: Your Aging Parents and Relatives

Organizations

- *The National Alliance on Mental Illness (NAMI)* is an organization that helps the families and loved ones of mentally ill individuals.
  - https://www.nami.org
  - Hotline: 800-950-6264, or text "Helpline" to 62640.

Podcasts

- *The Perfect Scam Podcast* with Bob Sullivan, produced by the AARP Fraud Watch Perfect Network.
  - https://www.aarp.org/podcasts/the-perfect-scam

Websites

- *Alzheimer's Association*
  - https://www.alz.org

- *American Association of Retired Persons*
  - https://www.aarp.org

- *Assistedliving.org*
  - https://www.assistedliving.org/assisted-living-near-me/assisted-living-options-low-income-elders

- *At Your Side Home Care*
  - https://www.atyoursidehomecare.com

- *Eldercare Directory: Essential Resources for Senior Citizens and Their Caregivers*
  - https://www.eldercaredirectory.org/

- *HUD: Department of Housing and Urban Development*
  - https://www.hud.gov
  - https://www.hud.gov/topics/homelessness/localassist

- Storytelling services guide older adults to recall and write or record stories from their lives. The services will then put these in a book format.
  - https://www.storii.com

- https://welcome.storyworth.com
- https://vitalifestory.com

- *211*. If you need assistance finding physical and mental health resources, food, paying housing bills, or other essential services, 211 can help. Available in most states, 211 provides a shortcut through what can be a bewildering maze of health and human service agency phone numbers. By simply dialing 211, those in need of assistance can be referred, and sometimes connected, to appropriate agencies and community organizations.
  - https://www.211.org online or by phone at 211.

Chapter 9: Your Friendships

Books
- *Find Your People: Building Deep Community in a Lonely World,* Jennie Allen
- *People Fuel: Fill Your Tank for Life, Love and Leadership,* John Townsend

Organizations
- *Meetup* website and app: People use Meetup to meet people, make friends, explore their interests, or find support. You can even start your own local group for these purposes using this platform.
  - https://www.meetup.com

- *Nextdoor* website and app, where people can connect with their neighbors and communities, exchange recommendations, and read the latest local news.
  - https://nextdoor.com

Video
- "Bosom Friends: Anne and Diana Moments from Anne of Green Gables," Sullivan Entertainment.
  - https://www.youtube.com/watch?v=_3IZyMbhAf0

Websites and Web Pages
- "14 Things we Learned about Friendships from 'Steel Magnolias,'" Melissa Locker, Southern Living website.
  - https://www.southernliving.com/culture/steel-magnolias-friendship

- "30 Questions to Deepen Your Friendship," Kathryn Wheeler, Happiful website.
    - https://happiful.com/30-questions-to-deepen-your-friendships

RESOURCES FOR SECTION 3:
YOU: INSIDE AND OUT

You can thrive mentally, emotionally, spiritually, and practically as you use these resources. Dig in and flourish!

Chapter 10: Your Mind and Emotions

Books

- *Aging with Wisdom and Grace,* Wilkie Au and Noreen Au
- *Atomic Habits: An Easy and Proven Way to Build Good Habits and Break Bad Ones,* James Clear
- *Boundaries: When to Say Yes, How to Say No To Take Control of Your Life, Updated Edition,* Henry Cloud
- *Changes that Heal: Four Practical Steps to a Happier, Healthier You,* Henry Cloud
- *Change Your Questions, Change Your Life: 12 Powerful Tools For Leadership, Coaching and Life,* Marilee Adams
- *Face It: What Women Really Feel as Their Looks Change,* Vivian Diller and Jill Muir-Sukenick
- *Outlive: The Science and Art of Longevity – Rethinking Medicine to Live Better Longer,* Peter Attia, M.D.
- *Rest for Your Soul,* Mary Henderson
- *Retrain Your Brain for Joy: 31 Mini-Adventures,* Mary Henderson

Phone Services

- *Institute on Aging Friendship Line:* 1-800-971-0016
  This phone service is designed to support people 60 and older and adults living with disabilities. Their trained volunteers specialize in active listening and friendly conversation with older adults. They provide emotional support, elder abuse reporting, well-being checks, grief support, suicide intervention,

resources, and referrals for isolated adults. It is available 24 hours a day, 7 days a week, for no charge.

- *The Samaritans HelpLine:* 1-877-870-4673
  This phone service provides compassionate support to anyone who is feeling anxious, depressed or isolated. They also offer online chats for those who prefer to use digital tools. You can call or text this toll-free number 24 hours a day, 7 days a week.

Organization

- *Americorps* is an organization that helps people find ways to help others. Go to their website and click on the tab at the top that says "Serve," then scroll down to Americorps Seniors. When you click that, it will guide you to find opportunities in your specific area. Even if you don't find what you want, it will give you ideas you can seek on your own.
  - https://americorps.gov

Podcasts

- "Obesity, Diabetes, Cancer and You," Dr. Peter Attia, *The Jordan B. Peterson Podcast.*
  - https://www.podcastworld.io/episodes/360-obesity-diabetes-cancer-and-you-dr-peter-attia-tymcl6dd

Websites and Web Articles

- *Calm* is a website and app to help you develop greater inner peace and well-being through mindfulness exercises. You can use their resources to have a mental break, develop calming mental patterns, or to get a better night's sleep. Their guided exercises are available in lengths of 3 to 25 minutes.
  - https://www.calm.com/

- "Beauty Will Save the World," Curt Thompson, Curt Thompson MD website.
  - https://curtthompsonmd.com/beauty-will-save-the-world

- "Erik Erikson's Stages of Psychosocial Development Explained," Jeremy Sutton, PositivePsychology.com website.
  - https://positivepsychology.com/erikson-stages

- *Headspace*, a website and app, helps people learn to manage feelings and thoughts by developing the lifelong skill of everyday mindfulness. Its guided relaxation and visualization exercises can assist people in achieving improved mental health.
  - https://www.headspace.com

- *Honey Good* is a website described as a "destination for women to come together from all over the world to find a rhythm to navigate life's passages with purpose and aspirational wisdom."
  - https://www.honeygood.com/

- "How the Aging Brain Affects Thinking," National Institute on Aging.
  - https://www.nia.nih.gov/health/how-aging-brain-affects-thinking

- "How to Stay Hydrated for Better Health," National Council on Aging.
  - https://www.ncoa.org/article/how-to-stay-hydrated-for-better-health

- Lumosity is a website and app with over fifty games to improve brain skills like memory, processing speed, problem solving, etc. Its exercises were developed by neuroscientists.
  - https://www.lumosity.com

Chapter 11: Finishing Well—Prepare to Leave This Planet

Books
- *Financial Peace Revisited*, Dave Ramsey
- *Peace of Mind Planner: Important Information about My Belongings, Business Affairs, and Wishes*, Margaret Rubiano

Websites and Web Articles
- *AARP Fraud Watch Network* is a free service designed to help you spot scams and get guidance from AARP fraud specialists.
  - https://www.aarp.org/money/scams-fraud/about-fraud-watch-network

- "Advance Care Planning: Advance Directives for Health Care," National Institute on Aging.

- https://www.nia.nih.gov/health/advance-care-planning-advance-directives-health-care#find

- *Alzheimer's Association*
  - https://www.alz.org

- American Association of Retired Persons (AARP)
  - https://www.aarp.org

- *Assistedliving.org*
  - https://www.assistedliving.org/assisted-living-near-me/assisted-living-options-low-income-elders

- *At Your Side Home Care*
  - https://www.atyoursidehomecare.com/

- "Eight Tips for Funeral Planning," American Association of Retired Persons.
  - https://www.aarp.org/home-family/friends-family/info-2020/funeral-planning-tips.html

- *Eldercare Directory:* Essential Resources for Senior Citizens and Their Caregivers
  - https://www.eldercaredirectory.org/

- *Eldercare Locator* is a public service website of the U.S. Administration on Aging. This website by the US government connects you to services for older adults and their families.
  - https://eldercare.acl.gov/Public/Index.aspx
  - Phone: 1-800-677-1116.

- Elizabeth Reynolds Turnage offers a variety of books and other resources on this website to help people prepare for the legacy they want to leave, including practical information for organizing your life, belongings, will, medical considerations, etc.
  - https://www.elizabethturnage.com

- "The 5 Stages of Palliative Care," Nurse Next Door.
  - https://www.nursenextdoor.com.au/blog/the-5-stages-of-palliative-care

- "How to Plan a Meaningful Memorial Service," American Association of Retired Persons.
  - https://www.aarp.org/caregiving/basics/info-2020/planning-memorial-service.html

- "How to Resolve Family Inheritance Conflicts," Empathy's Estates Specialists, Empathy.
  - https://www.empathy.com/will/family-inheritance-and-keeping-the-peace#

- "Living Wills and Advanced Directives for Medical Decisions," Mayo Clinic.
  - https://www.mayoclinic.org/healthy-lifestyle/consumer-health/in-depth/living-wills/art-20046303

- Ramsey: Dave Ramsey is a highly respected financial expert, and his programs and website provide helpful resources for planning and managing finances at every stage of life.
  - https://www.ramseysolutions.com/

- "7 Effective Job-Hunting Strategies for Older Adults," Maura Porcelli, National Council on Aging.
  - https://www.ncoa.org/article/7-effective-job-hunting-strategies-for-older-adults

- "10 Basic Facts About Writing a Will," Amend, Patricia, American Association of Retired Persons.
  - https://www.aarp.org/money/investing/info-2023/top-facts-about-writing-a-will.html

- "Things to Know About Being an Executor of Estate," Carole Fleck, American Association of Retired Persons.
  - https://www.aarp.org/money/budgeting-saving/info-05-2013/5-things-to-know-about-being-an-executor.html

Chapter 12: Your Spiritual Life

There are too many outstanding spiritual resources to list them all here. This is a sampling for your enrichment.

Books

- *Discerning the Voice of God*, Priscilla Shirer
- *Enjoying Your Walk with God: How to Live Above Your Everyday Circumstances*, Steve Douglass
- *Evidence That Demands a Verdict*, Josh McDowell and Sean McDowell
- *The Furious Longing of God*, Brennan Manning
- *God: Knowing Him by His Names*, Bill Bright
- *Jesus Calling*, Sarah Young
- *The Journey Home: Finishing with Joy*, Bill Bright
- *Life Application Study Bible*, Tyndale House Publishers, Inc.
- *The Practice of the Presence of God*, Brother Lawrence
- *A Praying Life*, Paul Miller
- *Sacred Pathways*, Gary Thomas
- *Sent: Living a Life that Invites Others to Jesus*, Heather and Ashley Holleman
- *77 FAQs About God and the Bible: Your Toughest Questions Answered*, Josh McDowell and Sean McDowell
- *Spiritual Disciplines Handbook: Practices That Transform Us*, Adele Calhoun

Websites

- *Bible Hub* provides a wide variety of tools and resources to study and understand the Bible.
  - https://biblehub.com

- "Bible Reading Plans," *Navigators*.
  - https://www.navigators.org/resource/bible-reading-plans/

- *The Bible Recap* website offers many resources and tools "to read, understand and love the Bible."
  - https://www.thebiblerecap.com

- *Christianity.net.au* provides a simple explanation of how to know God personally according to the Bible.
  - https://christianity.net.au/god

- *He Reads Truth* and *She Reads Truth* are websites and apps that provide a variety of ways to read or study the Bible. They have daily reading plans, as well as online conversations led by a vibrant community of contributing writers. You can choose from a variety of Bible books and topics.
  - https://hereadstruth.com
  - https://shereadstruth.com

- *Moms in Prayer International* is an organization that connects moms to pray for their kids of all ages. You can join a group in your area or start a group by filling out their online form.
  - https://momsinprayer.org

- *The Sage Forum* is a group whose purpose is "to equip, encourage and empower women over 40 to mature in faith and grow in wisdom."
  - https://thesageforum.com

- *The Significance Project* provides resources to help people grow spiritually, live out their purposes in life, and help others to do the same. There are also tools and guidance to lead group studies with their materials.
  - https://thesignificanceproject.org

The following websites feature answers to common spiritual questions:

- Everyperson
  - https://www.everyperson.com

- Got Questions
  - https://www.gotquestions.org

- He Gets Us
  - https://hegetsus.com

- Josh McDowell
  - https://www.josh.org

AFTERWORD

Remember when your mom or dad gave you a cookie, or helped you with a project, or fixed a birthday meal? They always waited a moment, and then asked, "What do you say?"

Remember doing the same with your children, or grandchildren? Or nieces or nephews? Or kids in a class you taught?

We all needed it and we all did it. We recognized the importance of saying "thank you," of giving thanks. And we understood that gratitude didn't come naturally; it took reminders and practice.

This was true in every season of our lives, and especially now in these later decades that include transition, confusion, and loss.

Over many years I have increasingly learned that gratitude is one of the most important values and practices for my life.

Some things are easy to be thankful for: loving relationships within your family, a job you enjoy, financial stability, continuing good health, faithful friends . . .

But with other realities—family tensions, hurtful memories, loss of a loved one, loneliness—life can be so challenging, making it difficult to be thankful.

Probably the most important practice I have learned—and cultivated—is learning to say "thank you" to my family, coworkers, friends, neighbors, service people, and others. Gratitude has become my "forward foot" in most circumstances. It's helpful for me as well as for those that I thank.

Gratitude has been a key part of my relationship with God, spurred on by the Bible's principle of giving thanks in everything. I have learned this practice contributes greatly to a life of peace, joy, and hope.

Here are some ways to grow in gratitude:

○ **Remember:** List some good things in your life every day. Also be thankful for the hard situations that make you stronger, the times you cried and how God rescued or changed you, and the ways he has been with you every step of the way.

○ **Read:** Find stories of people helping people, including those in your own family history. Read examples in the Bible about people being thankful, about encouragements to be thankful, and about the blessings that come with gratitude.

○ **Reflect:** Recall when God has been good to you. This can help you to say, "Thank you, Lord," in even the most painful situations. It is a way to remind yourself that God is good and wise, working in ways you may not see or understand.

○ **Repeat:** The most important way to cultivate a grateful heart is to practice. Do this over and over, in every situation, in your family, with everyone. Be intentional about learning to say "thank you" for all the good that surrounds you.

And in ways I don't fully understand, saying "thank you," especially to God, begins to open doors. It's as if those words said in hesitant trust give God a key to our hearts and minds. With that key he unlocks doors shut by our pain, our anger, our fear, our resistance. We begin to get glimpses of answers to our prayers, of more steps forward than backward, of new attitudes, and occasionally, of outright transformation.

This is my heartfelt encouragement to make these years truly be your best years: Give thanks.

—Judy Douglas

APPENDIX

1

BEGINNING A PERSONAL RELATIONSHIP WITH GOD

The simple truth is that God loves you and wants to have a close relationship with you.

But as in all relationships, conflict happens. As humans, we have offended God because he designed us to be like him: good, truthful, unselfish. Instead, we choose to go our own independent ways, either through passive indifference toward him, or by going against what he created us to be. For example, who hasn't lied, been self-centered, or worse?

To enter a true and honest relationship with God, we have to admit that we have fallen short of what he wants us to be. We must understand and acknowledge that Jesus came to the earth and died on the cross to pay the penalty for our wrong-doings. Just like in a court of law, in God's justice system, a penalty had to be paid for our offenses. We need to acknowledge and accept this payment to begin a new relationship with God, surrendering to live as he wants us to from now on.

If it's your heart's desire to do this, you can simply pray something like, "Lord, I acknowledge I've been living my own way instead of yours, which has offended you. I accept that Jesus paid the penalty for these wrongs, and I now want to live the way you want me to. Please make me into the person you created me to be."

When you express this to God, you start a new relationship with Him. This means that you begin an adventure with him of love, peace, joy, and fulfillment. Who wouldn't want that? For information on how to proceed further, check out the many helpful articles on https://www.everyperson.com/menus/existence.html

APPENDIX
2
GROUP LEADER'S DISCUSSION GUIDE

Whether your group consists of two or two hundred people, here are a few tips to help your group discussion flow more effectively.

Have your group members read one chapter each week and write their responses to the journal questions at the end of each chapter. Encourage them to also underline thoughts in the chapters that they find particularly meaningful or helpful.

If your group is large, divide them into smaller groups of five to eight individuals for better discussion and interaction.

If you are a faith-based group, begin your time by praying, asking God to guide and bless your group time.

Start by reading the introductory paragraph for the chapter you will discuss. Ask your group to look back through the chapter and talk about anything they underlined or that stood out to them. Invite them to share some positive things about what they read this week, what was particularly helpful, what was new to them, or what stood out.

Next, lead the group through the questions at the end of each chapter, inviting people to share their thoughts freely. If a question is long or has multiple parts, divide it so that one person isn't talking too long.

As a group, look through the resources in Section 4 for the chapter you are discussing. Ask people to name a resource or two that they would like to research further.

If you are a faith-based group, you could end your time by praying for each person, particularly for any struggles or goals they have mentioned. Don't forget to give thanks for the good things happening in your group members' lives.

Finish by assigning the chapters for the following week.

HOW OUR BOOK
CAME TO BE . . .

It was 2013 and Carol sat in a bistro in New York City with her childhood friend. As they talked about many things, Carol shared insights that she had learned through many decades. She responded, "How do you know these things? If you write a book with these life principles, I will share it with others." Carol began to ponder the possibility.

At the same time, Mary, living in Texas, was counseling people who faced the issues of life after fifty—issues she had experienced herself. She realized that there were limited books and resources regarding the multitude of questions people contend with in these years. As she studied, researched, and considered writing a book, Mary began to create a list of dozens of questions, which grew to be hundreds, that people ask in this season as they search for answers.

Lyn was launching her three children during this time, facing the same issues and conundrums. When she and Mary met, they became close friends and soon realized that their conversations centered around the topics and challenges of these decades. Together, they studied and worked on solutions to the problems they were experiencing, while joking, "We should write a book!" Not too long after that, the joke became a reality.

As Carol, Lyn, and Mary sat over lunch one day in late 2020, they talked about all they had learned in this phase of life and realized the potential of writing a book. That day, they committed to embarking upon this project together. And yet, there was one additional person they knew who embodied the wisdom and life experience that they hoped to convey. That person was Judy Douglass. But would she be willing and able to be part of this with all of her worldwide commitments? They were absolutely thrilled when she agreed, and Judy became a guiding light and source of encouragement every step of the way.

Our hope is that our readers can benefit from our combined ups and downs, our mistakes, our studies, our research, and our lessons learned. We are so grateful for the opportunity to share them with you!

OUR GRATITUDE

We are incredibly grateful to every person who has helped bring this book to life. As with most things, we need the help of others to achieve our dreams. We are so thankful to each one along our path with *Beyond*.

MARY: Thank you to my wise, insightful husband John, who continually provided his listening ear, intelligent perception, and loving support at each turn. I love you. Thank you to my darling grown children Austin, Matthew, and Alisa, who have been cheerleaders and allies in life, giving me so much pleasure through the years. My dear family, together we have learned and taught each other through the decades. You are my joy and strength.

CAROL: Thank you to my soulmate and love of my life, Stuart. Your discernment and ability to synthesize life has empowered me in this project and every day. To our delightful grown children, Rachel, Michelle, and Jared: our family openness, shared faith, and willingness to keep growing together through thick and thin has taught me much of the content of this book. You also chose well in your life mates. Lastly, to my precious Mom, who models a life of love. I love you all.

LYN: To Dan, my beloved: once again you have been the feather in my cap who always had my back as I joined these three sensible, shrewd, and sage women in this project—this calling. Together we have grown in knowledge and prudence throughout these trials and seasons. You, Dan, and my cherished children, are my closest friends and comrades. You all have my deepest respect and gratitude for walking alongside me as we traversed and solved the dilemmas of life.

JUDY: I never get over my husband Steve's constant encouragement for me to step into every opportunity God has given. This book is no exception. I believe he cheers me on from heaven. And I know what I have shared with our readers was mostly learned from Steve and our children.

In addition to these, we give our heartfelt gratitude to Becky Robinson and her outstanding team at Weaving Influence. Becky, you gave us more than your time and experience—which you provided in abundance. You also gave your sincere care and devotion to this project, treating us as friends and partners, working toward excellence in every aspect of our time with you.

Thank you, Lori Weidert, our book production manager at Weaving Influence. We couldn't have done this without your tireless efforts on our behalf. We appreciate how you stayed on top of each detail with excellence and grace.

Thank you, Wendy Haan, for your meticulous efforts and oversight in all aspects of our book's design. We loved having you as our collaborator and comrade.

Carla Kliever, Judy's dear friend who became ours as well—you gave unbelievable time, precision, and care to editing our original manuscript. We were fueled by your love, humor, and belief in us, making the process so enjoyable.

Becky Antkowiak, our copy editor with Weaving Influence, your input and suggestions made significant improvements to our work. We so appreciate the time and care you invested to make this project the very best it could be.

Thank you, Keri Hales, for your proofreading diligence and excellence. You ensured that our book would be clear and understandable for all of our readers,

Stephanie Jordan, you listened to us carefully and created a lovely cover, exhibiting the hopeful exhilaration of creating a life of beauty and purpose after fifty.

Karen Overall, thank you for being a dear friend and for creating our book's website. We love your attention to detail, expertise, and diligent work, creating a big something out of nothing. You are a kind and generous soul.

Rob Mata, you were so fun and gracious as our photographer. We are grateful for your time, skill, input, and delightful conversation during our session. Thank you for your beautiful photos!

We thank Encore in Austin, Texas, as various topics were presented in your meetings that became parts of this book. You were an encouragement to us.

Finally, our hearts overflow with thanks to God for his wisdom, care, and blessing at each turn in this book's process. His presence, friendship, and provision were obvious from the beginning. May others experience this abundance as they travel through these pages and beyond.

ABOUT THE AUTHORS

 **JUDY DOUGLASS** is the founder and host of Prayer for Prodigals, an online community for those who love someone who is making destructive choices. She works for Cru, a multinational nonprofit organization. Judy is the director of Cru's Women's Resources and speaks all over the world. She has written six books, including *When You Love a Prodigal, Secrets of Success: God's Lifelines, Shaped by God,* and *What Can a Mother Do?* She blogs regularly and her podcast, *When You Love a Prodigal,* is available on all platforms. Judy graduated from the University of Texas with a degree in journalism. She loves to encourage God's children to be and do all that he created them for. Judy has three children and ten grandchildren. Her website is https://judydouglass.com

 **MARY HENDERSON** is a Licensed Marriage and Family Therapist and Licensed Professional Clinical Counselor. She is a graduate of the University of Texas and Hope International University. Mary works with Cru and speaks on a variety of topics. She loves to teach and perform theatrical improv and hike with her husband. Mary has authored three other books: *Breaking Free: Journey with God Through Illness to Health; Retrain Your Brain for Joy;* and *Rest for Your Soul.* Mary and John have three children and two grandchildren. Her website is https://www.maryhenderson.org

CAROL DODDS has served alongside her husband, Stuart, with Cru and Athletes in Action since 1982. Carol is a speaker and a life coach. She is the founder and director of Encore, an organization in Austin for influential women over fifty. Carol is a graduate of the University of Texas, where she was a member of Kappa Kappa Gamma sorority. For fun, Carol likes to play pickleball, go on weekly dates with her hubby, and hang out with her Austin family and dear friends. Carol and Stuart have three children and one granddaughter.

LYN ALEXANDER served as the Executive Director of Tru-Care in Austin, Texas for seven years. She graduated from the University of Texas with a radio/television/film degree. Lyn then moved to Los Angeles where she held key positions at The Hollywood Reporter, Paramount Pictures, and McDonnell Douglas. Lyn is passionate about developing deep, lasting relationships with her family and those she mentors, helping women live to their fullest potential. Lyn and her husband Dan have three children and two grandchildren.